Union Theological Seminary

Christian Worship

ten lectures delivered in the Union theological seminary, New York, in the autumn

of 1896

Union Theological Seminary

Christian Worship

ten lectures delivered in the Union theological seminary, New York, in the autumn of 1896

ISBN/EAN: 9783337285418

Printed in Europe, USA, Canada, Australia, Japan

Cover: Foto ©Lupo / pixelio.de

More available books at **www.hansebooks.com**

CHRISTIAN WORSHIP

Ten Lectures

DELIVERED IN THE UNION THEOLOGICAL
SEMINARY, NEW YORK, IN THE
AUTUMN OF 1896

BY

CHARLES CUTHBERT HALL, D.D.; ALEXANDER V. G. ALLEN,
D.D.; EGBERT C. SMYTH, D.D.; CHARLES C. TIFFANY,
D.D.; HENRY EYSTER JACOBS, D.D., LL.D.; WILLIAM
RUPP, D.D.; WILLIAM R. HUNTINGTON, D.D.; ALLAN
POLLOK, D.D.; GEORGE DANA BOARDMAN, D.D., LL.D.;
THOMAS S. HASTINGS, D.D., LL.D.

NEW YORK
CHARLES SCRIBNER'S SONS
1897

University Press:
JOHN WILSON AND SON, CAMBRIDGE, U.S.A.

PREFACE

THIS volume contains a history of Christian Worship, and an exposition of the methods of worship in use in the chief religious bodies of Christendom. Ten representative divines, chosen from seven religious denominations, present the historic modes of worship from their different points of view. The result is a remarkable consensus of opinion on this great subject and a substantial unity in the midst of a rich variety of form and method.

A Director in the Union Theological Seminary generously provided for these lectures. They were delivered in the Adams Chapel of the Seminary during the months of October, November, and December, 1896. They attracted great attention not only in the city in which they were delivered, but also in other parts of the country. It is hoped that in their printed form they may interest a still wider circle and contribute to a richer, more expressive, and more uplifting Christian Worship throughout the Church.

CONTENTS

I

	PAGE
THE PRINCIPLES OF CHRISTIAN WORSHIP	3

By the Rev. CHARLES CUTHBERT HALL, D.D., President-Elect of the Faculty of the Union Theological Seminary, New York City.

II

PRIMITIVE CHRISTIAN LITURGIES 33

By the Rev. A. V. G. ALLEN, D.D., Professor of Ecclesiastical History in the Protestant Episcopal Theological School in Cambridge, Mass.

III

THE GREEK LITURGIES 77

By the Rev. EGBERT C. SMYTH, D.D., Professor of Church History in Andover Theological Seminary, Andover, Mass.

IV

THE ROMAN LITURGIES 107

By the Rev. CHARLES C. TIFFANY, D.D., Archdeacon of New York City.

V

THE LUTHERAN LITURGIES 137

By the Rev. HENRY EYSTER JACOBS, D.D., LL.D., Professor of Systematic Theology in the Evangelical Lutheran Seminary, Philadelphia, Pa.

VI

THE LITURGIES OF THE REFORMED CHURCHES . . . 179

By the Rev. WILLIAM RUPP, D.D., Professor of Practical Theology in the Reformed Theological Seminary, Lancaster, Pa.

VII

THE BOOK OF COMMON PRAYER 213

By the Rev. WILLIAM R. HUNTINGTON, D.D., Rector of Grace Church, New York City.

VIII

THE BOOK OF COMMON ORDER AND THE DIRECTORY FOR WORSHIP. 249

By the Rev. ALLAN POLLOK, D.D., Principal of the Presbyterian College, Halifax, Nova Scotia.

IX

WORSHIP IN NON-LITURGICAL CHURCHES 281

By the Rev. GEORGE DANA BOARDMAN, D.D., LL.D., Honorary Pastor of the First Baptist Church, Philadelphia, Pa.

X

THE IDEAL OF CHRISTIAN WORSHIP 311

By the Rev. THOMAS S. HASTINGS, D.D., LL.D., President of the Faculty of the Union Theological Seminary, New York City.

I

THE PRINCIPLES OF CHRISTIAN WORSHIP

BY THE REV. CHARLES CUTHBERT HALL, D.D.

President-elect of the Faculty of the Union Theological Seminary, New York

THE
PRINCIPLES OF CHRISTIAN WORSHIP

MY first duty, under the theme assigned, is to point out the relation which may be assumed to exist between this lecture and the lectures following in this course. The following lectures may be expected for the most part to deal historically with certain liturgical types which from time to time have contributed to the continuity of Christian Worship. By considering successively the Primitive Christian, the Greek, the Roman, and the later liturgies, the student-auditor will be encouraged to comprehend, within broad lines of treatment, dominant modes of expression through which the worship-sense of the Christian society has found utterance in the past. He will also be prepared to view the present in the rich light of history and tradition, and to estimate worthily the office and the methods of worship in contemporary life and the ideals of worship in the future.

That the broadest foundations may be laid for a course of thought which, even in outline, has great and solemn beauty, and that the chronological development of Christian Worship may be joined in the mind of the student with those Divine and human principles and laws antecedent to an intelligent liturgiology, the projectors of this series have intimated that the first lecture shall contain some account of those principles, intellectual, moral, and religious, which underlie the institution of Christian Worship, and by which it is commended to rational and devout minds.

With this explanation of the prefatory or introductory character of the present occasion, I shall proceed to treat of the Principles of Christian Worship.

In order to do this it becomes necessary to lay down a definition of the specific sense which we shall attach to the word "worship," as used in this lecture. For, upon reflection, it appears that the flexibility of language allows a variable use of the word, which at one moment may convey to the mind an impression differing from that given at another moment. Thus, three distinct applications of the word "worship" enter into our common speech. It is employed respectively to indicate a permanent state of consciousness, or the concrete expression of religious emotion by an individual, or, as on the present occasion, the common devout exercises of the Christian society. It is worth while to pause and briefly to examine these distinctions occurring in the variable use of the single word.

When Charles Kingsley uttered that most virile and suggestive sentence, "Worship is a life, not a ceremony," he conceived of worship as a permanent state of consciousness. Such does it become to the soul thoroughly alive unto God, — a life, not a ceremony. The operations of the Godward sense cannot in such a soul be limited to the prescribed functions of certain days and of certain places. Love, casting out fear, beholds God in the face of Christ, glorifying all life, and co-ordinating in the unity of the Spirit and in the bond of peace all times, places, duties, and relationships. The knowledge of redemption sheds upon life an almost eucharistic gladness. Prayer verges toward companionship, and the humble things that grow by the wayside gleam with the unconsuming fire of new and nobler meanings. Worship becomes a permanent state of consciousness.

But the term also and more frequently serves to indicate the concrete expression of religious emotion by the individual. That worship may be, as Kingsley finely said, a life, not a mere ceremony, does not invalidate the thought of times when the individual consciousness is moved to seek formal and concrete expression of its emotions toward God. In this, worship and love are alike. Love may be "a life," involving the entirety of a man's being, and sweeping like a tide "too full for sound or foam" beneath all his thought; but love has its times of demonstration, its resistless moments of the heart's outpouring, its sacramental hours and deeds wherein the inward passion fulfils itself in outward and visible signs. The heart of Christ was a shrine of perpetual worship. Concerning this permanent attitude toward the Father He said: "I do always those things that please Him." Yet Christ knew and obeyed that psychic law which accentuates the devout life with occasions of formal and concrete expression; and He who lived in the constant light of God's face would yet rise at daybreak to seek that face in prayer among the waking birds upon the mountain-side. Therefore we speak of worship as the expression of the devout life, when in the solitude of the closet, or in the companionable loneliness of nature, or at the family altar, or in the house of prayer, the heart which believes that God is, and that He is the rewarder of them that diligently seek Him, pours itself forth before Him with the consent of the will and the eagerness of the affections.

Another application of the word "worship" remains to be considered, and brings us immediately in touch with the specific end of this lecture. Worship is one of the primary functions of the Christian society, in the evolution of its common and corporate life. There are other primary functions named and described in the Apostolic letters of the New Testament. Evangelization is a primary function, the heralding, in the ears of every creature, of the gospel, the good news of God. Social tenderness is a primary function, — not an incident, but an ordained function. Love is the fulfilment of law, and love is to be the dominant note of progress in the brotherhood of the Son of God, — the sympathy of all the members in the sufferings of one. Government is a primary function. That is to say, the self-government of the society, under the counsel of the Spirit, through its own teachers; not as lords over God's heritage, but as interpreters of the Word and shepherds of the flock. Education is a primary function, — the edifying, the building up of the body of Christ, that membership therein may be not nominal but organic, membership of His flesh and of His bones. Separation is a primary function, at times, alas, more honored in the breach than in the observance; not cenobitism, not corporate seclusion, but spiritual differentiation, in motive, in conduct, in ideal, from the world that lieth in the Evil One. And so also in the constitution of the Christian society, worship is a primary function; worship not alone in the individualistic sense already considered, but worship distinctively regarded as service collectively rendered unto God; common prayer, common praise, common liturgical and sacramental usage. It is not enough that men shall pray everywhere, lifting up holy hands without wrath and doubting; not enough that the worshipper shall enter into the closet to commune apart with Him who seeth in secret. For reasons which may be plainly discerned, and which it is our intention presently to enumerate, there must be more than the devout consciousness, more also than the individualistic outpouring. There must be the worshipping assembly, the coming together, the convening of believers, for solemn transactions with God which shall be for a memorial before the Most High, for a testimony before the world, and for the nourishment and consolation of the body of Christ on earth.

Such is the place of Public Worship in the organic structure of historic Christianity; a primary function, an Apostolic rule, a permanent institution; not the ephemeral product of local excitement, but the steadfast, universal practice of the Church, to be continuously maintained during the undefined period of the Lord's absence, and to grow more intense and engrossing as the signs multiply that foretell the nearness of the Second Advent. The common worship is to have reached its maximum of power and earnestness, in the watchful Church, when the Parousia of the Lord is at hand. Perhaps the supreme example of the New Testament estimate of a common worship, as a constant and cumulative function of the Christian society, occurs in that most moving exhortation in the Epistle of the Hebrews, "Having therefore, brethren, boldness to enter into the holy place by the blood of Jesus, by the way which He dedicated for us, a new and living way, through the veil, that is to say, His flesh; and having a great priest over the house of God; let us draw near with a true heart in fulness of faith, having our hearts sprinkled from an evil conscience, and our body washed with pure water: let us hold fast the confession of our hope that it waver not; for He is faithful that promised: and let us consider one another, to provoke unto love and good works; not forsaking the assembling of ourselves together, as the custom of some is, but exhorting one another; and so much the more, as ye see the day drawing nigh."[1]

Having now defined the place of Public Worship in the structure of historic Christianity, and having discriminated between this specific use of the word "worship" and such other uses as may imply individual acts of devotion, or, more broadly, the general attitude of a life in its reverence for God, it is well to gain a more exact view of this great and venerable institution by noting what appear to be its essential contents. Not without some approximate agreement as to the contents of the institution of Christian worship can we hope to agree touching the fundamental principles upon which it rests. To treat adequately of the contents of Christian worship would be to explore the history of liturgies and to trace to the germ that extraordinary evolution, which has reached in our time a diversity extending from the stately cathedral use of the Greek, the Roman, and the Anglican orders, to the bold simplicity of the camp-meeting and the reverential liberty of the Plymouth Brothers. Such a *résumé* is, on the present occasion, impracticable. Nor is it neces-

[1] Heb. x. 19-25.

sary. For, overlooking the historic divergences of liturgical order, each one of which involves a chronicle of human aspiration (not to say of human suffering), we may repair directly to the Apostolic Scriptures, there to find, sketched in broad and free-hand outlines, not only the institution of Christian worship, but its essential contents. And what are these? It being granted that the Apostolic writings exalt public worship as a primary and perpetual function of the Catholic Church, witnessing on earth amidst coming and departing generations to Him who is ascended up on high until He come a second time, are there to be found, in these Apostolic writings, intimations of the fundamental elements of common worship sufficiently distinct to constitute what may be called a Catholic use for the body of Christ, thus providing a unity of devotion beneath the lamentable controversies and confusion of Ecclesiastical History? The question is intensely interesting; to the lover of Catholic Unity it is deeply reassuring; for he sees that amidst the doctrinal divisions and the governmental conflicts of eighteen centuries, and beneath the almost infinite variations of ritual, there has been maintained throughout the Christian society, presumably by the intervention and care of the Holy Spirit, a practically universal adherence to those elements of worship which form the Apostolic and fundamental contents of the institution. These fundamental elements may be readily found by grouping the Apostolic writings which bear upon the office of worship. Not now may we pause to cite the passages on which we base these remarks. And it may be assumed that these citations are unnecessary in the presence of a body of New Testament students. The fundamental elements of public Christian worship will be found enumerated in the pages of him on whose great heart came the care of all the churches daily. And, strangely enough, those elements are seven in number, — as it were a sevenfold gift from the Spirit to instruct the Church how to maintain through the ages of the Lord's absence the vital institution of a serious, suitable, and spiritual worship. The seven elements are these: The Hymn, the Scripture, the Belief, the Prayer, the Oblation, the Teaching, the Sacraments.

1. THE HYMN. Devout music is an eternal integer of the common worship, in heaven and on earth. They who believe in the redemption must sing. If these should hold their peace, the stones would immediately cry out. As soon bid the waves of ocean to break silently upon their coasts as think to hush the song, like the sound of many waters, from those who know that their Redeemer liveth, and that He shall stand at the latter day upon the earth. Music may be misused in Christian worship; it cannot be abolished. It is inseparable from the new creation, as it was from the first creation when the morning stars sang together, and all the sons of God shouted for joy.

2. The Scripture. The reading of the Holy Oracles is an indefeasible part of Christian worship. Christ reading in the synagogue the prophetic witness concerning Himself, while the eyes of all were fastened on Him, and men marvelled at the gracious words, exalts the Scripture to its supreme office as a vehicle of the Spirit's power in testimony to the eternal Son. At this time, when attention is so continuously and so properly called to the Bible as a field for devout research and criticism, it is well, perhaps peculiarly well, also to affirm the use of Holy Scripture as an instrument of worship. To those to whom the inspiration of the Scriptures is an unquestioned reality, the solemn reading of the Word in the Christian assembly is as truly an act of worship as it was in that impressive day of which we read in the Book of Nehemiah, when "Ezra opened the book in the sight of all the people; . . . and when he opened it, all the people stood up: and Ezra blessed the Lord, the great God. And all the people answered, Amen, Amen, with the lifting up of their hands: and they bowed their heads, and worshipped the Lord with their faces to the ground."[1]

3. The Belief. The most ancient of the Catholic creeds is a growth whose roots are in the Apostolic Age. The Belief, the Creed, the Confession with the mouth, is a fundamental element of Christian worship. The word of man should be the echo of

[1] Neh. viii. 5, 6.

the Word of God. The heart of man should reply to the outpourings of the heart of God. Confession of faith should ascend in answer to revelation of truth, as the blades of harvest rise and expand beneath the quickening floods of sunshine. So also the creed is for testimony. "God gave us not a spirit of fearfulness, but of power and love and discipline;" and the spoken belief, sounding forth with joy and power in the Christian assembly, is the historic continuance of that objective witness-bearing which marked the pioneers of Christianity, and which recruited the noble army of martyrs. Strange that the use of a Catholic creed in public worship should have been discontinued in any part of the Church, to be supplanted by inferior and ephemeral incidents of local custom. Strange that the speaking forth of the belief should ever be intermitted. May it be renewed and exalted in all our churches! Belief and speech are mysteriously interdependent. "I believed, therefore have I spoken," is more than a casual association of ideas. To believe without speaking is to imperil the faith. A silent church might soon become a skeptical church.

4. THE PRAYER. The place of prayer in Christian worship, while gaining the New Testament liberty and love, has lost none of the Old Testament glory and splendor. The Christian presbyter, standing or kneeling in the assembly of believers, and leading them in humble, lowly, penitent, and obedient approach to the throne of the heavenly

grace, occupies a station great as that of Israel's priestly king, interceding in the cloud-filled temple. If ministerial unspirituality and popular indifference have at certain melancholy periods of decadence co-operated to reduce the office of public prayer to thin and threadbare routine, such catastrophes but emphasize, through the force of a tragic contrast, the Apostolic conception of this most august function. The mind of the Spirit, as reflected, for example, in the Pauline consciousness, makes prayer the true altar of incense in the Christian *ecclesia*. There shall be presented the fragrant gifts of adoration, the incomparable blend of homage, faith, penitence, and thanksgiving. And there shall all the contents of the social order, and of the personal life, be daily consecrated in the mystery of intercession. "I exhort therefore, first of all, that supplications, prayers, intercessions, thanksgivings, be made for all men; for kings and all that are in high places; that we may lead a tranquil and quiet life in all godliness and gravity. This is good and acceptable in the sight of God our Saviour."[1]

5. THE OBLATION. In the New Testament conception of God the Father and God the Son the distinctive attitude of the Divine consciousness is represented as that of love expressing itself through *giving*. As to the Father: "He that spared not His own Son, but delivered Him up for us all, how shall He not with Him also freely give us all

[1] 1 Tim. ii. 1–3.

things." As to the Son, He is "the Son of God who loved us and gave Himself up for us; who for our sakes became poor, that we through His poverty might become rich." In perfect correspondence with this view of God is the direct and indirect teaching of the Apostolic writings which exalts the consecration of wealth, the oblation of substance, as an organic element of worship. The Divine giving is, in the Christian scheme of worship, the inspiration of the human giving. "Freely ye have received, freely give." As the Eucharist is God's sacrament for man, the outward and visible sign of the Divine self-oblation, so the cheerful offering of wealth on the scale of absolute ability is man's sacrament for God, the outward and visible sign of a self-oblation in human life prompted by an enlightened sense of the evangelic mercy.

6. THE TEACHING. Worship is contemplated by the Apostolic mind as no sporadic or temporary factor in the life of the Christian Society, but rather as the perennial harvest of faith and love ripening wherever the good seed of the Word is truly sown. But worship is ever regarded in the New Testament as an effect of knowledge, not as the tribute of ignorance and superstition. Thus said Christ to the woman of Samaria, "Ye worship that which ye know not, we worship that which we know." Hence the continuity of worship is maintained, and the normal level of worship is preserved by incorporating "the teaching" as a constant element. Worship is the

expression of faith, but the substance of faith must forever be recruited by growth of knowledge, else faith fades into a pallid and anæmic superstition, and worship sinks into the routine of materialism. In the economy of the Spirit, faith cometh by hearing, and hearing by the Word of God. And how shall they hear without a preacher? Hence in the new priesthood of believers teaching is above sacrifice, and the right dividing of the Word is more vital than the first-fruits of flock and field. Here, then, is the coronation of preaching as a means of grace. Through it is to come that perpetual increment of knowledge which is fuel for the altar-fire of intelligent worship. So the passion of the Apostle's heart was that his preaching might be a veritable teaching: "In the church I had rather speak five words with my understanding, that by my voice I might teach others also, than ten thousand words in an unknown tongue."

7. THE SACRAMENTS. If the teaching element in Christian worship may be described as that through which the reason and the conscience are enlisted in the approach to God, the sacramental element in worship is that through which, pre-eminently, an appeal is made to the imagination, to the memory, and to the affections. The two divinely constituted sacraments of Baptism and the Lord's Supper are profoundly imaginative and tenderly emotional. Holy Baptism, the sacrament of the blessed Comforter, Holy Communion, the sacrament of the suffering

Saviour, contribute to Christian worship an imaginative aspect and an emotional potency which not only perpetuate but nourish and stimulate the sense of that which is supernatural. Chiefly is this realized in the Eucharist, because of its recurrence in our experience. The thrilling contrast therein between the simplicity of the material substances employed and the vastness of the event and the personality which are by them sacramentally delineated, lays hold of the imagination, enchains the memory, kindles the affections with a sense of Christ's supra-naturalism, opens the inner life for the entrance of grace, and clothes with majestic realism that Apostolic thought of the witness to the infinite, the spiritual, and the unseen, accomplished by sacramental participation: "For as often as ye eat this bread and drink this cup, ye proclaim the Lord's death till He come."

We have now enumerated the seven fundamental elements of Christian worship, notice of which appears more or less distinctly in the Apostolic writings. We behold a rich and impressive unity. No element is redundant; none is irrelevant; each has its own logical and spiritual relation to the other; each contributes a specific force to the whole volume of energy. All, united, blend as the seven bands of the rainbow, in one radiant symbol of hope, spanning the present dispensation from the Ascension to the Second Advent, and revealing the existence of a substantial agreement (not to say an involuntary agreement) among Christians, historically maintained amidst innumerable sectional variations and local adaptations. As there is one Lord, one faith, one baptism, one God and Father of all, so also may we venture to say there is, among Christians, in the last analysis, one worship, — the Hymn, the Scripture, the Belief, the Prayer, the Oblation, the Teaching, the Sacraments.

The thought which we have now given to this branch of our subject has prepared the way for a statement of those broad principles which constitute the real foundations of Christian worship. And it is hoped that this statement of principle may be sufficiently clear to be of practical use to those whose life-work is to be closely connected with the great institution of worship now under review.

He who attentively regards the historic phenomena of Christian worship finds *à priori* reasons for believing that it is no fortuitous outcome of circumstances, but a divinely constituted force, operating in accordance with principles which may be ascertained and defined. Whether the powerful fact of worship be regarded in the light of its permanence, as abiding continuously through the politico-ecclesiastical upheavals of many centuries; or in the light of its substantial conformity to the Apostolic type, as we have already essayed to show; or in the light of its ethical effects as a prodigious contribution to the vigor and the purity of civilization; or in the light of its spiritual power as tending to produce in all times and countries qualities of human character spiritual in proportion to the spirituality of the worship, — from every point of view the attentive mind finds in the phenomena of worship suggestions of underlying principles fully accounting for the perpetuity and the immense influence of the institution itself. When we undertake to collect and to co-ordinate these principles we discover that they fall into two classes or groups, which we may conveniently describe as the subjective group and the Objective Group. The term "subjective principles underlying Christian worship" is intended to indicate those inward and constitutional relationships with the life of God and the life of man which are found to exist in the concept of worship. The term "objective principles underlying Christian worship" is intended to indicate those outward uses for the Church, and for society at large, which historically subsist in Christian worship normally administered.

Our attention is now given to the subjective group. The concept of worship, whether regarded in its generic sense, as involving the manifold religions of humanity, or in its specific sense, as an institution of Christianity, is found to be the outcome of two interior and constitutional ideas, — the one a belief concerning God; the other an experience concerning man. The belief concerning God is that the desire and will of the Divine Mind invite and enjoin worship on the part of created intelligences. The experience concerning man is that worship is an intuition of self-consciousness. As our Lord, when giving the first and great commandment, and the second which is like unto it, declared, "On these two commandments hang all the law and the prophets," so may we also declare with confidence concerning the two ideas just enumerated: on these two subjective principles, the Will of God, the intuition of man, rests, fundamentally, the institution of Christian worship. Consider the former, the Will of God. So far as God is known in the ethnic faiths, or is revealed in the Biblical Scriptures, He is known and revealed as desiring and willing the worship of created intelligences. If in the ethnic faiths the conception of God is often one of horror, a confused polytheism, or a lurid and vindictive monotheism, yet is the idea prevalent and even universal, that Deity desires and wills the tribute of worship to be paid by the mind and heart of humanity. When, from the ethnic faiths that lie outside of Biblical revelation, we advance to the religion of Israel, the keynote of the dispensation is the desire of Jehovah to receive that homage from the created intelligence which it is competent to give. This surely is the substantial basis of the Divine legation of Moses; this the meaning of that most extraordinary code wherein one looks in vain for any intimation of immortality, or for promise even of a future life, and finds, instead, a complex liturgical order for the life that now is. In the Israelitish code God is self-revealed as desiring and demanding worship from created intelligences. Had He not given subsequently, in Christ, a larger self-revelation along the same line, there would still exist, in the Hebraic Scriptures, clear and conclusive declaration that worship is not first of all a conception of man, but first of all an ordinance of God. But Christ gives us infinitely more than this. Christ, proclaiming Himself to be the revelation of the Father, and not only permitting worship to be addressed to Himself as God, but explicitly providing, in the sacrament of His body and blood, for a perpetual homage, declared, in the clearest terms, that the mind of God is not passive, but active, in its relation to those offerings of the intellect and of the affections which man is competent to bring to Him. "The hour cometh, and now is, when the true worshippers shall worship the Father in spirit and in truth; for such doth the Father seek to be His worshippers. God is a Spirit, and they that worship Him must worship in spirit and in truth."[1] It is not too much to say that the vitality of Christian worship is commensurate with the grasp of Christian minds upon this subjective principle, that God wills, desires, commands the approach of human intelligences to Himself. Let there be in minister and in people but a languid and traditionary assent to this proposition, and that which is called worship subsides to the level of religious routine; but let presbyter and

[1] Jno. iv. 23–24.

people feel that the will of the Eternal bespeaks their coming together, that the Spirit of the Eternal is operating on their human spirits to produce the emanation of worship for the joy of Him who is invisibly present in their assembly, and worship becomes transfused with extraordinary and soul-compelling awe, and (to adopt the very striking language of Professor Sohm of Leipsic, employed in another connection)[1] "the aim of Divine worship and its crowning glory is that feeling of the immediate omnipresence of the Divine Man which constrains the congregation to bow down in adoration."

The second and complementary subjective principle of Christian Worship is the intuition of man. It is complementary as seen in relation to the Will of God. God desires worship, and man, made in His image and for Himself, discovers in his own self-consciousness the intuitional impulse of worship. In the presence of voluminous evidence supplied from the history of religions, it is wholly unnecessary to consume time in pointing out the universality of that impulse which prompts man to the worship of Omnipotence.

The correspondence between the human intuition and the revelation of the Divine Will is too complete to be overlooked or to be explained away. The conclusion is psychologically necessary: Man is constituted a worshipping creature, and approximates to an absolutely normal state as his worship advances

[1] *Outlines of Church History*, p. 122.

toward ideal spiritual completeness. The evidence of this appears in the effects of worship on character.

He who knows the act of true worship, who has experience of what it is to gaze upon God with eyes of faith and holy fear, to pour out the soul toward God not only in petition and pleading, but in the contemplation of Himself, to say "Holy, Holy, Holy, Lord God Almighty, which was and is and is to come," he knows that worship mysteriously affects life. There is an intense incompleteness in him who knows not the meaning of worship. There is a lack of depth and of dignity in him who will not look upon God. His life seems curtailed and crippled. We give him credit for keenness, or talent, or courage, or maturity of mind, or whatever else he may possess, but we miss in him a certain glory which can be given only in one way, by the light of God's countenance. He is like a fruit that has ripened in the dark and not in the sunshine. We see not in him the reflection of God's face, for he has not lived looking on God's face. He has been intensely interested in earthly things; he has prayed hard and worked hard for success; he has studied himself; he has not studied God; he has not worshipped God. The decline of worship means the withering of man's spirit. If we no longer have that mystic blending of our spirit with God's Spirit, we lose the mysterious resultants of worship from our own life. The presence of the intuition of worship in man's organism is accounted for in the fact that worship is the true foundation of character and channel of power. "The fear of the Lord is the beginning of wisdom." God is the ideal. To ignore the ideal is to throw away the standard of character, and to leave only the conventional notions of morality. To worship is to think of God, to fasten the eyes upon Him until the heart is filled with the splendid vision as with the influx of the tide. The mystery of worship is that this contemplation of God founds and forms character. While the man is thinking of God, God is moulding him; and thus, with unveiled face, reflecting as a mirror the glory of the Lord, one is changed into the same image, as by the Lord, the Spirit. So also worship is the channel of power. Whence comes spiritual power? Whence come the courage of faith, the patience of hope, the gift of ministry? Whence are born those splendid abilities to help other souls in their distresses and humiliations? Spiritual power comes not through the study of self, albeit the study of self is an indispensable part of the Christian discipline. Spiritual power comes through the contemplation of God, which is worship. "They that wait upon the Lord shall renew their strength; they shall mount up with wings." This is the mystery of worship,—that when we forget ourselves in God, we receive most into ourselves; when we lose our lives in Him, we find them. When we break away from our own petty scale of thinking, cast from about us our network of worries and disputings, throw away even our knotted scourge of self-flagellation, and go out to look upon the wideness of God; when we cease from our small devices for self-improvement and our hair-splitting self-analysis, and cast ourselves down beneath the shining of God in His strength, as on some high foreland by the sea, beneath the blessed midday sun, —

> "To lie within the light of God,
> Like a babe upon the breast,
> Where the wicked cease from troubling
> And the weary are at rest," —

that is worship, and that is the channel of power. Our feebleness is swallowed in His strength; our fears are swept away by the torrent of His love. Our dwarfish notions are lost in the measure of the stature of the manhood of Christ;

> "God's greatness flows around our incompleteness,
> And round our restlessness, His Rest."

Having now noted what appear to be the two subjective principles conditioning the institution of Christian worship, namely, the will of God and the intuition of man, we advance to the final division of this lecture, and proceed rapidly to enumerate some of those objective principles which include the outward uses, for the Church and for society at large, which historically subsist in Christian worship, normally administered.

When we advance to this part of our subject, the territory presented to thought is so broad, we see at a glance the impossibility of making a complete statement of the objective principles of Christian worship. Our method of treatment must be elective rather than comprehensive, suggestive rather than exhaustive. Brief and concentrated references to *three* of the objective uses of worship may at least indicate the line to be pursued by the student in search of thorough knowledge of this great subject.

Christian worship, considered objectively, that is to say, not in respect of esoteric relations between man and God, but in respect of outward uses for the Church and for the community at large, is seen as ideally subserving the following, among other uses, and these several uses are to be regarded as principles underlying the institution: the affirmative use; the conservative use; the educative use.

The affirmative use contemplates Christian worship as testimony, comprehending the evangelical facts and uttering the same continuously and effectively, as a propagandism of spiritual light and hope, throughout a world lying in the Evil One. The glory of Christianity is its undebatable affirmation, whether men will hear or will forbear; whether men consent or protest, allow or forbid, — an undebatable affirmation, sounding in the generations, irrepressible, unsilenceable. Such is the method of Jesus. "Go ye into all the world, preach, proclaim the Gospel to every creature." The Gospel: What is that? Not a cautious scholastic argument, but an invulnerable assumption; still invulnerable, though sought out by sheaves of arrows from the bow of philosophic doubt. Christianity, in its relation to the world, is an affirmation, not a polemic, — a voice that cannot be hushed. It may be prohibited; it speaks above the prohibition. The ban of the State cannot stop it; the walls of the prison house cannot confine it; the clods of the grave cannot smother it. Most heroical and most suggestive is that sequence in the Acts of the Apostles, recorded without comment by the narrator, as being the natural order. The injunction from the council: "They commanded that they should not speak in the name of Jesus, and let them go;" the action of the Apostles under that injunction, "And they departed from the presence of the council, and daily in the temple and in every house they ceased not to teach and preach Jesus Christ,"— the undebatable, irrepressible affirmation! Christian worship is the perennial continuance of this affirmation. Every place of sacred assembly, from the buttressed cathedral, sumptuous with the spoils of time, to the frail and austere chapel of some out-station on the plains; every hymn sent upward to God by the rescued wanderers of the street, or by the snowy multitude of stoled priests and vested choristers massed before the shadowy splendors of the shrine, like Dante's white rose of Paradise; every eucharistic board, sweet with fair linen, august with elemental bread and wine, is worship in its affirmative use, proclaiming alike to the stolid ears of ignorance, to the sinister mind of unbelief, to the prostrate helplessness of despair, to the hallowed anguish of penitence, "the Lord's Death till He come."

The conservative use of Christian worship is discerned most impressively in the solemn light of history. Amidst vanishing empires and dissolving philosophies; amidst the incessant harvests of Death, gathering from the scene Apostolic and post-Apostolic defenders of the faith; amidst the relentless attacks in every age of that carnal mind which is enmity against God; amidst internal dissensions of the Church and partisan over-statements of truths which were thereby compromised through those who fiercely thought to do God service, — worship has been the great conservative of faith. It is more than fifty years since the brilliant and sympathetic man, Cleveland Cox, who as Bishop of Western New York has just departed to his rest, wrote words that perfectly express the conservative use of worship.

> "Oh, where are kings and empires now
> Of old that went and came?
> But, Lord, Thy Church is praying yet,
> A thousand years the same.
>
> We mark her goodly battlements
> And her foundations strong;
> We hear within the solemn voice
> Of her unending song."

It is through the "unending song" of a worshipping Church that the faith of Christ has been conserved upon the earth, rather than through the involved confessional creations that lie dormant in theological literature. They indeed bore their part, and out of them came many a glorious strophe and stanza for the Church's song: but the worship of the Church, far more than its scholasticism, has safeguarded, through warring centuries, the faith once for all delivered to the saints. The Apostles' Creed, the *Gloria Patri*, the *Gloria in Excelsis*, the *Te Deum*, the Nicene Creed, the Words of Institution at the Lord's Supper, have kept the Catholic faith unspotted from the world, unwarped by the Church.

The educative use of Christian worship, its reflexive influence on persons, on households, on schools, and on communities, makes worship a part of sociology. The religious nature must be reckoned with in all attempts to reconstitute the dignity of a fallen community, or to develop the powers of an inchoate life. Man is not normal until he worships. Upon the director of worship lies, therefore, the burden of an educator. To him much has been committed, and of him shall men, without injustice, require much. They have a right to the best, to the noblest forms of worship; to the most devout, the most studious, the most solicitous, the most reverential fulfilment of all the contents of that sacred institution founded upon the will of God, demanded by the intuitions of human consciousness. Worship is an education, the leader of worship a teacher of men. It is his so to serve with clean hands at the altar of God, so to live in all godliness and gravity, so to stand surrendered to the power of the Paraclete, that the eternal verities of worship shall become to many lives a revelation of truth, a voice from the unseen, a theophany of the Spirit, sublimating thought, moulding character, strengthening with might the wings of the soul's aspiration.

II

PRIMITIVE CHRISTIAN LITURGIES

BY THE REV. ALEXANDER V. G. ALLEN, D.D.,

Professor of Ecclesiastical History in the Protestant Episcopal Theological School in Cambridge, Mass.

PRIMITIVE CHRISTIAN LITURGIES

I PROPOSE in this lecture to discuss the liturgical motives which influenced the development of worship in the ancient Church, and were finally embodied in liturgies.[1] The impulse to liturgical development was Oriental in its origin. It is a familiar generalization that in the development of the ancient Church Greece contributed the intellec-

---

[1] LIST OF SOME OF THE MORE IMPORTANT WORKS ON ANCIENT CHRISTIAN WORSHIP.—The larger collections of Assemanni, Renaudot, Daniel, and Muratori. The Liturgies in the 2d, 7th, and 8th books of the Apostolic Constitutions. Cyril's *Mystagogic Catechisms*. Bingham's *Christian Antiquities*, B. XIV. c. 5, B. XVI. Dionysius the Areopagite in Migne, *Patrol. Gr.* ii. Swainson, C. A., *The Greek Liturgies, chiefly from Original Authorities*, 1884. Brightman, F. E., *Liturgies, Eastern and Western, being the Texts, original or translated, of the Principal Liturgies of the Church*, vol. i. 1896. Palmer, W., *Origines Liturgicæ*. Bunsen, Chevalier, *Christianity and Mankind*, and *Analecta Ante-Nicæna*. Smith and Cheetham, *Dictionary of Christian Antiquities*; articles on LITURGIES AND LITURGICAL BOOKS. Neale, J. M., *Introduction to the History of the Holy Eastern Church*; also *Essays on Liturgiology and Church History*. Stanley, *The Eucharistic Sacrifice* in " Christian Institutions," 1881. Freeman, *Principles of Divine Service*. Probst, *Liturgie der drei ersten christlichen Jahrhunderten*, 1870. Mone, *Lateinische und griechische Messen aus dem zweiten bis sechsten Jahrhundert*. Gottschick, *Der Sontagsgottesdienst der Christl. Kirche*, 1885. Körtlin, *Geschich. d. Christl. Gottesdienstes*, 1887. Duchesne, *Origines du culte Chrétien, Étude sur la Liturgie Latine avant Charlemagne*, 1889.

tual formulas of doctrine, and Rome her genius for law and government and administration. To this may be added that Oriental countries contributed the tendencies which to some extent influenced the aspect of worship. And by Oriental countries are meant Egypt, parts of Asia Minor, and Eastern Syria, where, although the influence of Greek culture had been felt, there were characteristics of temperament, religious traditions, a certain conception of man in his relation to nature, and theosophical tendencies also, which were never entirely overcome by Greek influence, and which finally left their mark on Christian worship. The time of liturgical preparation may be said to date from the age of Constantine, and to include the fourth and fifth centuries. During this period we may trace the origin and development of most of those principles which were afterward embodied in the cultus. The liturgies themselves did not assume their final shape, as we know them to-day, until a much later time. There are no manuscripts of liturgies which date earlier than the eighth or ninth centuries. The liturgy of Constantinople, called after Basil and Chrysostom, was not then in existence, nor was the Roman Mass. The sources for our knowledge of the worship of the fourth and fifth centuries are to be found in a so-called liturgy, which is contained in the eighth book of the Apostolic Constitutions. The exact date is uncertain, but I will assume that it was put forth about the year 340. The reason for this assumption is a certain tinge of Semi-Arianism which is to be detected in it, a theology which was then in vogue, whose influence may be said to have culminated at the Council of Antioch in the year 340 or 341. This so-called liturgy is commonly known as the Clementine, and as this is a convenient designation, I shall refer to it by this name in the frequent allusions which will be made to it. It was never used as a liturgy, nor was it intended that it should be; it is to be regarded as a private compilation, containing formulas of prayer which were never adopted into general use. But it also contains ritual directions which were adopted, and therefore serves in many respects as a model and type of the later Eastern liturgies. Other important sources for our knowledge of the worship in the fourth and fifth centuries are the Lectures on the Mysteries by Cyril of Jerusalem, who lived about the time of the Second General Council, in 380; the many allusions to the ritual, and comments on its significance, by Chrysostom, bishop of Antioch, and afterwards patriarch of Constantinople; and lastly, the order of worship given by the so-called Dionysius the Areopagite, who lived in the latter part of the fifth century.

The development of liturgical principles was contemporaneous with an age of doctrinal activity and controversy, with which are connected the names of Apollinaris and Cyril of Alexandria, Nestorius and Eutyches. When the Church grew weary of the incessant discussion, and losing its faith in the reason fell back upon tradition as the highest authority, ritual came to the front, as if a refuge from the distractions of controversy, as if the instincts of the heart might be trusted, when the Christian intellect seemed to have lost itself in a labyrinthine maze of contradiction and confusion.

In order to measure the ritual advance of the fourth and fifth centuries, we must keep in view the worship of the Church in an earlier age, our knowledge of which depends upon a few brief but precious fragments There is an account of the worship at the close of the Apostolic age, or about the beginning of the second century, which is given in the Didache. Another account is contained in the letter of the Roman governor, Pliny, to the Emperor Trajan, which belongs to the earlier years of the second century. Justin Martyr is our next authority, whose time is about the middle of the second century. Nearly two centuries intervene between Justin Martyr and the time of the Clementine liturgy, in which we are dependent upon allusions in various writers, but in which as a whole the ritual of the Church is like an underground stream, collecting its waters from sources which have not yet been fully traced, till at last it emerges a river, which no authority of council or hierarchy can control, which defies tradition and makes its channel at its will and pleasure. We seem to pass abruptly, and as if without preparation, from the simple eucharistic service as described by Justin, to the highly complex and elaborate worship, the stately ceremonial of the age of Constantine.

The word "liturgy" has undergone many changes. According to its etymological use and its earlier application, it meant a public service or function, and the name Leitourgos was sometimes given to the deacon as indicating his peculiar work. In its widest use, when applied to the worship, the liturgy included a public service, consisting of prayer, the reading of Scripture, and preaching. This may be called a homiletic service, whose aim was moral and spiritual edification. All classes of Christians were allowed to be present, — the catechumens, the penitents, and also the outside world of heathens and unbelievers. This service was given in the morning hours. There was also from the first an interior service for the faithful, in which was administered the Lord's Supper, and from which the public were excluded, as were also the penitents and catechumens. Ritual advance or development consisted in expanding the ceremony of the Eucharist, and enhancing its importance, till finally, somewhere after the fifth century, the homiletic worship ceased in the churches, the Eucharist was thrown open to the whole congregation, the communion of the Lord's Supper was practically discontinued, and the people were content to witness the impressive dramatization of the passion of Christ.

The earlier homiletic service now took refuge in the monasteries, where its development continued till it issued in what is known in the Latin Church as the Breviary, which, however intricate it became, still retained its original character as a service of prayer and song, readings from the Scripture, and the word of exhortation. At the Reformation it was reduced into the Morning and Evening Prayer of the English Church.

It is then with the development of the worship which is connected with the Lord's Supper that we are now chiefly concerned. The office of the Eucharist becomes the liturgy, — the only application which the term now has in the Greek and Latin churches. There is among us a popular use of the word "liturgy" to which I may refer in passing, which places a liturgical service in contrast with those forms of worship where the ministrant offers extemporaneous prayers. But this distinction was not made in the ancient Church. In the account of the worship found in the Didache, while formulas of prayer are given for those who may need them, it is also enjoined that the prophets are to be permitted "to give thanks as much as they will." In the liturgy of Justin Martyr no forms of prayer are mentioned, but the president of the congregation is said to pray at considerable length, and according to his ability. Even in the Clementine liturgy, while some forms of prayer are given in full, in other cases only directions are given as to the nature or contents of the prayer to be offered. According to Chrysostom of Antioch, there were three usages in prayer.

There were certain formulas pronounced by the officiant alone; there was the Litany, where the priest or deacon read the petitions and the people responded with *Kyrie Eleison;* and thirdly, there was a method of common prayer, which has since disappeared, in which, after the priest or deacon had declared the object of supplication and bidden the people to pray, there was silence in the church while the prayer was offered, followed by the injunction to pray more fervently, when silence again prevailed. To this custom Chrysostom alluded when he exclaimed, "Great is the power of the congregation." But so late as the sixth century, according to Duchesne, the Leonian Sacramentary, so-called, gives ground for supposing that improvised prayer was still practised, or at least the insertion of phrases prepared by the officiant himself.

I

The earliest accounts of Christian worship connect the Lord's Supper with the Agape, which may be defined as a common evening meal, in imitation of the last supper of Christ with his disciples, when "after supper he took the cup." It is possible not only that this arrangement was followed in the social meeting of the Christian community, but that in individual households the evening meal became a Christian agape, where after supper the head of the household presided, praying over the bread and taking the cup.

Traces of the agape are also to be seen in the Didache, and in the letter of Pliny to Trajan. Let me read here these two accounts, although you are already familiar with them. The service of the Didache is peculiar, and according to a type which has had no historical development.

"Now concerning the Eucharist, thus give thanks: first, concerning the cup. We thank thee, our Father, for the holy vine of David thy servant, which thou hast made known to us through Jesus thy servant; to Thee be the glory forever.

"And concerning the broken bread; We thank thee, our Father, for the life and knowledge which Thou hast made known to us through Jesus, thy servant: to Thee be the glory forever. Just as this broken bread was scattered over the hills and having been gathered together became one, so let Thy church be gathered together from the ends of the earth into Thy Kingdom; for thine is the glory and the power through Jesus Christ forever. But let no one eat or drink of your Eucharist, except those baptised into the Lord's name : for in regard to this the Lord hath said : Give not that which is holy unto the dogs.

"*Now after ye are filled* thus do ye give thanks: We thank thee holy Father for Thy holy name, which thou hast caused to dwell in our hearts; and for the knowledge and faith and immortality, which thou hast made known to us through Jesus thy servant; to Thee be glory forever. Thou Almighty Master did'st create all things for thy name's sake: both food and drink thou did'st give to men for enjoyment, in order that they might give thanks to Thee. But to us Thou hast graciously given spiritual food and drink and eternal life through thy servant. Before all things we thank Thee that thou art powerful: to Thee be glory forever. Remember, Lord, thy Church, to deliver it from every evil and to make it perfect in thy love, and gather it from the four winds, the sanctified, into thy Kingdom which thou hast prepared for it; for thine is the power and the glory forever. Let Grace come and let this world pass away. Hosanna to the Son of David! Whoever is holy let him come: Whoever is not let him repent. Maranatha. Amen. *But permit the prophets to give thanks as much as they will.*"

In Pliny's letter to Trajan, which contains information extracted from the Christians by the Roman governor, it is said that "they were wont to meet on a stated day before sunrise, when they offered a form of invocation to Christ as to a God, binding themselves also by an oath not for any guilty purpose, but not to commit thefts or robberies or adulteries, not to break their word, not to repudiate deposits when called upon. These ceremonies having been gone through, they separated and again met together for the purpose of taking food, — food that is of an ordinary and innocent character."

In consequence of the prohibition of Trajan against secret societies, the agape seems for a while to have been given up, and the Lord's Supper as distinct from the agape was transferred to the morning hours, where it followed the homiletic service. In the next description of Christian worship as contained in Justin Martyr's Apology, about the middle of the second century, the agape is not mentioned, but the Lord's Supper is described as following a service at which the catechumens were present, in which the Scriptures were read, prayers were offered, together with a sermon or exhortation.

There are two descriptions in Justin; they are short, and I will give them both.

"Having ended the prayers we salute one another with a kiss. There is then brought to the president or leader among the brethren bread and a cup of wine mixed with water; and he taking them, gives praise and glory to the Father of the universe through the name of the Son and of the Holy Ghost, and offers thanks at considerable length for our being considered worthy to receive these things. And when he has concluded the prayers and thanksgivings all the people express assent by saying Amen. And when the president has given thanks and the people have expressed assent, those who are called by us deacons give to each of those present to partake of the bread and wine mixed with water, over which the thanksgiving was pronounced and to those who are absent, they carry away a portion."

"And on the day called Sunday, all who live in the city or in the country gather together to one place, and the memoirs of the Apostles or the writings of the prophets are read, as long as time permits; then, when the reader has ceased, the president verbally instructs and exhorts to the imitation of these good things. Then we all rise together and pray, and as we before said, when our prayer is ended, bread and wine and water are brought, and the president in like manner offers prayers and thanksgivings according to his ability and the people assent saying Amen. And there is a distribution to each and a participation of that over which thanks have been given, and to those who are absent a portion is sent by the deacons. And they who are well to do and willing, give what each thinks fit, and what is collected is deposited with the president who succors the orphans and widows and those in sickness or want, the prisoners and the strangers among us."

Justin's account might be made the occasion of extended comment, which the limits of my time and subject will not allow. But the main points to be noted are that the Lord's Supper has been disconnected from the agape, and transferred from the evening to the morning, following the homiletic service, and we may also note the great simplicity of ritual direction and observance.

But the agape had left so deep an impression, and was also so beautiful an expression of Christian love, that it still continued for a time to be observed. Tertullian refers to it as still maintained about the beginning of the third century, and also Clement of Alexandria. Even so late as the Synod of Gangra, in the fourth century, those are reproved who speak disrespectfully of the agape. The rite, however, was doomed to disappear. It was incongruous with the splendid churches that began to be built after the accession of Constantine, and with the solemn and stately formalities of ritual. The relics of it may still exist, as in the Roman Church, in the small cakes called *eulogiæ*, which on certain occasions are distributed to the people; or in the Eastern Church, in the bread which has been blessed in the Prothesis, but not consecrated on the altar, and which, after the divine office is ended, is given to the people who are not deemed worthy of communing in the consecrated elements.

This union of the agape with the Lord's Supper, their subsequent separation, and the final suppression of the agape, have a deep significance for the development of Christian worship, because of the perpetuation in a modified form of one feature of the agape, which constituted one of its most potent charms. The people themselves furnished the material for the evening meal, which thus became, as it were, a kind of alms or offering, in which the poor participated, as well as a manifestation of Christian love. When the agape was discontinued, these contributions, which also included the bread and wine for the eucharistic feast, still continued to be made, but now they were enveloped with a new solemnity, and became in themselves as if meritorious acts of worship. This view, so far as it may be traced, first appears in the writings of Cyprian of Carthage, who seems to have been influenced by Jewish rather than by heathen analogies in his doctrine of oblation and sacrifice. The giving of alms he regards as a religious act, which is placed to one's credit in the records of heaven, and therefore contributes to salvation. The bread and wine brought for the Lord's Supper form what is called the lesser, or "lower oblation." After their consecration they are offered in a "higher oblation" which is presented to God as an acceptable sacrifice. Between the middle of the third century, when Cyprian flourished, and the middle of the fourth century, the date of the Clementine liturgy, this idea had come to prevail widely throughout the Church. In the liturgy as described by Justin, in the account of Christian worship in Pliny's letter to Trajan, or in the Didache, there is no such ritual act mentioned as an oblation. A prayer is made over the bread and the wine, but they are not presented to God as a sacrificial offering. If the later importance attached to the oblation had been assigned to it in this earlier age, it would surely have been mentioned.

Let me give at this point a summary of the Clementine liturgy to which I have referred. It is a picture of the worship as it was conducted in the age of the Emperor Constantius, the son of Constantine, and although somewhat uncertain in its theology, it is reverential toward Christ in the highest degree. It suggests a scene in which preparation is made as for some great solemnity.

"Let the children stand at the reading desk and let a deacon stand by them that they be not disorderly. Let the deacons walk about and watch the men and the women that no tumult be made and that no one nod or whisper or slumber. Let the deacons stand at the doors of the men and the sub-deacons at those of the women, that no one go out nor a door be opened even for one of the faithful at the time of the oblation. But let one of the deacons bring water to wash the hands of the priests, which is a symbol of the purity of the souls that are devoted to God."

When the injunction has been renewed which has ordered the departure of the unbelievers, the penitents, the catechumens, and the hearers, the faithful who remain are exhorted to have nothing against any one, to come in sincerity, and to stand upright before the Lord with fear and trembling to make the offering. "Then let the deacons bring the gifts of bread and wine to the bishop at the altar, and let the presbyters stand at his right hand and at his left, as disciples stand before the Master. But let two of the deacons on each side of the altar hold a fan made of some thin membrane, and let them silently drive away the small animals that fly about, that they come not near the cups. Let the High Priest pray by himself, and let him put on his shining garment, and stand at the altar, and make the sign of the cross upon his forehead with his hand."

At this point begins the *Anaphora* of the Greek liturgy, the *Sursum Corda* of the Latin Mass.

" Let the High Priest say, The grace of Almighty God and the Love of our Lord Jesus Christ and the fellowships of the Holy Ghost be with you all; to which all the people are to respond with one voice, And with thy spirit. The High Priest, Lift up your mind; and the people, We lift it up unto the Lord. The Priest, Let us give thanks unto our Lord God: the people, It is meet and right so to do. Then let the High Priest say, It is very meet and right before all things to sing an hymn to Thee, who art the true God, who art before all beings, from whom the whole family in heaven and earth is named."

Such is the beginning of the long prayer which, without any break, proceeds first to glorify God in his wisdom and goodness and power, next at some length and with much detail to commemorate the creation of the whole world and the goodness which is revealed in its adaptability to man; then the creation of man, the garden of Eden, and the fall are mentioned, and the beginning of the process of redemption. After the leading features of the Old Testament history in the successive stages of the process of redemption have been rehearsed, there follows the Cherubic hymn, as the preparation for the recountal of the story of the Incarnation: "For these things, glory be to Thee, O Lord Almighty, whom innumerable hosts of angels, archangels, thrones, dominions, principalities, authorities and powers with their everlasting armies do adore, saying, together with thousand thousands of angels and ten thousand times ten thousands of angels, saying incessantly and with constant and loud voices, — and let all the people say it with them. Holy, Holy, Holy Lord God of Hosts, heaven and earth are full of thy glory. Glory be to Thee, O Lord most High."

The incidents of the life of Christ are then given as they lead up to his crucifixion, and Christ is glorified in his redeeming work as a preparation for the culmination of the office, in the sacred words of institution of the mystery, when he broke the bread and took the cup.

The language of the prayer now grows more intense and intimate in the intercession which follows for the living and the dead, till it finally concludes with the angelic hymn, the *Gloria in Excelsis*, the preliminary to the distribution of the elements. To the waiting congregation in the attitude of standing, the bishop in turn gives the oblation, saying, "The body of Christ," and the deacon gives the cup with the words, "the blood of Christ, the cup of Life." And while the communion is in process, is said the thirty-fourth Psalm, and a more exquisite Psalm could not have been chosen: " O taste and see that the Lord is gracious. Blessed is the man that trusteth in him."

After the distribution of the elements a shorter prayer follows, and the office concludes with the benediction, which has a tendency, as in other Oriental liturgies, to expand itself, until it has been illustrated anew what the blessing of God may mean.

II

As we study this directory for worship, which is in many respects the model of the later Oriental liturgies as they appeared in the eighth and ninth centuries, it is seen to contain some marked divergencies from the worship of the earlier Church. In the earlier age the Christians came together in a spirit of gratitude to acknowledge a great work which had already been accomplished, some blessing which was continuously bestowed. But here the solemnity centers and culminates in a great act to be performed. Something is to be done by means of which a desired end is to be attained. That act is the oblation of the elements of bread and wine, the offering of them to God after they have been consecrated by the repetition of the words of institution: —

"We offer to Thee," so runs the formula, "Our King and God, according to His constitution this bread and this cup, giving thee thanks through Him that Thou hast thought us worthy to stand before Thee and to sacrifice to Thee; and we beseech Thee that Thou wilt mercifully look down upon these gifts which are here set before Thee, O Thou God, who standest in need of none of our offerings. And do Thou accept them to the honor of Thy Christ, and send down upon this sacrifice thine Holy Spirit . . . that He may show this bread to be the body of Thy Christ and the cup to be the blood of Thy Christ, that those who are partakers thereof may be strengthened for piety and may receive the remission of their sins, may be delivered from the devil and his deceits, may be filled with the Holy Ghost, may be made worthy of Thy Christ, and may obtain eternal life upon Thy reconciliation to them, O Lord God Almighty."

To comment fully upon the significance of this change in Christian worship is here impossible. But I must allude briefly at least to one of its aspects, which constitutes a supreme motive in the development of the ritual which was to follow. A change is taking place in the thought regarding God, by which what is called anthropomorphism is being substituted for the earlier conception of God as a spirit, whom they that worship must worship in spirit and in truth. Of course our language regarding God, from its inherent limits and deficiencies, must always have an anthropomorphic character. In our highest thought, He is infinite intelligence, to whom the universe lies open, and in whom, as in a focus, is concentred the unity and harmony for the sight of which we vainly strive. Because all things are known to Him, we speak of Him in anthropomorphic language as seeing whatever is done, as hearing prayer. We go further, and speak of His eye as fastened upon the children of men, His ear as always open to their supplication. Or again, in the manner of Hebrew prophets and psalmists, we speak of His right hand and His glorious arm. But it is important to guard our thought of God against

the imperfection of language. The eye and the ear
are the most spiritual of the avenues to the human
soul. The sense of smell, of taste, or of touch, are
more closely related to our material bodily organiza-
tion, and lend themselves less easily to the idea of a
spirit. It is of course hard to say in this, as in
everything else about which there is difference of
opinion or practice, just exactly where the line is to
be drawn which separates the higher from the lower;
but we generally know when the line has been
passed. The fathers and writers of the ancient
Church in the first three centuries were making a
desperate struggle to maintain the spiritual conception of Deity as a being who is "without body, parts
or passions," according to the very significant language of the first of the Thirty-nine Articles of the
English Church. But in the fourth century this
spiritual idea of God had begun to yield to an
anthropomorphism which conceived of Deity as existing in bodily form. The change was silent and un-
perceived, accomplished without discussion, and only
acknowledged after the transition had been made.
In the earlier Church there was also sacrifice and
offering, but it was what we call a spiritual offering,
the sacrifice of prayer and thanksgiving, and the
grateful consecration of one's self, after the likeness
of the offering of Christ once for all. It was therefore a momentous change from a spiritual sacrifice
to a physical or material one. From the higher
point of view, it is incongruous to offer to Deity the

physical or material sacrifice, because the whole world is His, and He needs none of these things. There is only one thing which God has not and desires to have, — the grateful love of His children, manifested in obedience to His will. In His mysterious economy, He has left men free to make this offering or not as they choose, while using His love and His power to persuade their choice. This offering of the consecrated will is seen and known to spirit alone. "Speak thou to Him, for He hears thee, and spirit with spirit may meet."

The introduction into the worship of what is called the "higher oblation," as the supreme act of Christian devotion, was accompanied with a change in the popular thought regarding God, of which, however, the traces are slight in the literature of the time. And yet no such change can be accomplished without some external evidence, and somewhere, if we look, we shall find the consciousness of an impending transition. In Christian history, it is those insignificant controversies, as they seem to us, which are obscure or scandalous, and do not seem as if they would repay our laborious investigation, which may be the turning-points on which hinge momentous results.

There was one such controversy in the latter part of the fourth century, not far from the time when this liturgy on which I am commenting was produced. It is known as the Origenistic controversy, and was felt in Alexandria and Constantinople,

Antioch and Jerusalem, those centres of church life, for each of which was afterwards claimed a liturgical interest and activity. I will not stop to describe it; one remark will answer my purpose. The controversy began with a complaint of the monks in Egypt against Origen, because he had written in his books that the Father did not see the Son, or the Son the Father, as with bodily vision. In other words, the communion of the Father and the Son was a spiritual fellowship. To this teaching, which had been almost universal in the Church of the first three centuries, some of the Egyptian monks now made opposition, raising the cry of the woman at the empty sepulchre, "They have taken away my Lord, and I know not where they have laid Him." Such was the beginning of the movement which finally ended in the condemnation of Origen and the discouragement of free inquiry in theology.

III

Again, there is to be noticed in this Clementine liturgy an increase in what may be called ceremonialism, as when the ministrant is directed to put on his shining garment in order to stand before the altar for the oblation. When compared with later liturgies, the amount of ceremony is yet small and rubrical directions are few. But compared with the simplicity of worship of the earlier Church, there has been a great change in this respect, which also marks the introduction of a new motive, controlling the development of the cultus. We shall not find any discussion over this motive in Christian literature, as there was over the theological opinions of the time; it was a silent change, tacitly accepted without being formally announced; it seemed fitting and proper that there should be an increase of form or ceremonial; it was not imposed by the authority of councils, but it spread rapidly from church to church, till it became universal. And yet again it would be strange if somewhere in the literature of the time some writer had not stated the principle which explained the motive of ceremonial, and attempted its defence and justification. There is a passage in the writings of Gregory of Nyssa to which I call your attention as being profoundly significant for the history of ritual development. He lived in the latter part of the fourth century, and was nearly if not quite contemporaneous with the production of the Clementine liturgy. He was a Cappadocian by birth, which means that he shared in the Oriental temperament to a certain extent, and although he had received the benefits of Greek training in the schools of Athens, and was a disciple of Athanasius, yet he had another element in his composition, and never escaped the sensuousness of Oriental influence. In his treatise on the Holy Spirit, Gregory of Nyssa writes as follows:—

"Inasmuch, as men when approaching emperors and potentates for the objects which they wish in some way to obtain from those rulers, do not bring to them their mere petition only, but employ every possible means to induce them to feel pity and favor towards themselves, adopting a humble voice and a kneeling position, clasping their knees, prostrating themselves on the ground, and putting forward to plead for their petition all sorts of pathetic signs to wake that pity, so it is that those who recognize the true Potentate, by whom all things in existence are controlled, when they are supplicating for that which they have at heart, some lowly in spirit because of pitiable conditions in this world, some with their thoughts lifted up because of their eternal mysterious hopes, seeing that they know not how to ask and that their humanity is not capable of displaying any reverence that can reach to the grandeur of that glory, they carry the ceremonial used in the case of men into the service of the Deity. And this is what worship is, that worship I mean which is offered for objects we have at heart along with supplication and humiliation."

Comment upon this passage is hardly necessary. The anthropomorphic conception of God is here seen as tending toward the acceptance of the Roman emperor, after he had assumed the arbitrary character of an Oriental despot, as the standard by which to adjust the formal manner of approaching God. The etiquette of an imperial court determines the external aspect of Christian worship. Since Deity is conceived as holding a reception on earth, there must be the same splendor of surroundings, the same regulations of attitude on the part of those who approach, while officials who represent or guard his presence must be clothed with becoming splendor in order to represent the dignity of the monarch dwelling in some remoter grandeur; whose secret, glorious shrine so intimidates and awes the worshipper that he loses his power of utterance, and must be content with the physical signs of abject humility and destitution. There may have been an educational influence in such a dramatization of piety towards God, and it was something after all that human souls, shut out from the vision or sympathy of the earthly king, were still able at their will to enter the presence of the King of kings. It may have done something also to check the exercise of arbitrary power in the earthly sovereign, at a time when there was no other check, that he should be represented in Christian worship as dwarfed by the majesty of the Eternal Potentate. But one also recalls the words of Christ: "I say not unto you that I will pray the Father for you, for the Father Himself loveth you." When the disciples asked how they were to pray, the answer was given, "When ye pray, say, Our Father." It was the heathens who thought to be heard by much speaking. But in the dramatization of the soul's relations with God, there is a danger of formality hardly compatible with the worship which is in spirit and in truth.

IV

There is one other peculiarity about the Clementine liturgy which is so important as to demand our special attention. The subject with which it is related is difficult and obscure, leading us to a field of inquiry which has not yet been thoroughly explored.

It is a prominent feature of this liturgy that not only in the eucharistic prayer given in the eighth book of the Apostolic Constitutions, but also found in the liturgical sketch given in the seventh book, there is an emphatic and beautiful commemoration of nature, external nature and this visible world. The story of the creation is rehearsed in detail, and the beauty of the kosmos is ackowledged in eloquent language. God is praised for having beautified the world, and for our comfort rendered it illustrious with sun and moon and choir of stars which forever praise His glorious majesty. The water is commemorated also for drink and for cleansing, the air for respiration and for sound, the fire for our consolation in cold and darkness, the navigable ocean, and the land with the animal creation, the sweet-smelling and healing herbs, the fruits of the earth, the order of the seasons, the courses of the clouds, and the winds which blow when commanded by God. For all these things praise is given to Him in the eucharistic prayer, as though it formed an indispensable element in worship to acknowledge the beauty, the glory, and especially the goodness of the visible world of external nature.

The commemoration of external nature forms a part of every Eastern liturgy. Cyril of Jerusalem, who lived in the later part of the fourth century, speaks of it as if an indispensable element to a true eucharist. After the *Anaphora*, as it is called, with which the divine office begins, Cyril remarks that the next step is to commemorate the creation: "We make mention of heaven and earth and sea; of sun and moon; of stars, and all the creation rational and irrational, visible and invisible." So also Dionysius the Areopagite, who lived at the close of the fifth century, in his outline of the eucharistic office, makes the Hierarch celebrate the works of God before proceeding to consecrate the divine gifts. In the words of Dionysius, or attributed to him: —

"The commemoration of Thy gifts, O Lord, exceeds the power of mind or speech or thought; nor can human lips or minds glorify Thee as Thou art worthy to be praised. For by Thy word the heavens were made, and by the breath of Thy mouth all the supernal powers, all the lights which are in the firmament, sun and moon, the sea and the dry land, and whatever in them is. Things which have no voice by their silence, and those endowed with speech, praise Thee perpetually through word and song, because Thou art by nature good, and in Thy incomprehensible essence above all praise. This visible creation related to the senses praises Thee, O Lord, as well as that higher intellectual world above the conditions of sensuous perception. Heaven and earth glorify Thee; sea and air proclaim Thee; the sun in his course praises Thee; the moon in its changes venerates Thee. Troops of archangels and hosts of angels, powers elevated above the world and above all human faculty, send their benedictions to Thy throne, — sweet songs and pure, free from all earthly strain; joining all in one eternal hymn of praise, — 'Holy, Holy, Holy.'"

Such was the way in which the Oriental Church met and satisfied the deep unquenchable instinct which in earlier ages had given birth to the nature-religions, and had generated the worship of sun and moon and stars. This worship the Church prohibited and overcame, resisting the fascination which it exerted. How deep and potent its charm for the Oriental mind is seen in the patriarch Job's cry for forgiveness, if ever he had been tempted to kiss his hand to the moon riding in her beauty.

But the commemoration of nature is not to be found in the Latin or Western liturgies, nor in the Sarum Use in England. While it is a most characteristic feature of Oriental liturgies, its absence from Occidental worship is also deeply characteristic of the Western civilization. The Western world has never felt the charm of nature as it has been felt in the East. Rather has it been called to resist and conquer nature, to subdue the powers of nature to the will and service of man. According to the Oriental interpretation of the miracle, it is wrought by sympathy with nature; according to the Occidental interpretation, the miracle is essentially a violation of the laws of nature, wherein lies its influence upon the elevation of human life and the development of personality.

It should be said, however, that the Latin Church has found a place, though a subordinate one, for the recognition of this view of nature, by incorporating in the Breviary the Benedicite, or the Song of the Three Children, which begins with the words, "O all ye works of the Lord, bless ye the Lord, praise Him and magnify Him forever." The English church also adopted the Benedicite as one of the Canticles in the office of Morning Prayer; retaining it there despite the objections of the Puritans, who requested that some Psalm or Scripture hymn be substituted for it. It is possible that the Puritan dislike of the Benedicite had some deeper root than the circumstance of its being taken from the Apocrypha.

But there is a further aspect of this subject to which we must now turn. It is in the environment of the Oriental Church that we must seek the explanation of its emphatic insistence upon the natural order as good, and as if alive and choral with the worship of God. Much more than in Western Europe had the influence been felt there of the great nature religions which prevailed till the coming of Christ. In Syria and in Egypt more particularly was the Catholic Church confronted with both the principle and the practice. If these worships had seemed to decline, yet there came to them a revival in the second century, when missionaries and priestesses of Isis, or of the Syrian mother, went forth throughout the empire to propagate their ancient cults. We know that they became popular, that they were eagerly received, the mysteries of Mithras in particular finding many and ardent votaries.

This missionary movement on the part of the old nature religions came at the close of a long *régime*, which Plato had initiated when he taught that matter was evil, that man was superior to nature, and had called man to the knowledge of himself as his highest study. Plato had no taste for the old mythologies which deified the forces of nature, but rather regarded them as immoral. Socrates had been put to death because he no longer believed in them. When Christianity came into the world, it almost seemed as if the nature worships were dead or dying. Nature no longer appealed to man as instinct with a divine life, or as worthy of worship. On the contrary, the Gnostics of the second century in their speculative systems denounced the natural order as evil, as unworthy of creation by God. They regarded it rather as the work of some evil or incompetent being, who was called the world-maker as distinct from the true and highest God. When the nature religions began to revive and reassert their old charm in the second century, Christian apologists had attacked them with all the power of satire and ridicule at their command. It is not impossible that Tertullian, before he entered the Catholic Church, may have been influenced by their teaching; and the same may be true of Justin Martyr, though in less degree. But even though Tertullian fought the nature worships with bitterness and vehemence, he also retained, even as a Montanist, traces of their inherent principle in his thought. In his doctrine of the magical efficacy of water and its latent spiritual potency, in his insistence on the sacredness of the flesh and the eternal permanence of the human form, in his doctrine of the spiritual efficacy of physical acts, may be seen the ancient conception of the relation between body and soul, between the material and the spiritual, which prevailed before Plato arose.

It was in the fourth century, in the latter part of the fourth century, the age of the Cappadocians and of Cyril of Alexandria, that an influence born of the reverence for physical nature began to tell most powerfully upon Christian thought and practice. This was also the age when the principles were reached which were to mould the worship of the Catholic Church. The line which divides Athanasius and the Nicene theology from the later theology, which came into vogue in the Oriental Church, is profoundly significant. Athanasius was the culmination of the Anti-Nicene age, not the founder of a new theology. We shall not understand the history of the ancient Church until we make the distinction sharp and clear that Athanasius belongs to the school of Origen, whatever departures from his teaching he may have made, while Cyril of Alexandria is the antagonist of the Origenistic principles, and helped prepare the way for his further condemnation. Cyril introduced into theology a physical material principle, by which the distinction between spirit and body was weakened and neutralized. He was seeking for some law by which the world of matter should be brought into organic relationship with spirit, by which matter and spirit should be fused into some higher form of organic life, by which matter should minister to the spiritual life. When this tendency came to prevail, as it did after the fifth century, is it any wonder that Origen should have again become the type and embodiment of all that was most false or obnoxious! Origen, it must be admitted, had gone too far; he had come very near conceding that the natural order was evil; he saw evil in external nature, and he drew the inference that man was placed in this world to expiate the sins of a former existence, that the human body was a prison-house in which the soul was confined.

It is outside of my province to attempt to show how this new motive, originating in an Oriental source, modified Christian doctrine. Hitherto the leading direction in theology had been the Platonic Philosophy. Now it became an Egyptian mysteriosophy, which, combined with kindred tendencies in the remoter Syria of the East, and planting itself upon a modified conception of the Incarnation, developed into the Oriental theology which commingles nature and spirit in organic fashion, and found its expression in Oriental worship. It is only with the latter that I am here concerned.

The recovery of the truth which had been endangered in the Church of the first three centuries, that the "world is good," that there is a divine life in nature, and that the natural order has been ordained for the service of man by a beneficent Creator, marks the greatest movement in the history of ritual development. But this remark refers mainly to the Eastern Church. The Latin Church in the West did not feel its influence until a later age, when it was too late for its incorporation into the Latin Mass. In the Eastern Church it was not only introduced into the liturgies, but it gave rise to a peculiar religious philosophy or theosophy, which pervaded every part of the cultus, and gave to it unity and coherence. So profoundly has the Eastern Church been influenced by this new motive, springing from the conviction that the natural order is good, and that of this order humanity forms a constituent part, that it rapidly became oblivious of the literature and life of the Church of the first three centuries, as if it were almost a barren and empty world. It was as if the Church began a new career in the fourth century with Basil of Cæsarea, Cyril of Jerusalem, Cyril of Alexandria. In the Russian Church to-day, it was true only a few years ago, there was no translation of any church father earlier than St. Basil. Origen has been dismissed and forgotten as an evil dream, even Athanasius is not so great a name as his successor Cyril of Alexandria, and no influence has been greater than that of Cyril of Jerusalem.

It was indeed an important gain for the cause of truth when the conviction of the sacredness of the natural order was achieved. For the foundation of revealed theology must be laid deep in natural theology. If the world were to be regarded as evil, it would not have been very long before faith in the goodness of God would have perished. Humanity is too weak to sustain its hope, when it cannot see the love of the eternal Father revealed in the visible creation. In the age, however, when this conviction began to prevail, that the world is good and closely related to the spiritual life, there was no longer any scientific study of nature. What the Catholic Church from the fourth century knew about nature may be seen in a little treatise of St. Basil, called the "Hexameron," which was widely read, and which contained a comment on the six days of the creation. It may be contrasted with Origen's allegorical treatment of the first chapter of Genesis, where facts are submerged in ideas, and where his obnoxious conception of the body as a prison-house of the soul was unfortunately advanced.

V

But now there were grave dangers connected with this doctrine of the divine life in nature, which were not slow in appearing. There was danger of a relapse into the earlier Greek attitude before Socrates, when man was conceived as part of the natural order, when there was no consciousness of personality as higher than nature, — the blissful unconsciousness, as it has been called, of that antagonism between man and natural law, out of which there has grown up in Western Christendom the higher civilization.

The doctrine of the Divine immanence was also in danger of a one-sided perversion. In the earlier Church the divine mind had been regarded as immanent in the human reason. But that conception was now yielding to the idea that the divine immanence was chiefly to be sought in the physical or natural order. The great bishop Theodore of Mopsuestia contended for the divine immanence in the *conscience* as that faculty of the soul where the human and divine most closely intermingled; but his teaching was of no avail. When we study the writings of Gregory of Nyssa or of Dionysius the Areopagite, whose thought is saturated with idea of the divine immanence, both of whom profoundly influenced the development of the cultus, it is an indwelling of the Deity in the physical order upon which the stress is laid rather than in the reason or the conscience. There was danger, therefore, that the Christian cultus would come to resemble the ancient Greek Mysteries, of which Aristotle had said "that their object was not to teach anything, but to produce an impression on the religious feelings and imagination."

The conviction of the sacredness of external nature which filled the Eastern Church in the latter part of the fourth century with a new enthusiasm, gave rise to the necessity for seeking some organic tie between the spiritual life in man and the latent potentiality of matter. The tendency was now to connect most closely body and soul, matter and spirit, natural and spiritual law. Already the germs were at hand for development in the cultus, in the symbol of water in baptism, the chrism in confirmation, the laying on of hands in ordination, and above all, the elements of bread and wine in the Eucharist. Cyril of Alexandria announced the principle of transmutation, transelementation, or transubstantiation, by which matter passes over into spiritual force, when, in speaking of the water of baptism, he declared that "by the power of the Holy Ghost the water perceived by the senses is metamorphosed into a certain divine and ineffable power." Cyril of Jerusalem and Gregory of Nyssa speak in a similar way of the action of the Holy Spirit upon the elements of bread and wine, by which they are metamorphosed into the body and the blood of Christ. The passage of Scripture upon which they chiefly rested in making the Holy Ghost the bond of unity between the physical and the spiritual, was found in the Mosaic account of the creation, where the Spirit of God is said to have brooded upon the face of the waters. Those words became almost the *locus classicus* in defending or expounding the sacramental mysteries. This word Mysteries, by which the Eastern Church designated the sacraments, may then be defined as a conjunction of the physical with the spiritual, operated by the action of the Holy Ghost. In every Greek liturgy the invocation of the Holy Ghost becomes the essential condition for the transmutation of the physical elements of bread and wine into food for the immortal soul. I can only here allude to the circumstance that this invocation of the Holy Ghost is wanting in the Roman liturgy. It has not merely dropped out; it never was there. In the Latin Mass, it is the enumeration of the words of Institution by the priestly ministrant that accomplishes the transmutation. From the point of view of the Greek Church, if it were strictly construed, the Roman sacrament of the altar is lacking in an element which is vital and indispensable.

This nature philosophy, which began to prevail in the latter part of the fourth century, found its strongest illustration and support in the doctrine of the Incarnation, which was strongly advocated by Cyril of Alexandria. In the thought of Cyril, the deepest importance attached to the body of Christ, as if therein were a common meeting-place of nature and spirit, as though the body of Christ were endowed with spiritual and supernatural power. Hence the essence of the Incarnation now came to be identified with the act of the miraculous conception of Christ, as if God and nature found their supreme point of conjunction in the womb of the Virgin, in order to the accomplishment of the transcendent work of divine revelation. An act of such supreme significance in itself, whose principle also covered the whole range of mysteriosophy, necessarily found recognition in the ritual, where the Virgin Mother was associated with its most solemn moment, — the time of the oblation, — as if her commemoration formed an integral part in the right performance of the mystery of the altar. The earlier view of the Incarnation, while accepting the miraculous birth as its unique initiation, had placed the emphasis, however, in the mind and teaching, the character and the life of Christ, as reflecting the inmost life of God. But from the end of the fourth century it was the body of Christ, rather than the spirit of Christ, which elicited the popular reverence; it was the sacrifice of the body, rather than of the will, which constituted the highest feature of divine atoning love. Along with this estimate of the body of Christ came the worship also of the bodies of the saints and martyrs, till in the adoration of physical relics, whether of Christ or Mary or the saints, the fervors of Christian devotion found their most intense and rapt expression.

VI

I have now only a moment left in which to allude to that strange mysterious personality who once tabernacled in the flesh, as we must believe, but concerning whom we know little more. The preparation for ritual development seemed to have been completed when Dionysius the Areopagite appeared, — a most profound religious thinker, a most beautiful spirit, whose soul was alive with love toward higher things, and burning with the flames of devotion, a man without a country, without beginning or end of days, the essence of whose being was so identified with his thought that all except his thought has perished. The first allusion to his books was made in the year 533, from which it is inferred that his time was the latter part of the fifth century. In his writings, the nature philosophy found fuller expression and a beautiful exposition. He brought together the teaching of the ancient Neoplatonism, modified as it had been by Egyptian influence and the purest Christian feeling. At the moment of the decline of the old civilization, he lighted up the gloom of the closing day with an unearthly light, which softened its dark and evil memories with its subdued reflection. He dwelt mainly on the good in the world and in man. In human sinfulness he saw mainly a weakness which attracted the divine compassion. He looked upon this world as some dim reflection, some feeble reproduction of a higher and more beautiful world, anticipating Swedenborg in his doctrine of a correspondence between things natural and supernatural, earthly and heavenly, human and divine. He dwelt much upon angels and archangels, and all the hosts of heaven, constituting them into a hierarchy of which the earthly hierarchy, its ministrants and its sacraments, was but a continuation, a ladder as it were let down from heaven, on which angels were ascending and descending. Physical objects became religious symbols, because they were a divinely given alphabet for spelling out eternal realities. A supernatural coloring was in consequence thrown about the ritual, so that every slightest act became significant of some spiritual meaning. Under his magic touch a new impulse was given to ritual development, the extent of which or the depth of which in the East and in the West can hardly be exaggerated.

It is difficult to estimate the exact nature of this influence, but, at least, it was of a twofold kind, one aspect of which neutralized or negatived the other. He seems at times so to identify the symbol with the thing signified, after the cruder fashion of an earlier age, that the symbol appears to become in itself an indispensable agency for man's salvation. But he also held that while God revealed Himself through the external sign, yet there was also in the symbol a concealment, as if by a veil, of his glory and his power.

Dionysius also seems to have had an exoteric faith in harmony with the Catholic Church, which was expressed in symbol and ritual for the common people, while for the clergy, the monks and enlightened souls, there was reserved a more direct approach to God, which no longer depended upon material media. In the description which he has left us of the ritual of the altar, as performed in his time and possibly by himself, there is little change or advance as compared with the order of the Clementine liturgy, beyond the introduction of the incense: —

"The hierarch having finished his prayer by the altar, begins by incensing it, and then makes the circuit of the holy building. Returning to the altar he begins to chant the psalms, all the ecclesiastical orders joining with him in the sacred psalmody. After this, the lesson from Holy Scripture is read by the minister; and when it is ended, the Catechumens, together with the penitents and those possessed, are ordered to depart from the sacred enclosure, those only remaining who are worthy of the sight and the communion of the sacred mysteries. Of the lower ranks of the ministry, some are standing near the closed doors of the sanctuary, while others perform some functions pertaining to their order. Those who hold the highest place among the deacons (leitourgoi) assist the priests in bringing to the altar the sacred bread and the cup of blessing, chanting at the same time, together with the whole assembly, the universal hymn of praise. Then the divine hierarch completes the sacred prayers and announces to all the peace; and when they have made the mutual salutation, then follows the mystic recital of the names inscribed in the holy diptycha. The hierarch and priests having washed their hands, the hierarch stands at the middle of the holy altar surrounded by those chosen from among the deacons, together with the priests. After the hierarch has celebrated the marvellous works of God, he consecrates the divine mysteries, and offers to the view the things celebrated beneath the symbols reverently exhibited. When he has thus exposed to view the gifts of divine power, he partakes of the communion himself and then invites the others; and when he has received and given to others the divine communion, he closes with a sacred act of thanksgiving. *But while the common people have seen the mysteries under the veil of the symbol, he himself is led, always by the Holy Spirit, through spiritual contemplation, and as becomes a hierarch, to the intellectual types of the ceremonial in their original purity.*"

The chief significance of this account lies, as I think, in its closing words, which are strangely prophetic, as if he were writing better than he knew. Wherever his influence was felt, it carried with it a double tendency; it led to increased devotion toward ritual observance, and it also relaxed the tie which bound the soul in bondage to the material symbol. It affected Thomas Aquinas and all the scholastic theologians of his age, giving also to the worship of the Latin Church a charm which it could never have originated. But it also inspired a Dante, and the mystic reformers who prepared the way for the Reformation, for the restoration of that spiritual worship which is now the common heritage and not the possession of a few, — a worship in which we are taught that even now we know God and see Him as He is, by means of faith, while yet we wait for a perfect fruition and bliss in the glory to be revealed. From this point of view the ritual of the ancient Church carried in it the seeds of its dissolution. It was rejected by the Protestant churches, but not until all that it contained of beautiful or good or true had been taken up by other agencies with richer and more ample possibilities of development.

III

THE GREEK LITURGIES

BY THE REV. EGBERT C. SMYTH, D.D.

Professor of Church History, Andover Theological Seminary, Andover, Mass.

THE GREEK LITURGIES

THE phrase "Greek liturgies," by which the topic on which I am asked to speak to you has been expressed, can be variously understood. It may apply to the rites of the Greek or Oriental Church, including not merely present uses but forms or types which have been earlier observed by churches now in its communion; or it may cover all liturgies written in Greek; or it may designate Eastern liturgies as distinguished from Western, inclusive of those which exist in other languages than the Greek, in so far as these are regarded as versions or derivatives, or as marked by Greek characteristics.

The attempt would be inadmissible, within the limits of this address, to notice individually the various distinguishable Greek liturgies, and wholly impracticable to include those in other languages more or less closely connected with them. I could present little more than what, in the present condition of liturgical investigation, must be at best an imperfect enumeration, and one that would leave only a confused impression. My aim will be a practical one, — the suggestion of a method of study, and of some incentives to it. For that acquaintance with the ancient rites which it is desirable that all whose office it is to conduct public worship should secure, and for that personal benefit which familiarity with them may bring in many ways and in rich measures, it is best to concentrate attention upon the great liturgies — first upon the liturgy of St. James, then upon that of St. Mark, then on the Byzantine rite (the so-called liturgy of St. Chrysostom, with that of St. Basil), in use to-day in many languages, and especially interesting because of this relation to the religious thought and life of so very great a number of disciples of our common Lord. If one desires to go further, he will naturally connect with the Syrian and Byzantine rites the Armenian liturgy, and with the Alexandrian the Coptic and Abyssinian. He will include also the Persian or Nestorian rite, and finally the Mozarabic and Gallican liturgies. In all this range of study the acquaintance of which I am now speaking will be with the accepted texts, if not in the originals (which for most of us, in several instances, would be, perhaps, impracticable), at any rate through such scholarly translations as are now available. This amount of reading could be done by every minister in his preparatory courses. And, if nothing more were attempted, important advantages would be gained. But something more, even from a purely practical point of view, is desirable, may I not say incumbent.

If I may speak from my own experience, the mere

reading of the leading liturgies, those which are translated, for instance, into English in a volume of the Ante-Nicene Library, whether in this rendering or in the original, leaves upon the mind, with a measure of enrichment and stimulus, an almost painful sense of a lack of clear and definite distinction and division, of order, proportion, and progress. We find ourselves in a strange land; the tones and accents we catch are unfamiliar. All this, apart from much that may be positively offensive from its apparent formalism, or its tendency to superstition, or its affinity with a magical interpretation of the spiritual and holy sacraments of our faith, or from the presence of corruptions of the truth and simplicity of the gospel.

For the best use, therefore, — and this because necessary to their true understanding, — for the best use of these developed, aggregated, compounded, and changed liturgies, these composites of many rites and many successions of religious conception and life, we need pre-eminently to study them by a right method. This means that we must deal with them as historical formations. Such a study is, in many respects, at present beyond the pursuit of any but special liturgical scholars. It is not yet brought up to the standards and requirements of modern historical scholarship. The criticism of texts, for instance, — their collection, publication, even their examination and collation, — demands much patient labor beyond that already expended. Liturgics is, it may fairly be said, and with very high appreciation of what has been achieved,— without this we should not have even the urgent pressure of a sense of our ignorance, — liturgics is, at present, the least developed department of theological science. So much especially needs to be done in order to the understanding of the genesis and growth of liturgies, that a complete or thorough scholarly discussion of them is not yet possible. Yet we may not let the best be the enemy of the good. We may, by a simple and practicable method, gain very much light upon the structure of these liturgies, and obtain some true insight into their significance and value. For such a fruitful study the revision of Mr. Hammond's helpful volume on "Eastern and Western Liturgies," now in course of publication by Mr. Brightman, of Oxford, through the Clarendon Press, is an invaluable aid. The first volume, the only one yet published, is limited to Eastern liturgies, and is confined to texts and bibliographical and other critical aids. It may be hoped that in the second volume the author will be able to make some systematic presentation of the genesis and literary dependence and inter-relations of the liturgies which he has classified in groups or families.

What, as already stated, I will now attempt, and this only tentatively and provisionally, is the suggestion of a method of approach to the greater liturgies, serviceable to their understanding and personal use; and then, so far as time permits, the presentation of some remarks on their value.

The earliest account which has come down to us of an order of worship is from Justin Martyr, writing about the middle of the second century.

I notice this testimony, and one which will follow, for their peculiar helpfulness to an understanding of the later developments. The simpler uses guide us when we come to the more complex. This advantage will excuse, I trust, my recalling what may already have been considered in the preceding lecture (of which I have seen no report), or which may be otherwise quite familiar.

Justin's account implies distinct services, or composite parts of one service. In one chapter of his first "Apology" he describes the baptismal rite. In another, the usual order of worship at the Sunday gatherings. Each of these is followed by the communion. We see here quite distinctly defined the later distinction between what is called the *Anaphora*, or Holy Communion, and the Proanaphoral or antecedent part. We have a suggestion also of what appears, from Cyril's "Catecheses," to have been the practice in Jerusalem two centuries later, namely, the substitution, under appropriate conditions, of the baptismal service for the ordinary more didactic observance which preceded the communion.

The essential parts of each order are substantially indicated. The baptismal portion is least described, noticeably so when compared with a representation half a century later. We observe, however, the two actions described in this subsequent account, — the ceremony at the water, or the administration of the rite, and the bringing of the baptized into the church or place of assembly, to join in the prayers of the brotherhood and in the communion.

Turning our attention to the other and ordinary Sunday service, including the eucharistic, we find this order:

1. The reading of Scripture, specified as "the memoirs of the Apostles, or the writings of the prophets." This continued as long as time permitted.

2. Instruction and exhortation by the προεστώς, or president.

3. Prayers. This included intercession for all the assembled "brethren," and "for all others in every place, that we may be counted worthy, now that we have learned the truth, by our works also to be found good citizens and keepers of the commandments, so that we may be saved with an everlasting salvation."

These prayers are described as earnest or intense. They were marked with power. They were offered not only at the ordinary Sunday morning service, but in connection with the baptismal, and contained distinct petitions for those now to participate in their first communion.

Probably the prayers already included the ἐξομολόγησις, or confession of sin, which became a permanent part of the Proanaphoral.

They are characterized as "common prayers." The phrase does not require the supposition of written or wholly fixed formulas. Yet this portion of the service would naturally be early elaborated, though without uniformity. One of the richest and most instructive portions of later liturgies is the so-called bidding-prayers. The ancient Church was an interceding church.

4. The kiss of peace. "Having ended the prayers, we salute one another with a kiss." This "seal of prayer," as Tertullian calls it, this sign of mutual forgiveness, peace, and unity, is recognized in all ancient liturgies, Western as well as Eastern. Its literal observance has now generally disappeared. It survives, however, in symbolic forms, and still more impressively in the injunctions, exhortations, and prayers belonging to all developed or even thoughtful communion services, whether written or unwritten, which emphasize forgiveness, mutual charity, brotherly love, as the indispensable prerequisites of fellowship with Him who is our peace, and its giver, and who has left to his disciples his repeated, emphasized, and sacred commandment that they love one another.

The position of the sign of this love in Justin's account of the early order is noticeable. It belongs to the Proanaphora, or at least to the portion of the service which precedes the communion. This, substantially, is the place assigned it in the earliest Western forms, as well as in all the Eastern. It is so in the Gallican liturgy and in the Mozarabic, — the latter, I may be permitted to say in passing, one of the richest of all. In the existing Roman order, in other closely related Western forms of perhaps the fifth or subsequent centuries, its position is later in the service, being a part of the portion pertaining to the immediate administration of the sacrament. Even here it precedes reception. Not unlikely the Gallican and Spanish customs reflect a use which once obtained at Rome also, this church having departed in this respect, as in others, from some tokens of its earliest catholicity.

5. The presentation of the elements, bread and wine and water, or wine mixed with water, the later offertory, and also the Great Entrance, so magnified and to some so magnificent in the developed Oriental rituals.

6. The eucharistic prayer,—further described as an offering by the προεστώς, to the extent of his ability, of prayers and thanksgiving, of praise and glory to the Father of the universe, through the name of the Son and the Holy Ghost, and of thanks that we are counted worthy to receive these gifts.

7. The response from the people, Amen.

8. The distribution by the deacons to the communicants, not forgetting the absent, of the bread and wine and water for which thanks had been rendered.

9. Communion.

Elsewhere, in the same "Apology," Justin refers to the use of hymns, and of solemn prayers, characterized by a certain dignity and splendor.

There can be no question that Justin describes a

service such as existed at Rome. This itself implies, on the Irenæan principle of the necessarily representative character of its church, a wide observance. Justin's own knowledge of the East points in the same direction, especially in connection with his evident aim to speak for Christians in general, and his explicit declaration in one of his reports that he is describing the worship of "all who live in cities or in the country."

The traces of freedom in the forms of worship are evident in the account. We have an outline, not a prescribed order. The bishop or celebrant composed, or poured out, if he chose, his own prayers. What the Abbé Duchesne happily calls the liturgy of the Spirit — a phrase I do not employ with the least intimation that such a liturgy exists alone in unwritten forms — was still present in the prayers that arose as the Holy Spirit, active in those who led and in those who joined in them, gave a measure of expression and sympathy which doubtless at times transcended in power anything attainable where all is prescribed. Yet we must admit that there are other demands and methods. The formation of prayers which, through sustained dignity and fit expression of the great common needs and of corresponding ministries of divine condescension and redeeming love, won a right to permanent use, was already in progress. It is plainly intimated in Justin's words: "With gratitude to Him to offer thanks by pomps and hymns" — stately and solemn prayers and rhythmical forms of devotion — "for our creation, and all the means of health, and for the various qualities of the different kinds of things, and for the changes of the seasons," the very substance of a portion of the great liturgies. It appears yet earlier in the prayer at the close of Clement's Epistle. Had it not long before begun, — in ancient Scriptures, in the worship of the synagogues, in Apostolic benedictions, in the prayer taught His disciples by our Lord? It is a poor freedom that cannot use the best.

With this general order or type of service derived from Justin's account in mind, we come to another document composed about half a century later, — the so-called "Canons of Hippolytus."[1] For our subject, and in some other respects, they are the most important recovery of recent criticism. Their authorship is not known. Some suppose that they proceeded from an ecclesiastical council, the least likely suggestion. Others attribute them to Hippolytus, whose name they bear. Mr. Headlam's suggestion is valuable, that they are an early composition of this copious author. On the whole, this is a probable view. The

---

[1] *Texte und Untersuchungen zur Geschichte der Altchristlichen Literatur* von Oscar von Gebhardt und Adolf Harnack. VI. Band. Heft 4. *Die Aeltesten Quellen des Orientalischen Kirchenrechts.* Erstes Buch *Die Canones Hippolyti* von Dr. Phil. Hans Achelis. Leipzig, J. C. Hinrichs'sche Buchhandlung, 1891. Rev. A. C. Headlam, B.D., Fellow of All Souls College, Oxford, has given an admirable account of these Canons in "The Guardian," Feb. 12, May 6, June 24, 1896, to which I am much indebted. I have followed mostly Mr. H.'s translations, so far as available. Mr. Brightman, as well as Mr. H., appreciates the importance of these Canons, and of Dr. Achelis's investigations. See *Liturgies, Eastern and Western*, vol. i. pp. xix-xxiv.

resort to an Anonymous is a confession of ignorance beyond what is absolutely required. In any event their date — not later than early in the third century — is reasonably clear, and we may assume that they are of Roman origin. What has been said of the representative significance of this fact still holds. They certainly found acceptance far away from Rome. They probably gave definite expression to what existed widely in practice or desire, and then they helped to fix and extend, in observance and theory, what had been so clearly formulated. They continue the pathway of development opened to our view in Justin's testimony, and which is broadened by the Coptic and the Æthiopic "Ordinances" and the "Apostolic Constitutions," and the liturgical notices in Cyril's "Catecheses" and Chrysostom's "Homilies," and which issues in the well-known liturgies of St. James, St. Mark, St. Chrysostom, and the Syrian, Egyptian, Persian, Byzantine rites.

It is of advantage, for our present object, still to keep to the simpler construction and forms presented in these " Canons."

They are instructive in their suggestion of the variety of the Christian services. The great liturgies are communion services. They have given to the word "liturgy" this specific sense, the order of the Mass or Eucharist. This celebration was from the beginning, doubtless, the centre and culmination of the Christian worship. All liturgical wisdom, fervor, devotion, conspired to its enrichment and development. Every other service found in it, or in connection with it, expression and power,— Lections, Homily, Psalmody, Charity, even ecclesiastical discipline and the orders of the clergy and the forms of spiritual training and the impulses and consecrations of an aggressive and sometimes contentious piety. Yet as we read the greater liturgies, and perhaps run over the many titles of others, the sacramental type becomes to our thought not only predominant but exclusive. We may be misled, also, by the fact that so many liturgies are simply *Anaphoras* in appearance,— that is, strictly sacramental prayers and rites, not realizing that to all these, in their varieties, belongs some Proanaphoral portion, not repeated, because common to many. We need to learn how rich a variety of services early appeared, and of what practical worth, and then to find in the later and technically denominated liturgies, deposits or appropriations from these distinguishable forms.

The "Canons of Hippolytus" are of much help here. Through them, in connection with other well-known sources, we gain a clearer understanding, not only of how manifold a ministration there was of sympathy and charity, but of Scriptural instruction, and of aids and utterances of devotion. There was a regular Sunday Agape, probably, early developed, — a second service, for I quite agree with Mr. Headlam in thinking that the great eucharistic service was probably held in the morning. There were also Agapae for the poor and for widows, and in memory of the departed. At these Agapae — held in private houses and on week days as well as on Sundays and in the place of common assembly — there was an opening prayer, followed by the breaking of the loaf and participation, the bread of exorcism, the sign and pledge of unity, offerings of thanksgiving and special intercession, remembrance of the departed, the singing or recital of psalms, probably Scripture lessons or the reading of other writings. Allusion is made to preaching by the bishop, sitting, and it is added naïvely that " when he thus sermonizes others will have profit, nor will it be without profit for himself." Daily services in the churches are also mentioned, although it is implied that they were not everywhere established.

Specially interesting to us is the recognition of a service for the Word of God, — *conventus propter verbum Dei*, — a Biblical and expository lecture, attendance upon which is urged upon all. Business men are somewhat particularly exhorted to be present, that they may strenuously expel hatred of an enemy. Those who can read, the educated especially, should attend. The Lord is present in the place where His majesty is thus brought to remembrance, and the Spirit descends upon the assembly and pours out His grace upon all.

But I may not linger upon these details; they are here relevant only to correct any misunderstanding of the strictly liturgical services, and also for the suggestion of their contribution to these. For instance, as has been pointed out by Mr. Headlam: "The funeral banquet in memory of the departed, whether at the time of death or on the anniversary of the death, was a custom taken over from heathen surroundings; to this was added the definitely Christian ceremony of the Eucharist; gradually the heathen element was allowed to fall into disuse, and the purely Christian portion of the commemoration survived." It survived in one of the richest and most impressive portions of the liturgies, the Great Intercession for quick and dead, in which, in the grandest sense, the Church realized its spiritual unity.

Looking now more closely to these Canons for what they reveal of that order of service which underlies the Liturgies, we are struck with the resemblance to that described by Justin.

I pass by the baptismal portion, and notice only the regular Sunday morning worship. We have for its order: —

1. The Reading of Scripture.
2. A Sermon.
3. Prayer with Confession of Sin.
4. The Kiss of Peace.
5. The Oblation.
6. The *Sursum Corda*, — known henceforth to every liturgy: —

> "And let the Bishop say, —
> "'The Lord be with [you] all.'
> "Let the people reply, —
> "'And with thy spirit.'

" Let him say,—
" ' Lift up your hearts.'
" Let the people reply,—
" ' We have, unto the Lord.'
[" The Bishop —]
" ' Let us give thanks unto the Lord.'
" Let the people reply,—
" ' It is meet and right.' "

7. The Eucharistic Prayer, — still free.
8. The Blessing of the Oil and First-fruits.
9. The Communion.
10. When baptism had preceded, the tasting of milk and honey. The presbyters, or, in their absence, the deacons, are instructed at the Communion to "bear cups of milk and honey, that they may teach those who communicate that they are born again as little children, because such partake of milk and honey." They are received after the bread and cup, " in memory of the life to come, and of the sweetness of good things which are the desire of him who doth not return to bitterness. . . . Now, indeed, they are made perfect Christians, who enjoy the body of Christ and advance in wisdom, that they may adorn their lives [*mores*] with virtues, not only in their own presence, but also before all nations, who, not without envy, will admire the progress of those who glory that their lives [*mores*] are higher and more excellent than the lives [*mores*] of other men."

The use of the formula of benediction appears; also, as the text stands, of the *Gloria*, in the form,

" through Whom to Thee be glory, with Him and the Holy Spirit, for ever and ever, Amen."

The administration of the sacrament is thus appointed: The deacon having brought in the sacred elements, the bishop with the presbyters lays his hand upon them, and then, standing at the table, communicates the people. "Let him give them of the body of Christ, saying, 'This is the body of Christ.' But let them say, 'Amen.' And let those to whom he gives the cup, saying, 'This is the blood of Christ,' say, 'Amen.'"

Here is a basis of the later sacramentarianism, yet also a corrective of its superstition. The language is still Biblical. One should bring it to the reading of the later formulas and of the prayers connected with it.

The leading divisions of the later liturgies are already represented, with one important exception, — the Invocation of the Holy Spirit upon the oblation and those who partake of it. This becomes a marked feature of the developed liturgies, and also evinces an important difference between the Eastern conception and the Western of the relation of the officiating priest to the change, which, though not in the same way, the Greek Church as well as the Roman supposes to take place in the elements.

There is, however, some reason to suppose that the service represented in the "Canons of Hippolytus" contained other liturgical forms than those that now appear. In the "Æthiopic Church Ordinances," as in the later Clementine liturgy and in the liturgy known to St. Chrysostom, we find the Invocation. It is in a form so free from elaboration, so simple and brief, as to suggest antiquity. The Æthiopic liturgy may in this respect as in others depend on the " Canons." In any event it is likely that the Invocation early became a part of the eucharistic service, whether embodied in a written prayer or left to be formulated by the celebrant. It is precisely a portion of the service most likely to become substantially fixed as early as its conception was accepted. The form in which it appears matches, both in definiteness and latitude, the stage of thought we have reason to suppose had been reached as early as the close of the second century.

I will read the prayer from the *Anaphora* of the " Æthiopic Church Ordinances;" it follows the recital of the words of institution : " Remembering therefore His death and His resurrection, we offer Thee this bread and cup, giving thanks unto Thee for that Thou hast made us meet to stand before Thee and do Thee priestly service. We beseech Thee that Thou wouldest send thine Holy Spirit on the oblation of this church ; give it together unto all them that partake [for] sanctification and for fulfilling with the Holy Ghost and for confirming true faith, that they may laud and praise Thee in thy Son Jesus Christ, through whom to Thee be glory and dominion in the holy church both now and ever, and world without end, Amen." [1]

[1] Brightman, *Liturgies, Eastern and Western*, vol. i. p. 190. Cf. Achelis, *Die Canones Hippolyti*, pp. 54, 55.

The only rite of the Church here expressed is that given in the Roman Symbol, whose existence scholars have carried back into the first half of the second century.

It is of no little interest to compare this form with that in the present Greek liturgy, that of St. Chrysostom.

But I may not pursue this special doctrinal line, nor, which would be more relevant, dwell upon the order which appears in this important connecting link between the earliest and the later liturgies. Bunsen, not unreasonably attracted by its purity and simplicity, refers it to the second century. A soberer judgment, founded on more critical study, puts it in the line of sources between the "Canons" and the Clementine liturgy, in the eighth book of the "Apostolic Constitutions." It deserves the special attention of all who would study in the way I am commending the current texts of the Greek liturgies, especially that now in use throughout the Greek Church, the so-called liturgy of St. Chrysostom.

The Clementine liturgy just referred to has long attracted attention. It is a private composition; so far as known, it never was the accepted order of any church. It helps fill out our conception of the general order of service in the last half of the fourth century, especially at Antioch, and may not be neglected. Its forms of prayer, however, are far inferior, even apart from doctrinal considerations, to those of the public liturgies. For the ends and uses

I now have especially in mind, — for liturgical training and personal edification, — one may pass at once to the current rites.

What can I say of these in the few moments that remain ?

First of all, their expansion. Every part is greatly elaborated. Antiphonal singing, a large use of psalms and hymns, has enriched the worship. Most of all, the conception has been developed of a service which shall represent, even to ear and eye, not only the action of the original institution, and the sacrificial import of the Eucharist, with all its elements of passion, triumph, heavenly sustenance, impartation and reception of eternal life, but, including the preparatory services, the history of Redemption from the creation of light to the Incarnation, the holy life of our Lord from the nativity to the public ministry, his teaching and works, the passion, death, burial, resurrection, and ascension, the descent of the Spirit and the eternal reign, — a symbolic, scenic, and even dramatic representation of all that the Church understands to be given to it in that life, and an appropriate utterance of its peace and joy, its gratitude and adoring praise, in view of such deliverance and triumph.

This is the informing idea of the whole service, giving relation and unity to its several parts, from the vespers of Saturday, through matins, to the eucharistic climax. All that is splendid in vestments and processions, suggestive in ikons or images, impressive in variety of scenes and actions, of postures and participators, all that can be gained by musical responses, and flowing accompaniments to low and modulated prayers, or melodious settings of the highest expressions of a worship which embraces and emphasizes all the notes of a universal peace and fellowship and victory, combine to impress the meaning of the Incarnation and the glory of the Cross, and of the Triune God from whom all blessings flow, and who is both now and through eternal ages to be adored.

Much may be said in criticism, not only of special parts, but of the conception as a whole, — much certainly from a doctrinal and Biblical point of view, much no less from the only true liturgical point of view, the ultimate test, ministry to a worship in spirit and in truth. Liturgy is ministry.

But I pass all this by; we shall inevitably bring to these liturgies our Western and Protestant preconceptions. We are not likely to forego our inherited gains in the apprehension of true worship. Perhaps we are more in danger of not appreciating enough the value of symbolism, the legitimate aid of form and even ceremony. But, waiving all this, what have these liturgies to give us to help us in our own work, in the line of our own best traditions, in our ministry of public prayer?

Something in the way of diction. Not so much, indeed, as the Western liturgies, which alone have collects as we have come to understand the term, and whose simple and even severe expression constitutes a discipline never so much needed or so useful as for those who, in the freedom of our services, are exposed to the dangers of diffuseness. Yet something, — examples, illustrations not unneeded, of how invocations, reverential titles, representations of divine perfections, all in close and fitting connection with specific supplications, may be varied, amplified, made conducive to supplication, intercession, adoration.

Not a little in the suggestion of ways by which a certain brightness and fitting splendor can shine forth in the Church's worship of Him who is the Light of the world, and of all life, and the Sun of Righteousness.

Much, in helping to a realization of what forms of thought are at the minister's command to bring the realities of faith to the multitudes of men wearied with the pressure of secular cares, tempted by the successes as by the failures of life to a sickening and palsying sense of its vanity, men needing sorely the refreshments and solaces of a devotion that reflects the peace and joy of those who have overcome. This note of triumph! It is the strongest anywhere struck, as you find it in these old Greek liturgies. Catch it there, in its beauty and strength, and you can never lose it.

Connected with this is the objective character and quality of the worship. Grant that it is not so deep as the Western in its fundamental tone. Admit the need of something that more adequately expresses the guilt of sin and its remedy. Recognize all the need that comes in with modern introspection and subjectivity, with changed standards and tests of historic truth, with clearer perceptions of the method of divine revelation, with the "pale cast of thought" or new outlooks in science or visions in philosophy. Still, after all, the early Church was right in introducing into its baptismal confessions those clear, evident, abiding revelations which centre in the manifestation of God in the person of His Son, those events which are at once eternal truths and facts of history, idea and fact in the highest mode and form of being and life, a perfect and perfected Personality, human and divine, the Son who reveals the Father, and through whom the Father sends the Spirit, who is their bond of union and from whom springs the holy Church, whose office it is to proclaim and declare the forgiveness of sins, and who is the pledge and power of the risen and eternal life. Ever to these springs must faith repair. Ever must such facts of being and life, those fundamental verities which are revelations of a historic Person and through Him of the personality of the one only God, be in the forefront of the Church's confession of its faith, ever no less the substance of worship, its inspiration, and the sign and seal of its purity and power.

From this point of view even the sacramentarianism of the liturgics may have, not merely in a negative way, or as a warning, a great lesson for us, but positively and inspiringly. Through the method of study I have endeavored to trace we can see where and how error came in, and the pathway of a tremendous exaggeration of early misconceptions was entered on and pursued. But is there not some danger that in the recoil from sacerdotalism, and all that interpretation and use of sacraments which is a part of it or affiliated with it, we may underestimate the true place, in our worship, of the communion service, and beyond this of that conception and appreciation of the gospel which flows from a true and spiritual discernment of the Lord's body and of His blood, and of what is symbolized and pledged to us in this sacrament, and which should give a key and note to all our praise?

I may not dwell upon this, yet may be pardoned for expressing the thought that we are not only inheritors of our great Puritan traditions, but heirs of the Christian centuries. Lotze has recognized that all progress is attended with some loss. It belongs, however, to the imperfection of the process, even though practically necessary or inevitable, if any true value is lost. History, from the religious point of view, is the pathway of prophecy, the movement of a divine purpose; it is fulfilment. When we think and see how early to appear, how perpetual, is the sacramental aspect or appreciation of Christianity, how widespread is its influence to-day, how realized it is in saintly lives, how manifested and evident where superstition and formalism are not among its elements or characteristics, how sustaining to piety and associated with and ministrant to types of Christian character, forms and forces of life, in which whatever is pure, lowly, reverential, sacrificial, beneficent, finds an expression no less energetic and mighty than serene and beautiful, we cannot help raising the question, whether, with the retention of our antagonism to mere externalism or to every substitution of ceremony and form for simplicity and truth and spirituality, we have not something to recover, as well as to retain and hold, and that to this end a thorough understanding and appreciation of the great liturgies, which are sacramental services, may be of inestimable advantage.

The life of an eminent scholar and most devout Christian has but recently closed. From his biography I take these words. They are a part of a letter from him to a clergyman who had questioned him about the meaning of a "call" to the Christian ministry. The whole letter is well worthy of the attention of all who are preparing for this sacred office. It goes to the heart of a Christian minister's distinctive service, the clergyman's "primary work." "He must have a desire to set forth the glory of God simply and directly, in those forms which show it forth most nakedly. He must not only act it out but speak of it, make men know it and consciously enter into it. None of the phenomena of life are primarily his province, but the glory and the love which underlie them all. He is not simply an officer or servant of God or workman of God, but His ambassador and herald to tell men about God Himself. He must bring distinctly before men the reality of the heaven of which the earth and all that it contains is but the symbol and vesture. And, since all human teaching is but the purging of the ear to hear God's teaching, and since the whole man, and not certain faculties only, must enter into the divine presence, the sacraments must be the centre and crown (I don't mean central *subject*) of his teaching, for there the real heights and depths of heaven are most fully revealed, and at the same time the commonest acts and things of earth are most closely and clearly connected with the highest heaven." [1]

This, as I understand it, is the vital truth which has given what we call sacramentarianism its perpetuity. We may see in the Eastern liturgies something of the perversions and abuses of this truth. We may discern, also, its presence and power. This — this beyond all else — is the reason for their study, a study which penetrates to their secret, a use of them which appropriates their unwasted values, which brings the soul under the influence of their tranquil beauty, and into the peace which flows through them like a river of God, and to the fountains of strength and life.

[1] *Life and Letters of Fenton J. A. Hort*, vol. i. pp. 279, 280.

BIBLIOGRAPHY.

For a general list, see Prof. Cheetham's in *Dictionary of Christian Antiquities*, vol. ii. pp. 1036-1038; C. E. Hammond's in *Liturgies, Eastern and Western*, pp. lxxvii-lxxx. For Eastern liturgies, see the "description of materials" in Brightman's *Liturgies, Eastern and Western*, vol. i., *Eastern Liturgies, Introduction*, and subsequent special Introductions.

I. TEXTS.

A. GENERAL COLLECTIONS.—J. A. Assemani: *Codex Liturgicus ecclesiae universae . . . in quo continentur libri rituales, missales, pontificales, officia, diptycha, etc., ecclesiarum Occidentis et Orientis*, Rom., 1749-66, 13 vols. II. A. Daniel: *Codex Liturgicus Ecclesiae Universae in Epitomen Redactus*, Lips., 1847-1853.

B. SPECIAL COLLECTIONS AND EDITIONS.—F. E. Brightman: *Liturgies, Eastern and Western, being the Texts, original or translated, of the Principal Liturgies of the Church, Edited, with Introductions and Appendices, . . . on the Basis of the Former Work by C. E. Hammond . . . vol. i., Eastern Liturgies*, Oxford, at the Clarendon Press, 1896. C. E. Hammond: *Liturgies, Eastern and Western, being a Reprint of the Texts, either original or translated, of the most representative Liturgies of the Church, from various Sources, Edited, with Introduction, Notes, and a Liturgical Glossary*, Oxford, 1878. C. A. Swainson *The Greek Liturgies, chiefly from original authorities. . . . With an Appendix containing the Coptic Ordinary Canon of the Mass from two manuscripts in the British Museum. Edited and translated by Dr. C. Bezold*, London, 1884. J. M. Neale: *Tetralogia Liturgica: sive S. Chrysostomi, S. Jacobi, S. Marci divinae Missae, quibus accedit Ordo Mozarabicus*, London, 1849; *The Liturgies of S. Mark, S. James, S. Chrysostom, S. Basil* [in Greek and in English], London, 1868. J. Goar: Εὐχολόγιον, *sive Rituale Graecorum Complectens Ritus et Ordines divinae Liturgiae, Officiorum, Sacramentorum, Consecrationum, Benedictionum, Funerum, Orationum, &c. . . . Juxta Usum Orientalis Ecclesia*[e]. *Cum selectis Bibliothecae Regiae, Barberinae, Cryptae-Ferratae, Sancti Murci Florentini, Tillianae, Allatianae, Coresianae, et aliis probatis mm. ss. et editis exemplaribus collatum. Interpretatione Latina, nec non mixobarbararum vocum brevi Glossario, aeneis figuris, et observationibus ex antiquis PP., et maxime Graecorum Theologorum expositionibus, Illustratum* [the Byzantine Rite], Paris, 1647 (Venice, 1740). Guliel.

THE GREEK LITURGIES 103

Morelius : Λειτουργίαι τῶν ἁγίων πατέρων Ἰακώβου τοῦ ἀποστόλου καὶ ἀδελφοθέου, Βασιλείου τοῦ μεγάλου, Ἰωάννου τοῦ χρυσοστόμου. Paris, 1560. [*Textus receptus.*] W. Trollope: Ἡ τοῦ ἁγίου Ἰακώβου Λειτουργία. *The Greek Liturgy of St. James, Edited with an English Introduction and Notes; together with a Latin version of the Syrian copy, and the Greek text restored to its original purity and accompanied by a literal English translation,* Edinburgh, 1847. Amb. Drouard: Ἡ θεῖα λειτουργία τοῦ ἁγίου ἀποστόλου καὶ εὐαγγελιστοῦ Μάρκου μαθητοῦ τοῦ ἁγίου Πέτρου. . . . Paris, 1883 [*Textus receptus.* Editor, Jo. a S. Andrea]. Αἱ θεῖαι λειτουργίαι τοῦ ἁγίου Ἰωάννου τοῦ χρυσοστόμου, Βασιλείου τοῦ μεγάλου καὶ ἡ τῶν προηγιασμένων. . . . Rome, 1526. ["This is the *editio princeps* of these liturgies, published with the license of Clement VII., and, according to the colophon, edited with the co-operation of the Archbishop of Cyprus and of Rhodes. Beyond this the source of its text is unknown. The text is reprinted in Swainson, pp. 101-187 (bottom)." See Brightman, p. lxxxiii.] J. N. W. B. Robertson : *The Divine Liturgies of our Fathers among the Saints, John Chrysostom and Basil the Great, with that of the Presanctified, Preceded by the Hesperinos and the Orthros,* London, 1894 [Greek and English]. C. C. J. Bunsen : *Reliquiae Liturgicae* [In *Analecta Ante-Nicaena*, vol. iii. pp. 67-300, London, 1854. Contains Liturgy of S. Mark, as the editor supposes it to have been observed in the time of Origen, pp. 107-127 ; that of S. James restored, as nearly as possible, to the form supposed to have been observed in the fourth century, pp. 107-127 ; and the Liturgies of SS. Basil and Chrysostom, according to the Barberini Codex, pp. 195-236. See, also, *Ibid. Hippolytus and his Age,* vol. iv. pp. 233-434, London, 1852]. E. Renaudot: *Liturgiarum Orientalium Collectio,* Paris, 1716 [Frankfort, 1847].

II. INTRODUCTIONS, DISSERTATIONS, ENGLISH TRANSLATIONS, AND OTHER HELPS IN STUDY.

[See previous titles. For Latin, German, and other versions, see Brightman, pp. xlviii, lxiii, lxxvii-lxxix, lxxxi-lxxxiii.] J. M. Neale: *A History of the Holy Eastern Church. Part I. General Introduction,* vols. i., ii., London, 1850 [contains, with other information, a full account of the *Arrangement and details of an Eastern Church,* and of the *Vestments; Translation and parallel arrangement of the proanaphoral portion of S. Chrysostom, Copto-Jacobite S. Basil, the Armeno-Gregorian rite, the Mozarabic rite, and of the anaphorae of S.*

Chrysostom, S. Basil, S. James, S. Mark, Copto-Jacobite S. Basil, Lesser S. James, Theodore the Interpreter, the Armeno-Gregorian rite, the Mozarabic rite; Disquisitions on the foregoing proanaphorae and anaphorae; The Liturgy of the Presanctified]. J. M. Neale and R. F. Littledale: *The Liturgies of SS. Mark, James, Clement, Chrysostom, and Basil, and the Church of Malabar. Translated with Introduction and Appendices.* London, 1868 [Revised 1869, and often reprinted]. *Ante-Nicene Christian Library*, vol. xxiv. *Early Liturgies and Other Documents*, Edinburgh, 1872 [contains the Liturgies of S. James, S. Mark, and the Blessed Apostles (Adæus and Maris)]. Same, *American Reprint*, vol vii., Buffalo, 1886. T. Brett: *A Collection of the Principal Liturgies used in the Christian Church in the celebration of the Holy Eucharist, particularly the Ancient, viz., The Clementine, . . . The Liturgies of St. James, St. Mark, St. Chrysostom, St. Basil, &c. Translated into English by several hands. With a Dissertation upon them, showing their usefulness and authority, and pointing out their several corruptions and interpolations,* London, 1838. C. E. Hammond, *supra, Preface and Introduction.* W. Smith and S. Cheetham: *A Dictionary of Christian Antiquities*, London, vol. i., 1875, ii., 1880: Liturgical Articles. C. W. Bennett: *Christian Archæology* [vol. iv. of Crooks & Hurst: *Library of Biblical and Theological Literature*], New York, 1888. W. Palmer: *Origines Liturgicae*, with a *Dissertation on Primitive Liturgies*, 2 vols., London, 1832 [Later Editions]. P. Freeman: *The Principles of Divine Service*, Oxford and London, 2 vols. 1855-1857 [Cheaper Reissue, 1871-1873]. P. Schaff: *History of the Christian Church*, vol. iii. pp. 517-531, New York, 1884. F. Probst: *Liturgie der drei ersten christlichen Jahrhunderten*, Tübingen, 1870. *Id.: Liturgie des vierten Jahrhunderts und deren Reform*, Münster i. W. 1893. H. A. Koestlin: *Geschichte des Christlichen Gottesdienstes, ein Handbuch für Vorlesungen und Übungen im Seminar*, Freiburg i. B. 1887. J. W. Richard, F. V. N. Painter: *Christian Worship: Its Principles and Forms*, Philadelphia, 1892. L. Duchesne: *Origines du Culte Chrétien. Étude sur la Liturgie Latine avant Charlemagne*, Paris, 1889. H. C. Romanoff: *Sketches of the Greco-Russian Church. The Divine Liturgy of St. John Chrysostom*, London, Oxford, and Cambridge, 1871. Lechmere, J. Gennadius: *Synopsis or a Synoptical Collection of the Daily Prayers, the Liturgy, and Principal Offices of the Greek Orthodox Church of the East. Translated, with Assistance, from the Original, and Edited by Katharine Lady Lechmere. With an Introduction by J. Gennadius, Envoy Extraordinary and Minister Plenipotentiary of H. M. the King of the Hellenes at the Court of St. James's,* London.

IV

THE ROMAN LITURGIES

BY THE REV. CHARLES C. TIFFANY, D.D.

Archdeacon of New York City

THE ROMAN LITURGIES

I AM, I believe, the only lecturer in this course on Christian Worship who is not an adherent of the liturgy he expounds. My desire is, and my attempt shall be, to be as accurate and fair as though I were. I am quite sure I should not have been chosen to this task had not those appointing it been convinced that I should be thus impartial and charitable. There is, of course, an infelicity in not being an advocate as well as an expounder of the subject assigned me. Points may be inadvertently overlooked which a loving eye would detect, and a bias may be manifest unsuspected by the writer. In studying the subject, therefore, I have chiefly confined myself to Roman Catholic authorities.[1]

[1] *The Decrees* and *Catechism* of the Council of Trent; The *Missale Romanum ex Decreto S. S. Concilii Tridentini Restitutum* itself; Prochiron, *Vulgo Rationale Divinorum officiorum*, Gulielmo Durando, 1551; Bellarmine, *de Sacramento Eucharistiæ*, especially the 5th Book "de Missa;" the *Hierurgia, or the Holy Sacrifice of the Mass*, by Daniel Rock, D.D.; Martene, *de Antiquis Ecclesiæ Ritibus;* Morinus, *de Sacris Ecclesiæ ordinibus;* and Muratori in his collection of the Earlier Missals, — the Leonine, Gelasian, Gregorian, and that of the Apostolic Constitutions, — have all been inspected at first hand, as

The sources from which I have drawn are almost exclusively devoted to the doctrine and delineation of the Mass, a term applied from very early times to the service of the Eucharist or Lord's Supper, as well as to other services of the Church, and derived, first from the words "*ite, missa est,*" used to dismiss the catechumens and other non-communicants before the consecration of the elements of bread and wine; and afterwards, to dismiss the communicants when the service of communion was over. I must confine myself, also, to the Roman Liturgy in the strict and restricted meaning of the word,—that is, as the Eucharistic service; because the time assigned me would be insufficient even to enumerate and superficially describe the great variety of services which the Roman Church has provided for the use of her children. Moreover, the Mass dominates all these other services. The service of Benediction is the blessing of the people with the Consecrated Wafer exposed in the Monstrance and held before the congregation by the priest, as he waves it in the sign of the cross above their bowed heads and prostrate bodies. Vespers are sung before the altar whereon the reserved Sacrament is kept, surrounded and confronted with the mystic glow of tapers. Matins, lauds, prime, tierce, compline,—

well as what Cardinal Newman in his various writings has stated. I have used also, of non-Roman writers: Maskele, *Monumenta Ritualia Ecclesiæ Anglicanæ;* Palmer, *Origines Liturgicæ;* Bingham's *Antiquities of the Christian Church,* and Smith's *Dictionary of Christian Antiquities,*—all reliable sources. Besides these, I have found in various of them valuable references to Bona and Le Brun on the Mass.

these offices contained in the Breviary, the use of which is obligatory every day by every one in orders, from the Pope down to the latest sub-deacon, have, as it were, been crowded out of the sanctuary, and have become, in using, private services. Of the Breviary we may remark in passing that it is the Reformed Breviary of Urban VIII., published in 1631, which is now in use. Up to the Reformation almost every diocese and monastery had its own Breviary; one hundred and fifty different uses were to be found in Western Christendom up to that time. After various efforts of various Popes to revise and reduce these uses, from Gregory VII., in the middle of the eleventh century, to Pius IV., in the middle of the sixteenth century, Pius V., after the failure of the Council of Trent to complete the task imposed upon it by Paul IV., ordered a number of learned men to compile a Breviary for general use. This reformed and condensed Breviary was published in 1568, preceded by the bull "*Quod a Nobis*," forbidding the use of any other. Subsequently amended by Clement VIII., and finally by Urban VIII., it is now (with the addition of some services for saints since canonized) of obligation, and in universal daily use by all in orders of every kind, conventual and ecclesiastical. It is divided into four parts, corresponding to the seasons; winter, spring, summer, and autumn. It consists of portions of the Psalter, Collects, Prayers, Commemoration of Saints and Martyrs, Ave Marias, and Litanies, and requires one hour and a half at least for the daily recitation.

It corresponds to the Order of Daily Morning and Evening Prayer in the Common Prayer of the Episcopal Church, which has largely drawn from it, by a condensation and amalgamation of its various parts.

But while this brief passing notice of a daily service, required *de rigueur* of all ecclesiastics, seemed necessary as indicating the Roman discipline of worship, it is the Mass or Liturgy which dominates to-day all the public services of the Roman Communion; and to this we must confine our chief attention.

And I speak of the Roman liturgy rather than Roman liturgies, because the time would fail me to delineate and differentiate the various forms of the liturgy such as the *Ambrosian*, the very ancient use of Milan and Northern Italy. This is still used in Milan, though not exactly as of old or without changes as edited at various times, since the second oblation or the oblation of the elements after consecration, which exists in the Roman liturgy, was not in it, as late as the ninth or tenth century (see Palmer, vol. i. p. 127); the Mozarabic liturgy compiled or edited by Isidore Bishop of Seville in the seventh century and used in Spain till the time of Gregory VII., when the Roman was substituted. Cardinal Ximenes in the fifteen century renewed its observance in Toledo and published an edition of it Anno Dom. 1500; the various Gallican liturgies of which there were many, though based on one original, probably to be traced to Lyons and through Lyons to

Asia and the tradition of St. John (since Irenæus, a disciple of Polycarp, who was a disciple of St. John, became Bishop of Lyons about A. D. 177). This differed in some measure from the Roman in the sixth century, as seen by the fact that Augustine, first Archbishop of Canterbury, writes to Pope Gregory to inquire " why one custom of liturgy prevails in the church of Rome and another in those of Gaul." The Roman rites were introduced in the place of the ancient Gallican in the time of Charlemagne, who ordained by an imperial edict that every priest should celebrate the liturgy in the Roman manner. He meant to unify the religious uses of his vast empire and please the Pope who crowned him. Nor need we dwell on the various English uses or customs, as of York, Sarum, Hereford, Bangor, Leicester and Aberdeen, for these had all been derived from the sacramentary of Gregory, though the Sarum Use, dating from Osmond, Bishop of Salisbury, 1078, became the common Use, the whole of England, Wales, and Ireland adopting it. These various missals and rituals differed very little from each other, the sacramentary of Gregory being used with various small additions. The rites, however, of the English churches were not entirely uniform in the middle of the sixteenth century, and therefore the Metropolitans of Canterbury, at the request of Edward VI., edited and compiled the English Ritual and produced the First Prayer-Book of Edward VI. in 1549. Of the liturgy of the British Church before the mission of St. Augustine, there are no traces in any known manuscripts. That it differed from the Roman, we learn from Bede, who quotes an address of Augustine to the British bishops as follows: "In many respects you act contrary to our customs, and indeed to those of the universal Church, and yet if you will obey me in these three things,—

1. To celebrate Easter at the proper time.
2. To perform the office of baptism, in which we are born again to God, according to the custom of the Holy Roman and Apostolic Church, and
3. With us to preach the word of God to the English nation, —

we will tolerate all your other customs, though contrary to our own (quamvis moribus nostris contraria)."

As the Roman and Gallican were the only two primitive liturgies in the West of which there is any record, it is probable that the early British bishops (who existed early in the fourth century) derived their orders from Gaul, the nearest Christian province, and used the Gallican liturgy, which, as we have noted, was superseded later by the Roman through the edict of Charlemagne.

The variations of various liturgies derived from the same source is to be accounted for by the fact that, while the substantial part, or more strictly the Canon, was preserved in nearly identical form, the Bishop of each church appears to have possessed the power to improve his own liturgy by the addition of new ideas and rites. While the Roman and Gallican liturgies and those derived from them, as the Italian and Mozarabic or Spanish, preserved an identity of order and the same series of parts, variety of expression is found for every particular feast. It is in these missals that we find the variations, and they grow with the development of dogma, or, as our Roman friends would perhaps prefer to say, with its more explicit definition. Thus, as an illustration, it was in the eleventh century, according to Rock, that the great elevation of the consecrated Host and the chalice, for the adoration of the faithful, was instituted to emphasize the received doctrine of the presence, in opposition to Berengarius, who about 1047 called the commonly accepted view (not decreed as dogma until 1215) " inepta vecordia vulgi." His excommunication was accompanied by this addition of the Elevation to the Roman Missa. And it is from these Missæ or rubrical directions, and the ceremonies derived from them, that we deduce the special Roman doctrine of the Mass, and not from the words of institution, which are largely scriptural and so accepted by all, though not interpreted alike by all. Of course the Nicene creed must be an addition of the fourth century to the liturgy. Before this no creed seems to have been used in any liturgy. In the Eastern churches it was introduced before it found a place in the Roman, being found in the liturgy of Constantinople about 511, while Berno says the creed only began to be sung in the Roman churches about 1062, though Martene thinks it was used — or said

— earlier. Still, the Roman liturgy, like all others, in its present form is a growth, and it is in the growing portions that we read its history and comprehend its meaning.

Now, though the liturgies are traditionally ancient, according to all authorities, not one appears to have been *written* before the fourth or fifth century. The one which appears in the Apostolical Constitutions is probably as ancient as any written form, and that stands about the middle of the fourth century, but "it is not known [to quote Dr. Rock] to have been used, as compiled in the ' Constitutions,' in any church service whatever." "The early liturgies of the various churches were transmitted solely by tradition;" so that Martene, in his work "De Antiquis Ecclesiæ Ritibus," says of the so-called Liturgies of the Apostles, that "learned men admit none of them as genuine productions of their reputed authors." The most ancient sources of the Roman Liturgy of to-day are the Leonine Sacramentary, that of Pope Gelasius, and the Sacramentary of Gregory the Great. But neither Pope Leo I. (451) nor Pope Gelasius (492), nor Gregory the Great (590) are supposed to have composed liturgies anew, but only to have improved, abridged, or in parts amplified, uses which had already obtained in the Church. But this usage of adding to the Missæ indicates how the Roman Liturgy has developed to its present form. The fact, moreover, " that the primitive liturgies were not committed to writing at first but to memory, indicates that many variations would be introduced, while the principal substance and order might be preserved.[1] And it can be readily seen that accretions would accumulate, according as circumstances (such as that alluded to at the time of Berengarius, in regard to the Elevation of the Host) would indicate the advisability of emphasizing, or making ritually apparent, a phase of doctrine which had obtained credence, but which had come into dispute.

Another cause for variations in the various Missæ is the fact that until the eleventh century the offices of the Holy Communion were not bound up in one volume, but were contained in *four*. These were:

1. The *Antiphoner*, or parts to be said or sung antiphonally.
2. The Lectionary, or the Books of the Epistles, also called Epistolarium.
3. Book of the Gospels, also called Evangelisteria, containing portions of the four Gospels.
4. The Sacramentary, or the Canon of the Mass, which is the missal proper.

In all of the separated portions of the service, annotations and changes would creep in, and variations would afterward appear, for which the cause or occasion would have lapsed from memory. After the eleventh century, up to the fourteenth and fifteenth centuries, the whole service bound in one volume could be found, and was more secure from variations. But

---

[1] Palmer, vol. i. p. 121.

as has been previously said, the Canon, or strict order of the Mass, preserved its essential features in all the liturgies with considerable uniformity. Martene gives as the order of the older Sacramentaries in which they essentially agreed, the following: —

1. Prayers for the Church and the conversion of Infidels.
2. The Kiss of Peace.
3. Oblations of Bread and Wine, mixed with water.
4. Consecration of the same.
5. Communion, or distribution of the Sacrament.

Around this nucleus the elaborated services of later dates have formed themselves. Martene also gives as the order of the service in the Apostolical Constitutions (a rite, as we have noted, proposed, if never performed, at some time not later than the fourth century) the following: After three lessons, — one from the Old Testament, one from the New Testament, and one from the Gospels, followed the *oratio*, or sermon. Then the catechumens were dismissed, and then followed the *Post Oblata*, or prayers over the oblations of the people; then the Kiss of Peace; the Prayer for all Men; the Consecration of the Elements; the Communion. Professor Swainson, of Cambridge University, in his exhaustive article on "Liturgy" in "Smith's Dictionary of Christian Antiquities,'' adds the following description of the Ordo of the Canon (which is wanting or simply indicated in the Gelasian Sacramentary). The Canon commences with the *Sursum Corda,* "Lift up your hearts," with its responses; then a Eucharistic address to God for the gift and work of his Son; passing at once to the words of institution, which are given in the simplest form. The prayer proceeds: "Calling to mind, therefore, His death and His resurrection, etc., we offer to Thee this bread and cup, rendering Thee thanks that Thou hast made us worthy to stand before Thee and to perform the functions of Thy priesthood." The Holy Spirit is invoked upon the oblations, but there is no prayer that He will make them the body and blood of Christ. The prayer is that those who partake of the gifts "may be fulfilled with that Spirit." The words "Sanctum Sacrificium immaculatam Hostiam" are by Walafridus Strabo (dec. 849) said to have been added to the Canon by Leo I.[1] It is difficult to get an accurate view of the Sacramentary of Gregory the Great (A. D. 590). Muratori says, "No one can believe that we have the book as it came from the hand of Gregory."[2] For in the four or five manuscripts known to Muratori the Masses vary in the several editions, the Festivals vary, and all are said to include the Commemoration of Gregory himself. Yet Palmer,[3] after diligent comparison and investigation, gives the following as an approximate exhibition of the service as revised and established by Gregory the Great:

[1] See Smith, *Dictionary of Antiq.* vol. ii. p. 1183, Art. SACRIFICE.
[2] See Smith, vol. ii. p. 1033. [3] *Origines Liturgicæ,* vol. i. p. 123.

" It began at first with a collect and lesson from Scripture, among which a psalm was sung. Then came the sermon, followed by the dismissal of the catechumens and silent prayer made by priest and people, after which the oblations of the people, consisting chiefly of bread and wine, were received while the offertory was sung. The elements being selected from these and placed on the altar, the priest read the collect called 'secreta' or *super oblata*, and then began the Preface, — a Thanksgiving with the form 'Sursum Corda,' etc., — at the close of which the people chanted the hymn 'Tersanctus.' The Canon now commenced with commending the people's gifts and offerings to the acceptance of God and prayers for the King and the Bishop, with a commemoration of the living and especially of those who had offered liberally. This was succeeded by a prayer that the oblation of bread and wine might 'be made to us the body and blood of Jesus Christ, our Lord and God." The commemoration of our Saviour's deeds and words in celebrating the Eucharist followed. After which came an oblation of the Sacraments, as a sacrifice of bread and wine, and a petition that they might be presented by the angels on the altar in heaven. Then followed a commemoration of the departed faithful, and prayer for communion with them. The canon being now completed, the bread was broken and divided into portions for distribution, and then the Lord's Prayer was recited. After this the clergy and people interchanged a kiss of peace and all communicated and the priest concluded the office with a short prayer." This was the order and substance of the Roman liturgy in the fifth century.

Having thus traced the Genesis and Method of growth of Roman liturgies, we turn to consider some of its salient features to-day and to indicate by the exposition of its essential idea an explanation of its elaborate and splendid ritual and the supreme place which it occupies in the worship of the Church.

One of the salient features of the Roman Mass to-day is that it is performed in all countries in the Latin tongue. Dr. Rock gives as the reason, that, being first originated in Latin (the language of the day and country), and that by the use of St. Peter at Rome, reverence for so august an origin and an aversion to innovation has continued the use, which secures uniformity in public worship throughout the world and makes the worshipper of whatever clime and tongue feel at home in the Church in every place. Then the preservation of the one language prevents variation in the meaning of terms incident to frequent translations of them, and so is conservative of orthodoxy; and, moreover,[1] " in the performance of this sacred service no office is assigned to the people. The sacrifice is offered up by the priest in their name and on their behalf. The whole action is between God and the priest. So far is it from being necessary that the

---

[1] I quote now the exact words of Dr. Rock (see *Hierurgia*, vol. i. p. 314), though it anticipates what will follow concerning the Roman idea of the nature of the service.

people shall understand the language of the sacrifice, that they are not allowed even to hear the most important and solemn part of it. . . . They do not act, they do not say the prayers of the priest, they have nothing to do with the actual performance of the Holy Sacrifice."

Such, then, being the reasons, we understand that peculiarity of the Roman communion which distinguishes it from that of all other churches, in that its principal service is conducted in a language not "understanded by the people."

Another peculiarity of the Roman Mass is that all save the officiating priest receive in one species only, that of bread, from the Pope down, *i. e.*, when there is communion of the people, which is by no means universally the case.

It was only towards the commencement of the twelfth century, according to Rock, that the public administration of the Sacrament in one kind began. It is held that previous to this the administration in *private* to the sick had been in one species only. But nothing was *authoritatively* promulgated by the Church concerning this regulation until A. D. 1414, when the Council of Constance (in opposition to Huss, who asserted, contrary to what had been the custom, that the use of the cup was necessary) decreed that the custom of communicating in one kind should be received *as law*, which no one without the authority of the Church might reject or alter. This decree, among other objects, was meant to buttress and emphasize by a ritual observance the doctrine, afterward decreed by the Council of Trent, under pain of anathema, that "as much is contained under one species as under both; for Christ whole and entire is under the species of bread, and under any part soever of that species; likewise the whole Christ is under the species of wine and under the parts thereof."[1] Earlier (A.D. 492) Pope Gelasius had made a similar dogmatic use of a ritual observance in a contrary direction, by insisting that the communion should be received by all the faithful, under *both* kinds, in order to confute the Manichæans, who abstained from the cup from superstitious reasons.[2] The administration hence now is universally in one kind, though it is a matter of discipline which might be changed, but which is observed as a guard against possible irreverence in spilling of the chalice, and on the principle enunciated by Rock:[3] "In the *sacrifice* it is by divine institution necessary for the sacrificing priest to consecrate and drink of the chalice in order to complete the sacrifice, — the mystic oblation of Christ's body and the shedding of his blood upon the Cross. In the *sacrament* this not required of the communicant." And this is confirmed by the words of the Council of Trent,[4] that "the whole and the entire Christ and the true sacrament are taken under either kind, and therefore, as to the fruit, that they who thus receive are deprived of no necessary grace."

---

[1] See *Canons of Council of Trent*, sec. xiii. chap. iii.
[2] Rock, *Hierurgia*, vol. i. p. 285.
[3] Vol. i. p. 288.   [4] Sec. xxi. chap. iii.

The practice of non-communicating attendance at Mass is not ordered or favored by the Council of Trent, nor by the most recent commentators on the Mass. Mochler[1] remarks: "The unseemliness of the congregation no longer communicating every Sunday (as was the case in the primitive Church), and of the priest in the Mass usually receiving alone the Body of the Lord, is not to be laid to the blame of the Church (for all the prayers in the Holy Sacrifice presuppose the sacramental communion of the entire congregation), but it is to be attributed solely to the tepidity of the greater part of the faithful; yet are the latter earnestly exhorted to participate at least spiritually in the communion of the priest, and in this way to enter into the followship of Christ." And this is borne out by the direction of the Council of Trent,[2] which speaks in this wise: "The Sacred and Holy Synod would fain indeed that at each Mass the faithful who are present should communicate, not only in spiritual desire, but also by sacramental participation of the eucharist; . . . but not therefore, if this be not always done, does it condemn, but approves of and commends those Masses in which the priest alone communicates sacramentally."

There are many kinds of Masses receiving many names from the objects for which they are celebrated, but they may all be reduced to two kinds, which are in themselves one, namely, High Mass and Low

---

[1] *Symbolism*, p. 236.
[2] Sec. xxii. chap. vi.

Mass, which are distinguished from each other, not so much by their contents, though they vary a little in subject matter, as by the amount of ceremonial attending their performance. High Mass is sung, and is accompanied with music, many attendants, more splendid vestments, and some additional ceremonies. Pontifical High Mass is a supreme function of this class. The Low Mass is read and is devoid of music, and is altogether a shorter and plainer service. But the variety of Masses, of which I have seen a list of thirty-six, are simply Masses on different occasions and for special needs; as Requiem Masses for the departed, Nuptial Masses for the newly wedded pair, A Votive Mass, formerly a Mass for some special blessing, temporal or spiritual, though now it means any Mass not of the day. In all these the ordo or Canon of the Mass is fixed and the same, the rest or the Proper of the Mass differs on different occasions. In all these services everything is prescribed. There is nothing individual, but all is official in action as well as in expression. The vestments in shape and color, the lights in number and size, the inclinations of head and knees, the motions of the hands and the eyes, all have significance; and much of this claims a remote antiquity for its origin. Dr. Rock sees the precedent for lights at Mass in the many lights in the upper chamber where St. Paul at Troas preached unto the Brethren as they came together to break bread, and continued his speech until midnight. He remarks that, "The numerous lamps particularly noticed here were no doubt employed to give splendor to the sacred institution;"[1] and claims that the vision of St. John as recorded in the first chapter of the Book of Revelation, beginning, " I was in the Spirit on the Lord's Day," and speaking of the Seven Golden Candlesticks, was an animated picture " which we may presume either represents the Liturgy as it was then celebrated, or became the model according to which it was afterward arranged " (p. 263). I do not allude to these arguments from Scripture either to fault or favor them, for my province to-day is not that of a critic, or of an expositor, but merely to show that scriptural and apostolic precedent is sought and claimed for all the general and essential features of the Mass, as it is performed to-day.

To enter into a minute description of the service of the Mass would take more time than the whole hour appointed for this lecture, nor could it seem other than cumbersome, intricate, and unedifying in its detail, unless the doctrine on which it is founded were thoroughly understood. Then it at once becomes plain and congruous; and though its varied features were elaborated during a long period, in which stately and splendid ceremonial, as witnessed at the courts of princes and emperors, was deemed the noblest and truest external homage to the King of kings, still these features become intelligible and interpretative of the great idea which underlies the

[1] Rock's *Hierurgia*, vol. i. p. 263.

service. It is not obnoxious to the charge that it is unmeaning. It is clear when the conception of the function is clear. There is not an osculation of the altar, nor a sign of the cross, the lighting of a taper, nor the swinging of a censer, not an attitude, nor a voice, nor a silence, but what has its meaning as an illustration and instrument of the action of which it forms a part.

In every Mass there is: 1. The Ordinary of the Mass, from the introit (Ps. xlii.) to and including the Sanctus, as well as the oblation and elevation of the Host and the chalice (as yet unconsecrated, but called in the prayer attending Elevation, a sacrifice); also the Epistle, Gospel, and Creed with the *graduale* before the Gospel. 2. The Canon, or words of consecration (which for the bread are, "For this is my body," without the addition " which is given for you " in St. Luke's account; and for the Cup, " This is the chalice of my blood of the New and Eternal Testament, the mystery of Faith which shall be shed for you and for many for the remission of sins "), and the Elevation of the consecrated Host and chalice, and then follow prayers for living and dead, and the commemoration of certain great saints, beginning with the Virgin Mary; then the commixture of a particle of the consecrated Host in the consecrated chalice, with the communion of the priest in both kinds; after this comes the communion, a short prayer of thanksgiving; then if there be communicants, they receive. Then follows the post-communion, thanksgiving and prayers and benediction, then "ite, missa est," and finally the first chapter of St. John's Gospel.

This rapid survey of the principal words and ceremonies of the Mass gives no adequate idea of the stately and intricate service, which is calculated to impress upon the worshipper the transaction of a transcendent mystery. It is explicable only on the Roman idea of the Church and Sacrament. Let me elucidate this out of their own authors and conciliar decrees.

The Church is regarded by Rome not chiefly as the authoritative witness to Christ, but rather as his personal embodiment. "In one point of view," says Moehler,[1] "the Church is the living figure of Christ manifesting himself amid and working through all ages, whose atoning and redeeming acts it in consequence eternally repeats and uninterruptedly continues. The Redeemer not merely lived eighteen hundred years ago, . . . he is, on the contrary, eternally living in his Church, and in the Sacrament of the altar he hath manifested this in a sensible manner to creatures endowed with sense. . . . If Christ, concealed under an earthly vail, unfolds to the end of time his whole course of actions begun on earth, he of necessity eternally offers himself to the Father as a victim for men; and the real permanent exposition hereof can never fail in the Church, if the historical Christ is to celebrate in her his entire imperishable existence. . . .

[1] *Symbolism*, p. 231.

"Christ on the cross has offered the sacrifice for our sins," but "the sacrifice of Christ on the cross is put only for a part of an organic whole. His whole life on earth . . . constitutes one great sacrificial act expiatory of our sins, consisting indeed of various individual parts, yet so that none by itself is, strictly speaking, the sacrifice. . . . The will of Christ to manifest his gracious condescension to us in the Eucharist forms no less an integral part of his great work than all besides, and in a way so necessary indeed that . . . without it the other parts would not have sufficed for our complete atonement. . . . Hence the sacramental sacrifice is a true sacrifice — a sacrifice in the strict sense, yet so that it must in no wise be separated from the other things which Christ hath achieved for us. . . . In this last part of the objective sacrifice, the latter becomes subjective and appropriated to us. Christ on the cross is still an object strange to us; Christ in the Christian worship is our property, our victim. There he is the *universal* victim, here he is the victim *for us* in particular . . .; there he was *only* the victim, here he is the victim acknowledged and revered; there the objective atonement was consummated, here the subjective atonement is partly fostered and promoted, partly expressed." "Now the sacrifice appears propitiatory and the Redeemer present enables us to be entirely his own children." "With faith in the real existence of Christ in the Eucharist, the past becomes the present. He is present as that which he actually is and in the whole extent of his actions, to wit, as the real victim . . ." so that " it is not the interior acts of thanksgiving, adoration and gratitude which it (the Church) offers up to God but it is Christ himself present in Sacrament."

These are not simply the words of an individual theologian, but of one eminent for his genius, and approved and sanctioned by Roman theologians. They are the philosophic exposition of the dogmas of the Roman communion as expressed in the decrees of the Council of Trent, and of the Catechism of that Council, which is of authority. For, as the following extracts will concisely show, the Church holds to not only the real presence of the flesh and blood of Christ, born of the Virgin Mary, but that in this flesh and blood he is immolated daily on the altar by the priest as his representative, *i. e.*, that in the Eucharist Christ immolates himself on the altar as he once immolated himself on the Cross.

From the third and fourth chapters of Session Thirteenth of the Canons of the Council of Trent we make these extracts: —

Ch. III. "Immediately after the consecration the veritable body of the Lord and his veritable blood, together with his soul and divinity, are under the species of bread and wine by the force of the words; and by the consecration [Ch. IV.] of the bread and of the wine, a conversion is made of the whole substance of the bread into the substance of the body of Christ our Lord, and of the whole substance of the wine into the substance of his blood, which conversion is by the Holy Catholic Church suitably and properly called Transubstantiation."

Also, in Question XXVI. of the Catechism of the Council of Trent (which is of authority), it is stated:

"There are three things which the Catholic faith unhesitatingly believes and confesses to be accomplished by the words of consecration:

" The *first* is, that the true body of Christ the Lord, the very same that was born of the Virgin and sits at the right hand of the Father in heaven is contained in this sacrament.

" The *second*, that however alien to and remote from the senses it may seem, no substance of the elements remains therein.

" The *third*, that the *accidents* which are discerned by the eyes or perceived by the other senses, *exist* in a wonderful and ineffable manner, *without a subject*. All the accidents of bread and wine we indeed may see; they, however, inhere in no substance, *but exist by themselves;* whereas, the substance of the bread and wine are so changed into the very body and blood of the Lord, that the substance of bread and wine altogether ceases to exist."

And *Canon VI.:*—

"If any one saith that in the Holy Sacrament of the Eucharist the Only begotten Son of God is not to be adored with the worship even external of latria, let him be anathema."

So much for the real presence, or Transubstantiation. In regard to the *sacrifice* of the Mass, treated in Session Twenty-two of the Council of Trent, we find this statement: —

Ch. II. "In this Divine Sacrifice which is celebrated in the Mass, that same Christ is contained and immolated in an unbloody manner, who once offered himself in a bloody manner on the altar of the Cross. This sacrifice is truly propitiatory. . . . For the victim is one and the same, the same now offering by the ministry of priests, who then offered himself on the cross; the *manner* alone of offering being different."

Therefore *Canon III.:* —

"If any one saith that the sacrifice of the Mass is only a sacrifice of praise and thanksgiving, or that it is a bare commemoration of the sacrifice consummated on the Cross, but not a propitiatory sacrifice, or that it profits only him who receives it, and that it ought not to be offered for the living and the dead, for sins, pains, etc., let him be amathema."

Again in Questions LXXIV., LXXV., and LXXVI. of the Catechism of the Council of Trent we find the following: —

"The sacrifice of the Mass is, and ought to be considered one and the same as that of the Cross, — as the victim is one and the same, namely, Christ our Lord, who immolated himself once only after a bloody manner on the altar of the Cross. For the bloody and unbloody victim are not two victims, but one only — whose sacrifice is daily renewed in the Eucharist."

Q. LXXV. "But the Priest also is one and the same, Christ the Lord, for the ministers who offer sacrifice, when they consecrate his body and blood, act not in their own but in the person of Christ . . . and thus *representing* Christ, he changes the substance of the bread and wine into the true substance of his body and blood."

Q. LXXVI. "And the Holy Sacrifice of the Mass is not a sacrifice of praise and thanksgiving only, or a mere commemoration of the sacrifice accomplished on the Cross, but also a truly propitiatory sacrifice, by which God is appeased and rendered propitious towards us . . . We *immolate* and *offer* this most holy victim . . . As often as the commemoration of this victim is celebrated, so often is the work of our salvation being done."

This, which might seem to be a literally physical sacrifice, is thus spoken of as a spiritual sacrifice by Dr. Rock[1]: —

"It (the Mass) is a spiritual sacrifice where the victim, though identically present, still is not observable excepting to the eye of faith only; where the sword of the sacrifice is the word of Christ, pronounced by his Ministering Priest, and which works the mystic separation of the body from the blood — where this blood is not poured out or spilled except in mystery, — and where there is no death, except by representation. Still it is a sacrifice, in which Jesus Christ is verily contained and immolated to God under this figure of death."

In view, then, of such a doctrinal basis is the ceremonial of the Mass illogical? If the Sacrament is

[1] *Hierurgia*, p. 254.

Christ's continual reacting of the sacrifice on Calvary, — here mystically as there physically slain — if this is the essential completing and application of that sacrifice to the individual, and if not ruling and reigning, not intercession and benediction, but sacrificial immolation on the altar is Christ's perpetual action for and before his people, is it strange that John Henry Newman should have written thus of this great function to his former brethren of the English Church:[1]—

"The idea of worship is different in the Catholic Church from the idea of it in your Church, for in truth the religions are different. They differ in kind, not in degree. Ours is one religion, yours is another. It (the Mass) is not a mere form of words, it is a great action. It is not the invocation merely, but (if I dare use the word) the *Evocation* of the Eternal. He becomes present on the Altar in flesh and blood before whom angels bow and devils tremble. This is that awful event which is the scope and is the interpretation of every part of the solemnity. Words are necessary, but as means, not ends; they are not mere addresses to the throne of grace, they are instruments of what is far higher, of consecration, of sacrifice. They hurry on, as if impatient to fulfil their mission. Quickly they go — the whole is quick; for they are all parts of one integral action. Quickly they go, for they are awful words of sacrifice — they are a work too great to delay upon, as when it was said in the beginning, 'What thou doest, do quickly.' Quickly they pass, for

[1] See *Loss and Gain*, p. 328.

the Lord Jesus goes with them, as he passed along the lake in the days of his flesh, quickly calling first one and then another. Quickly they pass, because as the lightning which shineth from one part of the heaven unto the other, so is the Coming of the Son of Man. Quickly they pass, for they are as the words of Moses, when the Lord came down in the cloud, calling on the name of the Lord as he passed by, 'The Lord, the Lord God, merciful and gracious, long suffering and abundant in goodness and truth.' And as Moses on the mountain, so we too make haste to bow our heads to the earth and adore. ' So we all around, each in his place, look out for the great advent, waiting for the moving of the water.' Each in his own place, with his own heart, with his own wants, with his own thoughts, with his own intention, with his own prayers, separate but concordant, watching what is going on, watching its progress, uniting in its consummation — not painfully and hopelessly following a hard form of prayer from beginning to end, but like a concert of musical instruments, each different, but concurring in a sweet harmony, we take our part with God's priest, supporting him, yet guided by him. There are little children there, and old men, and simple laborers and students in seminaries, priests preparing for Mass, priests making their thanksgiving; there are innocent maidens and there are penitent sinners, but out of these many minds rises one Eucharistic hymn, and the great Action is the Measure and the scope of it."

With these eloquent words of the great convert of the century, I close this sketch of the origin, growth, and doctrinal significance of the Roman liturgy.

They depict in glowing language the service which so enchanted his imagination and commanded his faith; and it is fitting that we should not only see what the Mass means, but understand its appeal to the devout Roman Catholic.

In this exposition — brief, though I fear too long — of a subject on which volumes and folios have been written almost without number, I have abstained from criticism, for that was not my office; but as a Protestant minister, addressing Protestant students, I may perhaps be permitted to say, in closing, that, to me, the reading of the simple statements of the Gospels in their account of the institution of the Lord's Supper, and of the Epistle to the Hebrews in its treatment of the nature and meaning of our Lord's sacrifice, taken together with the silence of St. Peter, Paul, and James and John concerning any such view of the Eucharist as forms the foundation of the Roman Mass (which view had they held, it must have appeared and imparted its tone to their writings), in fine, to me, the New Testament, in its voice and in its silence, is the one conclusive argument against the validity of the Roman liturgy.

V

THE LUTHERAN LITURGIES

BY THE REV. HENRY EYSTER JACOBS, D.D., LL.D.

Professor of Systematic Theology in the Evangelical Lutheran Seminary, Philadelphia, Pa.

THE LITURGIES OF THE LUTHERAN CHURCH

IN estimating the principles of Christian worship, as they have been applied in the Lutheran Church, the thoroughly conservative character of the Lutheran Reformation must always be kept in mind. Luther did not break abruptly with the past. The movement which claims him as its chief representative was no iconoclastic effort to demolish venerable institutions, as though the entire history and experience of the Church for the preceding fifteen centuries should be expunged.

The hand of God in the Reformation is not denied, when we trace its course in the true line of the historical development of principles inherent in the Church throughout her entire existence. The Lord was never untrue to His promise to be with His people to the end of time. Ever since the day of Pentecost, the Holy Spirit has been a living power within them. Side by side the twofold process may be traced, by which, on the one hand, the truth was corrupted, and, on the other, it was continually brought to clearer apprehension and statement.

Had there been no Mediæval Church, there would have been no Protestant churches. Had there been no Scholastic Theology, there would have been no Theology of the Reformation. The religious experience of Luther was the product of the purest form of the religious life of the Church, as he had received it from his parents and teachers. The evangelical principles were all present, even when the errors which directly contradicted them seemed to be received. More superficial natures could not be so sensitive to the conflict; but with Luther it was a matter of life or death. If the one class were true, the other was necessarily false. If the one class were to be accepted as bringing life, the other was to be rejected as soul-destroying. Without condemning predecessors, who had not appreciated the extent of the antagonism, he who, in his heart-struggle after certainty of faith, had passed through the severest anguish could not be silent. Nevertheless, even in his protest and open conflict, he was only the true and consistent son of the Church, who always maintained that his teaching was that of the Catholic Church, and that it was his opponents who had broken with the past. If in the Ninety-ninth of his Theses of Sept. 4th, 1517, on the Scholastic Theology, he declares, "In these statements, we believe that we have said nothing that is not in harmony with the Catholic Church and the Church's teachers," the Augsburg Confession repeats the same statement as the conviction of all the churches that had followed

Luther, in the words: "Nothing has been received on our part against Scripture or the Church Catholic."

Hence the entire work of Luther and his associates was determined in the liturgical sphere, as in other departments, by constant regard to well-established usage, in so far as this usage was found not to conflict with New Testament teaching and practice.

With the public services of the Church of his day, Luther was thoroughly familiar. He knew them long before he knew his Bible. He learned to know Scripture passages through them, long before the entire volume was first opened by him in the library at Erfurt. No one had been more diligent in the observance of the Canonical Hours, — the foundation for the matin and vesper services. From his boyhood, as a chorister, he had sung their words, until they became a part of his very life. As a most zealous and scholarly monk and priest, he was thoroughly at home in the Mass. His thorough philosophical training had accustomed him to a precision in the use of terms, that made the words offered him as the channels of his devotion the subjects of constant criticism. He sought to say no more than he meant, and to mean every word that he said. The Book of Psalms, so constantly used in these services, was a favorite subject of study, in which, as his cotemporaries, especially Matthesius, tell us, he weighed carefully and with protracted attention every word. His first lectures, as a theological professor, consisted in a verbal explanation of the

Psalms, and throughout his succeeding career their fuller treatment was a favorite occupation, even when the din of controversy was raging all around him. The same intellectual habits and spiritual necessities impelled him to a close attention to other parts of the service. The Collects, the Antiphons, the Responsories, the Graduals, the Tracts, were not regarded as mere forms to be perfunctorily sung or repeated, but as Church rites, that were to be used only as they were the expression of Scriptural teaching, adapted to the wants of the worshipping congregation or of the individual believer.

In this searching examination of all the prescribed Orders, his faith was refreshed by the preponderantly Augustinian character of the Collects, and the fervor and unction of many of the metrical compositions that were found in Missals and Breviaries, and which were afterwards translated or made the foundation of some of his great hymns. At the same time, the worship of saints, especially the Mariolatry, and the centralizing of the main church service around the so-called Sacrifice of the Mass, were unspeakable abominations.

In the hope, however, that the protests made against prevalent abuses would yet be heard, and a reformation of the worship, as well as of doctrine and church government, would be accomplished by the regularly appointed authorities, there was considerable delay in attempting any change. Luther appreciated the difficulties before him in transforming the service from a mere spectacle which the people witnessed, to one in which, as spiritual priests, they could all participate, and in providing for the change from the Latin to the language of the worshippers. Repeatedly did he express his dread of the extremes into which the people might be led, unless all changes were made with the greatest caution.

"I have done nothing forcibly or arbitrarily," he says, "neither have I changed old things for new. There are two classes of persons, because of whom I have always hesitated and dreaded a change: first, the weak in faith, from whom a mode of worship, so long and well-established, cannot be suddenly removed, nor for whom can one so recent and unusual be suddenly introduced; and, secondly, and especially, the trifling and fastidious spirits, who rush forward, without faith and without intelligence, impelled solely by the love of novelty, and who are weary as soon as the novelty ceases. In other spheres, nothing is more troublesome than this class of men; but in holy things, they are particularly offensive and intolerable. Nevertheless I am forced to bear with them, unless I want the gospel to be entirely suppressed."

The principles, however, of public worship, according to which the reformation was to proceed, he outlined as early as 1520, in his "Sermon concerning the New Testament." It is an earnest plea for simplicity in all the external regulations of the worship, upon the ground, "the less law, the better justice; the fewer commandments, the more good works."

The chief thing in worship is declared to be the Word of God; and man's chief part is not to bring something to God, but to receive what God brings him. "If man is to deal with God and receive anything of Him, the mode of procedure is, not that man makes the beginning and lays the first stone; but God alone, without any of man's seeking or desire, must first come, and make a promise. This word of God is the first thing, the foundation, and rock, upon which all the works, words and thoughts of man are to be built. This word man is to thankfully receive, and is to confidently believe the divine promise; and not doubt that it is and shall be precisely as it has been promised." This word of promise is embodied in the Lord's Supper, called "the New Testament in Christ's Blood." Hence, in order that the Lord's Supper be properly used, the words of which it is the seal must be kept in mind and laid to heart. The aim of the entire service is to awaken and confirm in every communicant faith in the redeeming work of Christ, and in its saving application to all who feel themselves to be sinners.

It was Carlstadt's radicalism, during Luther's absence at the Wartburg in the winter of 1521-22, that offered the occasion for the revision, that could be delayed no longer. Early in the year 1523, a revised Order was introduced, under his advice, into the *Stadtkirche* at Wittenberg, and, almost cotemporaneously, a similar Order appeared at Leisnig in Saxony, whose pastors had obtained from Luther a memorandum, "On the Order of Divine Service in the Congregation." In this paper he asserts, first of all, that, in the reformation of the Church, the provisions for public worship should be treated precisely in the same way as those for the preaching of the Word. As preaching should not be abolished, because of the many defects and abuses in the sermons of unevangelical preachers, but should be so reformed and regulated as to become an efficient means of applying the gospel in its purity, and with the utmost simplicity, to the people, so the current Orders, both of Daily Morning and Evening Service, and of the Sunday Chief Service, were only to be purged of their false teaching and to be readjusted to the highest edification of the worshippers.

Three abuses, he tells us, have heretofore prevailed: *first*, the frequent disuse of the sermon, and the confining of the service to the reading and singing of its prescribed portions; *secondly*, the introduction into what is read, sung, and preached, of much for which there is no foundation in God's Word; and *thirdly*, the regarding the service as a meritorious work, by the performance of which man hopes to secure or enjoy more of God's favor. For boys in school, and for all others who in the spirit of Christian Freedom may be disposed to attend, he recommends the continuance of the daily matins and vespers. These services had their value in the fact that from beginning to end, in the Psalms, the Responsaries, the Antiphons, the Chants, and the Lessons, they consisted almost entirely of the repetition of the very words of Holy Scripture. The Sunday services, however, are assigned a still higher position, since they claim the presence of the entire congregation.

The main service was known then as the Mass; as, to the present day, the same term is employed in the Scandinavian countries, after the designation of the service in the ancient Church, as a *Missa catechumenorum* and a *Missa fidelium*. So also the Augsburg Confession declares: "Falsely are our churches accused of abolishing the Mass; for the Mass is retained on our part, and celebrated with the highest reverence" (Art. XXIV.). It was the service held near mid-day on Sundays, in connection with which provision was always made for the administration of the Lord's Supper. All emphasis, in this service, Luther declares, must be placed upon the Word, which then, as well as at the Sunday vespers, must be preached to the whole congregation. At the Mass, the Gospel for the day, and at vespers, the Epistle for the day is to be expounded, unless the preacher prefer to preach upon particular books of the Bible consecutively. At the former service, the Lord's Supper is to be administered to those desiring it.

The principles thus laid down were more fully elaborated in his *Formula Missæ*, written a few months later. The Mass and the Communion, he declares, are rites that were instituted by Christ himself. Both under Christ, and afterwards under the Apostles, they were observed with extreme simplicity. Afterwards so many additions had been made that, besides the name, scarcely anything of the Mass and communion had come down to our times. After an historical examination of the various additions, he considers what parts of the Mass may still be retained. The reading and chanting of the Psalms, the *Kyrie*, the Gospels and Epistles for the day, the *Gloria in Excelsis*, the *Graduals*, the *Hallelujah*, the Nicene Creed, the *Sanctus*, the *Agnus Dei*, etc., are accepted, as contributing to edification, provided they be not required as essentials; that is, as commanded by God, but only as useful ecclesiastical forms. "If different men use different rites," he says, "let not the one judge or despise the other, but let every one abound in that which is according to his judgment. Even though we practise diverse rites, let us hold to the same thing; and let the rites employed by one please the other, so that our diversity of rites may not be followed by diversities of opinions and of sects. For the kingdom of God consists in no particular rite, but in the faith that is within." With characteristic severity he attacks the prevalent thought in the "Canon of the Mass," which had perverted the Holy Supper into the offering of the body of Christ for the sins of the living and the dead. The central truth, which the Lord's Supper was intended to proclaim and seal, was thus utterly denied.

Each element of the Service is then separately criticised. Instead of the *Introits*, he preferred the chanting of the entire Psalms from which they had been taken. In the use of the *Kyrie*, the music should vary according to the season of the Church Year. The use of the *Gloria in Excelsis* was recommended; but was left to the discretion of the bishop. So Scriptural are the *Collects*, that they commend themselves; nevertheless, reverting to the Gregorian usage, he directs that not more than one be used at one time. The selection of lessons from the *Epistles* he criticises for their preponderance of legal elements, styles their compiler a "remarkably ignorant man," and hopes for an ultimate revision which will introduce selections from St. Paul touching the doctrine of faith. The suppression of the *Hallelujah* at Lent, and at other penitential seasons, he disapproves, as this is contrary to the joyful spirit of the Gospel. Even when under the cross, the child of God should be ready to sing songs of triumphant thanksgiving. *Hallelujah enim vox perpetua est Ecclesiæ.* Much thought was given to the proper position of the sermon. Nor, on this subject, did he come altogether into the clear. He suggested, as a very appropriate place, that it introduce the Service, and thus directly precede the *Introit*. " For the Gospel is a *vox clamans in deserto et vocans ad fidem infideles.*"

In the year 1524, Dr. John Bugenhagen, Luther's colleague, and pastor at Wittenberg, embodied these principles in a pamphlet with the title: "Of the Evangelical Mass; what the Mass is, how and by whom and wherefore it was instituted; also how it is to be heard, and the Holy Sacrament received," and containing, as its third part, "An Order for the Evangelical Mass, translated from the Latin." The succession of parts is retained, as in Luther's *Formula;* but after the Epistle a direction is given that a Psalm translated into German, or a German hymn concerning Christ, is to be sung. A formula for "Confession" and a "Declaration of Grace" before the Service is also provided. The express statement is given that this Order must not be regarded as a law, but its use must be left free.

The Strassburg *Kirchen-Amt* of the same year, prepared by Köpphel, also introduces a Confessional Prayer, to be used by the congregation while kneeling, followed by the words: "This is a faithful saying, and worthy of all acceptation, that Christ Jesus came into the world to save sinners; of whom I am chief." This is followed by *Introit, Kyrie, Gloria in Excelsis, Salutation and Collect,* etc., as in the old Orders.

Cotemporaneously appeared an Order for the churches of St. Sebald and St. Lawrence at Nürnberg (Döber's Mass), following the same arrangement of parts, except that, instead of the *Introit,* a German hymn paraphrasing a psalm may be sung, while the minister enters the church. Instead of isolated selections from the Gospels and Epistles as found in the pericopes, a preference is expressed for the *lectio continua* of these two portions of the New Testament.

In 1526, another classical liturgical treatise was published by Luther in his *Deutsche Messe.* The use of the vernacular in the public worship is especially urged. God is to be addressed by the worshippers only in such language as they themselves understand. But wherever a language is intelligible to the congregation or a portion of it, whether that language be German or Latin, its use is appropriate. "Were I able," he says, "and the Greek and Hebrew were as common as the Latin, and had in them as much fine music and song, as the Latin has, Mass should be celebrated, one Sunday after another, in all four languages,— German, Latin, Greek, and Hebrew." Luther's hymns, therefore, have their origin in his efforts to translate and popularize the church service. Instead of mere spectators and listeners, he sought to make the people actual participants in the worship. Psalms, Canticles, Graduals, and even the Creed, that had heretofore been chanted by those trained for the purpose, were paraphrased into German verse, and set to familiar or easy tunes. Within the single year, 1524, the most of Luther's hymns were written. Their aim was not so much to supplement as to popularize the service. Even the Ten Commandments appeared in verse, each stanza ending with the *Kyrie*. Instead of the *Introit*, a versified paraphrase of a psalm, in German, was often sung. *Nun bitten wir den Heiligen Geist* was a popular adaptation of the *Gradual*, while the Nicene Creed appeared in *Wir glauben all an einen Gott*. A paraphrase of the Lord's Prayer was the first form of the prayer after the sermon.

As time progressed, there was a similar reformation of the service in every principality of Germany that had accepted the Lutheran faith. The principles laid down by Luther in his *Formula Missæ* and *Deutsche Messe* were consistently applied; and that, too, with the assertion of Christian Freedom in justifying diversities according to circumstances of time and place.

The Lutheran Church has peculiar capacities for adaptation to diverse gifts, and degrees of culture, and preferences of men, with respect to the externals of worship. Laying all stress upon unity in faith and confession, it is thankful that it is able to express this one faith in so many diversified forms both of government and cultus. What is often regarded as the very strictest of the Lutheran Confessions declares: "We believe, teach, and confess that no Church should condemn another, because one has less or more external ceremonies, not commanded by God, than the other, if otherwise there be agreement among them in doctrine, and all its articles, as well also as in the right use of the Holy Sacraments" (*Formula of Concord*, chap. x.). Lutheranism knows how to discriminate between what is desirable and what is essential. Uniformity in worship, if attainable, is often highly desirable; but there are greater questions at stake than that of mere external conformity to a given model. Augusti, accordingly, has stated that no less than one hundred and thirty-two Lutheran orders were published between 1523 and 1555. Nevertheless this does not indicate general confusion. In every respect, many of these orders are identical, and may be regarded as substantial reprints. A very few became the standards, which some with more, and others with less, revision, followed. They have been classified according to three distinct types: —

1. The *Ultra Conservative*, where the effort is the greatest to reproduce the Mediæval Service, with only such changes as seem to be imperatively demanded for doctrinal reasons. Of this type, the Mark-Brandenburg Order of 1540, the Pfalz-Neuburg of 1543, and the Austrian of 1571, are types. In the first of these, the chants are sung in Latin; the prayers are made in German; the Gospel and Epistle are first chanted in Latin, and then read in German, with the preface: "This is the Epistle, beloved, which you have heard sung in Latin." In the consecration, both the bread and the cup are elevated *cum modica inclinatione*. The words of Institution and the Lord's Prayer are sung in German; while, following the *Agnus Dei*, are three Collects, said in Latin, for the forgiveness of sins. The service ends with a German, followed by a Latin, Collect. The latter is subject to the just criticism of transcending the Lutheran doctrine of the Real Presence, by the use of language that, even if though meant in a figurative sense, admits of the interpretation of a permanent union between the bread and the body of Christ, and of that Capernaitic eating thereof, which the Lutheran Church afterwards confessionally repudiated in the Formula

of Concord: "*Quod nos peccatores sumpsimus et calix quem potavimus adhæreat visceribus nostris, et præsta ut ibi nulla remaneat peccati macula, ubi tam pura et sancta introierunt sacramenta.*" The *Pfalz-Neuburg* Order follows the Mark-Brandenburg in this.

While in 1539, Luther declares his indifference as to the extent to which external conformity with Roman ceremonies may be carried, provided only that the gospel be purely preached, the sacraments be properly administered, and no invocation of saints, or consecration of holy water, or Masses for the dead, or sacramental processions be admitted, nevertheless, at other times, he speaks freely concerning his apprehensions as to whither merely archaistic tendencies may lead. Problems were presented by the *Leipzig Interim* of 1548, concerning which the *Formula of Concord* had to make a definite statement as to the limitations with which ceremonies should be regarded as mere *adiaphora*. Rites which, of themselves, are matters of indifference, may become marks or badges of a false Confession. Times there are when it makes a difference whether we wear a blue or an orange ribbon, a white or a red rose, though this of itself be an *adiaphoron*. "We believe, teach and confess," says the Confession just cited, "that, in time of persecution, when a bold confession is required of us, we should not yield to the enemies in regard to such *adiaphora*. . . . For in such case, it is no longer a question concerning *adiaphora*, but concerning the truth of the gospel, Christian Liberty and sanctioning open idolatry, as also concerning the prevention of offence to the weak, in which we have nothing to concede, but must boldly confess, and then suffer whatever God allows the enemies of His Word to inflict upon us."

2. The *Conservative* type, following the principles set forth by Luther in his liturgical treatises. The general structure of the Gregorian Order which underlies the Latin Mass is here retained, but with important changes and adaptations. Of these, the most influential, probably, was the Brandenburg-Nürnberg, prepared by Osiander and Brentz in 1533, and revised by the Wittenberg Faculty. The Orders prepared by Bugenhagen for a number of States and cities in Northern Germany, as Brunswick (1528), Hamburg (1529), Lübeck (1531), Pomerania (1535); the Hanover Order (1536), prepared by Regius ; and the Order prepared in 1536 for Duke Henry of Saxony by Justus Jonas, belong to the same class. So also do the Swedish Order, and the Danish Order, prepared by Bugenhagen. Another most important Order of this type was the one prepared by Melanchthon and Bucer in 1547 for Archbishop Hermann in his proposed Reformation of Cologne. It was based upon the Brandenburg-Nürnberg Order, and, although never introduced, lives in the Prayer Book of the Church of England, through the first Prayer Book of Edward VI., which drew largely upon it, and which we claim as one of the members of this group of Lutheran liturgies.

3. The liturgies of Southwest Germany, the Bran-

denburg-Nürnberg excepted. While Lutheran in doctrine, they show the influence of the earlier efforts of Dr. John Brentz, the Würtemberg reformer, in the revision of the service, in which he had less regard for historical precedents than at a later period. With all his endeavors afterwards, to conform the Würtemberg Orders to the type that had been established in Saxony, the most he could do was to effect a compromise. These liturgies are recognized, therefore, as mediating between the Lutheran and Reformed types. They assume a fixed form in *The greater Würtemburg Order* of 1553, providing for two orders, one for communion days, and the other for other occasions. On communion days, the order is: 1. Hymn to the Holy Spirit, a German Psalm, or any hymn suitable to the time. 2. Sermon, followed by the General Prayer. 3. Creed (German). 4. Admonition concerning the Lord's Supper. 5. Brief prayer read. 6. Chanting of the Lord's Prayer. 7. Words of Institution. 8. Administration, a hymn being sung while communicants go to the altar. 9. Prayer of thanksgiving. 10. Patriarchal Benediction. For other Sundays: 1. A Latin Introit or a German Hymn. 2. Sermon. 3. Reading of the General Prayer. 4. Psalm or Hymn. 5. Benediction. Some elements are omitted in the enumeration, clearly because the pastors were assumed to understand that they were inseparable from elements that are mentioned, as, for example, the reading of the Gospel, before the sermon. Here the responsive features of the service have vanished, except that the Litany may be used for the General Prayer, or at special services on appointed days.

In all these Orders, however, even in those of the first class, provision is made for a considerable degree of flexibility, by express directions in the Rubrics, that, in the country churches and villages, a much simpler form might be followed, without destroying the organism of the worship, while a more elaborate rendering of the service was desirable in the cities, where the necessary musical resources were accessible. In thus seeking to adapt the principles of the service to the conditions of the people, while at the same time preserving all its parts, Bugenhagen's Order provides for no less than seven hymns, as *Introit*, *Gloria in Excelsis*, and *Agnus Dei* assume a hymnal form.

Underlying the Lutheran conception of the service are certain principles, necessary to be kept in mind in order to appreciate the mutual relations of its several parts. All true worship is the communion of man with God, in response to an assurance of favor and a divine invitation encouraging such approach. Upon some word and promise of God every prayer must rest. Two factors, therefore, are found in all true worship; namely, the divine invitation and the human response. God is ever graciously giving, and man is ever thankfully receiving. The former is the sacramental, and the latter the sacrificial, element of worship. A clear statement of this distinction is made by Melanchthon in the Apology of the Augsburg Confession.[1] The sacramental element is not limited to the two Sacraments, but, in a general sense, comprises every act in which God brings man a blessing, and thus belongs to the preaching and reading of the Word, as well as to Baptism and the Lord's Supper. A sacrifice, however, is any act whereby man brings something to God, in order to afford Him honor. Sacrifices are of two kinds. The propitiatory sacrifice, whereby God's wrath is appeased and His favor gained, is found only in the sacrifice of Christ for us on the Cross. But eucharistic sacrifices of prayer, praise, and thanksgiving are to be continual, offered by those who, through the one propitiatory sacrifice once offered, are reconciled to God.

Examining the three main types of Christian worship, it is claimed that these three factors, the sacramental, the propitiatory-sacrificial, and the eucharistic-sacrificial, distinguish three forms of Christianity. Romanism, and, to a less degree, Greek Catholicism, obscure or deny the doctrine of the completion of Christ's sacrifice on Calvary as the sole propitiation for our sins. The worship centres, therefore, around the Bloodless Sacrifice of Christ in the Mass, for the sins of the living and the dead. By being converted into a sacrifice, the sacramental force of the Lord's Supper is lost. The assurance of forgiveness, of which it is the pledge, has vanished.

---

[1] *Book of Concord* (Jacobs), i. 262.

God no longer is recognized as approaching His people with the words of pardon and comfort. But instead, the priest, in order to shelter the people from the divine wrath, offers the body of Christ to an angry and as yet unappeased God. Nor in the Holy Supper do we find, according to this conception, a divine act; but Masses are multiplied, as works whereby man brings something to God.

The Reformed and Lutheran conceptions of the public service are alike based upon a combination of the thought of the eucharistic sacrifice with that of the sacrament. The proportion, however, is different; or there is a variation in the side emphasized. The question involved is, as to whether the main end be the rendering to God of the sincere offering of grateful hearts, or the receiving of God's riches of forgiving, renewing, enlightening, and strengthening grace. Are the hearing of God's Word and the reception of the Holy Supper chiefly incentives to prayer and praise? Or do prayer and praise only prepare for and accompany Word and Sacrament, and help us to receive them? Is the Lord's Supper principally an act whereby man professes his faith, or one whereby God comes, with a peculiar blessing, to man? Which part of the minister's duty is the more important, — that whereby he stands before God as the leader of the congregation, or that whereby he stands before the congregation as the representative of God?

According to the Lutheran conception, the sacramental is the main element. Not the prayers and chants and hymns of the people, or even the word of the pastor, testifying from the depth of his Christian experience, but the Word of God, is itself the chief part of every service. The reading and repeating of this Word have a sacramental force; as with the Word, and only through the Word, comes the divine blessing. The Lord's Supper is no sacrifice that the worshipper offers, or that any priest offers for him. He thanks God for the sacrifice made for him, once for all, ages ago, when his Lord declared: "It is finished." Of this complete redemption he finds a sure pledge in the gift to him, with the bread and wine, of the very Body and Blood that have paid the price for his sins, and bought him back from the bondage of Satan to the sonship of God. Luther, in expounding the true character of the Lord's Supper as a sacrament of the New Testament, says in his sermon concerning the New Testament of 1520: " A testament receives no benefit from us; but brings a benefit to us. Who ever heard of a man doing a good work by receiving a testament? Man does nothing but take to himself the benefit that is offered. In the Lord's Supper, therefore, we give Christ nothing; but only receive from Him the blessing."

The entire life of the service is dependent upon the reciprocal action of these two elements; just as the life of the body continues by the twofold process of inhalation and expiration. God speaks. Man responds; and then God speaks again. In the eucharistic sacrifice the heart turns to God, and opens for the blessing, which is immediately followed by the word of divine grace. But no sooner is the blessing received than it immediately awakens new emotions. The heart overflows with gratitude, with the sense of unworthiness of the blessings received, and with the desire for closer union with God, and a more worthy service of so gracious a benefactor. The expression of this is another eucharistic act, to which God responds in a new blessing.

Thus the entire service is a conversation between God and man; a continual giving and receiving. Now the pastor acts as the representative of the people before God, when he leads their prayers; and then, as the representative of God to the people, as he reads or proclaims the Word, or administers the sacrament. Now the people exercise the function of their spiritual priesthood, in their united hymns and prayers, — the eucharistic act; and then, again, stand and speak in God's name, as, in their responses, they announce to one another the consolations and admonitions of God's Word, — the sacramental act.

So also the various parts of the service are directed towards a common end. The entire plan of salvation, from its beginnings in the counsels of eternity to its completion in the new heavens and the new earth, is gradually unfolded. A portion of the service, like the needs of the Christian life and their supply, is permanent; while another portion is variable with the change of times and seasons; yet so as to present each year (such, at least, is the aim) the leading features of the life of Christ, all the doctrines of the Christian faith, and all the duties of the Christian life. Not in advance was this organism of the service determined. Gradually and spontaneously it emerged from the experience of believers, as, from generation to generation, they assembled to hear and worship. Even where a fixed liturgy is discarded, or no attention is given to any scientific expression of principles, it reappears, without law or prescription, as to its main features, from the necessities of a common religious experience.

The ideal of congregational worship in the minds of the Lutheran reformers could not be realized within a single generation. Luther's introduction to the Small Catechism (1529) may be read, if we desire to learn the standard of intelligence and the extent of the religious knowledge among the most of the congregations with which they had to deal. A people unaccustomed to participate in the service were to be gradually trained to be more than mere spectators who "attended Mass." This had to be accomplished without hymn or prayer-book in their hands as to-day. The time was in the Lutheran Church when a book, even of hymns, in the hands of a member of the congregation was regarded as formalism. All hymns that were to be sung, it was thought, should be committed to memory, in order that men could sing from the heart what had first been learned by heart.

But before the complete revision of the service throughout the Lutheran churches of Germany could be attained, a new period came. Scholastic Lutheranism burdened the service with labored attempts at dogmatical precision of statement. Gradually the freshness and warmth of the sixteenth century vanish. The overwhelming preponderance of what was purely didactic in sermon, prayer, and hymn hinders the free movement between the sacramental and sacrificial elements. Then came the scourge of the Thirty Years' War, reducing the population of Germany to one fourth, and devastating alike city and country in many regions where the Lutheran faith was most unequivocally confessed. Then came Pietism, with its standard of what subserves the purposes only of individual and temporary devotion. The Common Prayer and common testimony of the Church were overshadowed by the individuality of the one who professed to lead the devotions. Then came Rationalism, which regarded sermon and service purely with respect to moral ends, and not as a means of the united communion of the children of God with their Heavenly Father, upon the ground solely of their redemption, as lost sinners, by the blood of Christ. No wonder that the orders of the sixteenth century were depreciated by those whose preaching was directly contradicted by their Scriptural teaching.

Both in Germany and America, during the last half century, there has been a widespread return to these orders, accompanied with the recognition of the necessity of certain adaptations to circumstances of time and place. In so doing, the Lutheran Church in

America has only reverted in the liturgical sphere, as she has generally done in the confessional sphere, to the foundations laid by her great organizer, Henry Melchior Muhlenberg, — a man who united the best elements of Pietism with thorough fidelity to the Lutheran Confessions, and who, as a Hanoverian, came from a portion of Germany where the Lutheran service of the Reformation period had been retained in its purity. At the first meeting of the first Lutheran Synod in America in 1748, an Order, prepared by him, was adopted, which, when the condition of the Lutheran churches of that period is considered, is remarkable for its fidelity to liturgical principles. The order is: A hymn to the Holy Spirit; an exhortation to Confession; the Confession of Sins; the *Kyrie;* a versified paraphrase of the *Gloria in Excelsis;* Salutation and Collect for the day; Epistle for the day, followed by a hymn; Gospel for the day; Paraphrase of the Creed, in verse; Sermon; General Prayer, according to a prescribed form, than which "nothing else shall be read," save only that the Litany may be used instead, followed by special supplications, as circumstances suggest; the Lord's Prayer; Hymn; closing Collect; Benediction; Hymn verse.

In 1783, Muhlenberg expressed his great desire that all the Lutheran congregations in North America should be united with one another, and use the same Order of Service and same Hymn Book. Within the last decade, all the so-called General Bodies of the Lutheran Church in this country, upon the motion of the United Synod of the South, have either adopted or indorsed the "Common Service," — an order embodying the consensus of the pure Lutheran liturgies of the sixteenth century. "The aim has been," we quote from an official statement, "to furnish the full Lutheran service for all who wish to use it. But if, at any time or place, the use of the full service is impracticable or undesired, it is not contrary to Lutheran principles or usage to follow a simple form, in which only the principal parts of the Common Service, in their order, are retained."

Briefly following the various parts of this "Common Service," the *Confession of Sins*, with which it opens, is demanded by the necessities of the Christian heart. For the very first thought that arises, as we come into the Divine Presence, is that of the contrast between God's holiness and our sinfulness. In the Orders that were followed, it is, indeed, true that the weight of authorities would have begun the service with the *Introit*. But this occurred, where there was a confessional service, late on the preceding evening (*Beicht-Vesper*), or early in the morning before the chief service began. The absence of a confession, where these subordinate services do not occur, would have been a violation of the principle. Accordingly after the example of Bugenhagen's Order and the Strasburg Order (both 1524), and the Brandenburg-Nürnberg (1533), the private prayers that, before this, were prescribed for the use of the priest, as he came to the altar, were adapted to the general wants of all present, and made the prayer of the entire congregation.

But when *The Confession* has been made, the heart yearns for some assurance of forgiveness. Hence it is followed by a *Declaration of Grace*, announcing in three sentences the mercy of God in the gift of His Son, the sending of the Holy Spirit, and the institution of the means of grace, and praying that what God has thus provided may be savingly enjoyed by all present. This declaration differs from an absolution in two respects, since the absolution is administered to an individual, and not to an entire congregation; and, secondly, the absolution is not the prayer for forgiveness, but the absolute impartation of God's pardoning grace to a penitent and believing man.

Joyful in the consciousness of the love of God thus pledged, the congregation can now enter upon what is properly *The Service*. As each Sunday presents its peculiar message of divine grace, and has its peculiar part of the plan of salvation to unfold, it is the office of the *Introit* to announce the main thought of the day. Many of the Sundays are known by the opening words of the Introit. Thus we have in Lent, *Invocavit*, *Reminiscere*, *Oculi* etc., and after Easter, *Quasimodogeniti*, *Misericordias*, *Jubilate*, *Cantate*, *Rogate*. The Introits, in their present form, appear first in the Gregorian Order. They have their origin however, in the Psalms, with which not only in the Apostolic Church, but also in the synagogues, the services began. Two parts belong to every Introit:

first, the scriptural words announcing the thought of the day, generally taken from the Psalms, and rendered at first antiphonally; and, secondly, the psalm verse, which is generally the first verse of a psalm, that probably was once sung throughout when thus announced. Then followed the *Gloria Patri*, which belongs to the Introit, because taken from the Psalms. The *Gloria Patri*, as used in our church services, at the close of every psalm, shows that the psalms have acquired a new meaning in the light of the gospel, and that we use them not as Jews, but as Christians.

But no sooner has the *Gloria Patri* been called forth in gratitude for what has been heard in the psalm, than there once more arises in man's heart the sense of his sinfulness and unworthiness. As even the apostle who had leaned on Jesus' breast fell as dead at the manifestation of the divine glory in the beginning of the Apocalypse, so the devout worshipper, after learning of God's favor, remembers that, even though he be a forgiven child of God, rejoicing in the consciousness of his sonship, nevertheless he still lives upon earth, and sin still exists within and around him. Hence there arises the plaintive *Kyrie, Eleieson* ("Lord, have mercy upon us;' Christ, have mercy upon us; 'Lord, have mercy upon us"), which is not simply a Trinitarian formula, but which looks back towards the fountain of all mercy as existing before the world, then to its historical manifestation in time; and finally, through all the stages of applying grace, to its full fruition in the world to come.

Then, as always in the Christian life, the cry for mercy is succeeded by the triumphant celebration of what we are and have in Christ, as the *Gloria in Excelsis* is chanted, — a hymn of which Luther declared: " It did not grow ; nor was it made on earth ; it came down from heaven." In it, the spirit of devotion, under the electric thrill of intense feeling, has blended many Scriptural passages, so that every clause of this, the greater *Gloria*, uses a new Scriptural phrase as the vehicle of its adoration and worship. It is truly termed a summary of all the hymns of thanksgiving and praise, both in this world and the world to come, that follow the contemplation of God's glory in the incarnation of Christ. May not its foundation be " the hymn to Christ as God" which the famous letter of Pliny to Trajan says that the early Christians chanted in their early morning worship?

The first part of the service, thus concluded by the *Gloria in Excelsis*, is chiefly sacrificial; for it consists mainly of prayer, praise and thanksgiving. The second part is chiefly sacramental; for in it, God approaches man with His Word, to bestow His blessing. The worshippers, before active, now become receptive. The transition, however, is gradual. Wherever God comes to men with His Word, they meet His approach with prayer. Hence the reading of the Word is preceded by a Collect. In uniting in the *Collect*, the pastor first prays for the people in the *Salutation*, and the people, for the pastor in the response: *And with Thy Spirit;* and then their combined petition arises in the brief and condensed language of these simple, but at the same time profound and comprehensive, prayers, through which the children of God have, for ages, been carrying to the throne of Grace the deepest felt aspirations of their hearts. That the most of them are a thousand years earlier than the Reformation, and cannot be claimed as the exclusive property of the Lutheran Church, only renders them the more precious to us. While drawn chiefly from the Leonine (A. D. 440), Gelasian (A. D. 492), and Gregorian (A. D. 596) sacramentaries, they were embodied there as formulas already approved, and we may, therefore, assume that some of them are much older than the book in which we first find them. Most clear and vivid expressions of the Augustinian theology, they adopt, at times, the very language of the great expounder of the doctrines of the utter nothingness of man, and the sovereignty of divine grace. Some of the very oldest came forth from a period when the Nestorian controversy was still fresh, and the Church gave the simplest and most direct expression to the doctrine of incarnation, with its unfathomable depths, upon which its mind had been greatly exercised. Their deep spirituality is the reflection of a period, when the vanity of earthly things was especially impressed by the decay of the Roman Empire, the inroads of the barbarians, the growing insecurity, the siege, the capture, the pillage of Rome itself, and when, where all was confusion and desolation, men turned to God, and found in Him that peace which the world could not give.

After the *Collect*, come the Scripture Lessons, where the practice of the ancient Church is retained in changing the synagogue lessons of the Law and the Prophets into those of the *Epistle*, the New Testament Law, and the *Gospel*, the fulfilment of the prophets. The selections themselves are those which the Reformers found already made for them. But various portions of the Lutheran Church have guarded against excessive rigidity in their use, by providing schemes of supplementary and even alternative lessons. So well-adapted, however, are the Gospels for the day to the end of presenting, in methodical order, within the year, the chief events of our Lord's life on earth, and the words which he left to be proclaimed, that they have a hold upon the hearts of the people which, without the urgency of any ecclesiastical regulation, creates the demand that they be, in general, followed, and renders any system of instruction unpopular among us, that attempts to completely revolutionize this order.

The *Sermon* is the application of the Word that is read. The lessons are not determined by the sermon that is to be preached; but the sermon that is to be preached is, as a rule, determined by the lessons. The sermon is supplementary and subordinate to the reading of the Holy Scriptures.

But, before proceeding to the sermon, and dwelling upon the one particular aspect of truth and duty presented by the day, in the repetition of *The Creed*, a survey is first taken of the entire scope of Christian doctrine. While theoretically the preference is given to the Nicene Creed, as the *regula fidei* of the ancient Church, nevertheless, in general usage, except, on the Chief Festivals and Communion Sundays, it gives place to the Apostles' Creed, as that which is better adapted to popular use. Following it, is a hymn, known as "*the* Hymn" of the service, as it is intended to particularly express the thought of the Lessons.

While, as a rule, the *Sermon* is upon the Gospel or Epistle for the day, free texts are often used as circumstances may suggest or the edification of the congregation may require.

The sermon preached, the minister descends from the pulpit, where he has stood as the representative of God to man, and goes to the altar, where he stands as the leader of the congregation and one of their number, in their approach to God.

What is called *The Offertory* has nothing, except its relative place, in common with the portion of the Roman Mass which is so designated. The Fifty-first, or another penitential psalm is chanted here, after a custom still more ancient than the Roman Offertory, as the expression of the sense of sin and of need of forgiveness, called forth by the Word of God proclaimed in the sermon, and as the declaration of the entire consecration of the people to the Lord, whose rights have just been asserted.

The General Prayer, which follows, is not a mere

résumé or application of the sermon, or even a prayer whose chief contents are the necessities of the worshipping congregation. At every stage of the service up to this point, these necessities have found expression. ¡The purpose of the General Prayer is that through it, the congregation may ask God that others may obtain the blessings which through the Word have been brought to them, and for which they have given thanks. It is not a prayer of the officiating minister for the congregation to which he has preached, but a prayer of the congregation itself.ˈ It is the common prayer of the whole people, expressed in simple and well-known words, and free, as far as possible, from such individual peculiarities as, by inviting criticism, would interfere with the intelligent adoption of all its petitions by every man, woman, and child in the audience, in whom God's Spirit has enkindled the flame of devotion. In it, the wants of all classes and conditions of men are recalled, and recounted before God.

The "Long Prayer," made in some of the Reformed churches before the sermon, has a different scope, since the adoration, thanksgiving, confession of sin, and supplication for pardon for which it provides, have been previously offered to God in the Order which we are explaining. It is peculiarly the Intercessory Prayer of the service. A place is found in this "General Prayer" for the introduction of "special supplications, intercessions, and prayers," as peculiar circumstances may suggest; but as to other parts, in order that the people may enter with the least distraction into the prayer, it is urgently recommended that, whatever variety may be employed in adapting prayers to individual wants at other times, in this prayer they should know beforehand not only for what, but also in what words, they are to pray. The aim of the Lutheran Reformers of the service, in this respect, is stated in the Würtemberg Order (one of the least conservative), where it is said : " Although the Lord's Prayer is in itself a General Prayer, and should always have the preference, as a brief summary of all other Christian prayers, nevertheless, since the other prayers comprised in the Holy Scriptures, and especially in the Psalms, or, according to present necessities derived from passages of Holy Scripture, are an explanation and exposition of the Lord's Prayer, they should not be rejected, but be used, at the proper time, in connection with the Lord's Prayer."

The entire structure of "the General Prayer," and, to an extent, its various petitions, have reached us by a clearly traceable historical process. When Luther substituted "The Lord's Prayer" for "The Offertory," and prefaced it by a paraphrase, explaining its petitions in detail, he was only returning to an older practice. In some of the ancient Oriental liturgies, of which that of St. James was a type, it was customary to comply with the Apostolic command that "supplications, prayers, intercessions, and giving of thanks be made for all men" (1 Tim. ii. 1), by a series of exhortations, specifying at length the various objects to be prayed for, as in the Bidding Prayer, to which the people replied in the words, " Lord, have mercy." So in some of the earlier Lutheran Orders, a very full exhortation of a similar character is used as a preface to the Lord's Prayer. Thus, in the Brunswick Order, prepared by Bugenhagen in 1531:

"Let us pray for his Imperial Majesty, and all who bear the temporal sword. Pray also for the ministers who feed us with the Word of God. Pray also for temporal peace, for the sick, the weak, the sorrowing, the tempted, women with child, for our enemies, for all necessities of body and soul. Let us pray for one another that all may be saved. Let us unite in the Lord's Prayer."

These exhortations, however, being themselves embodied in particular collects with which the Church was familiar, these collects were first said successively, as in the Brandenberg-Nürnberg Order, and, afterwards, by a very natural process, were combined in the continuous prayer, which is found, almost as now used, in the Würtemberg Order of 1553.

The *Consecration* consists of The Lord's Prayer, the Words of Institution, and the *Pax*. The consecration itself lies in the use of the words of Institution, the Lord's Prayer either preceding or following them, as consecratory of the communicants in their approach to this mystery, while of the *Pax* (" The peace of the Lord be with you alway "), Luther says: "It is the voice of the Gospel, announcing the forgiveness of sins, and is the only and most worthy preparation for the Lord's Table."

The communicants then approach the altar while the *Agnus Dei* is sung. In this chant, there is nothing to justify the objection that it is connected with the doctrine of the sacrifice of Christ in the Mass. It has been used as a part of the *Gloria in Excelsis* at the beginning of the service; and its repetition here, where the minds of communicants are thus directed to the Lamb of God that taketh away the sin of the world, is most appropriate and edifying. In the *Distribution*, each communicant receives directly from the pastor the consecrated elements, with the words: " Take, eat; this is the Body of Christ given for thee. Take and drink; this is the Blood of Christ, shed for thy sins." The words, " Given for thee," were added by Luther to the formula of distribution, in accordance with his statement that in them lay the chief stress of the sacrament.

The rest of the service is a gradual descent from this exalted place, where weak and sinful man has been admitted into the holy of holies, and conversed almost face to face with his Redeemer and reconciled Father. He has the highest joy that earth can afford, and his lips pour forth the song of Simeon, " Lord, now lettest thou thy servant depart in peace," and, after a thanksgiving collect composed by Luther, he receives the patriarchal benediction, " The Lord bless thee and keep thee," which was precious to Luther, because the pronoun is in the singular number. As the congregation disperses, each individual departs with the peace of God in his heart, and the light of God's countenance resting upon him.

The other church services hold a subordinate character, and follow the Orders for matins and vespers. Their aim is to provide for the systematic continuous reading of the Holy Scriptures, accompanied by Psalms, hymns, and a brief exhortation. They transfer to the New Testament the main features of public worship, in which our Lord himself frequently participated in the synagogues of His people. The structure of the two services is essentially the same. They differ chiefly in the Psalms used, and in the tone of the worship. In the Matin Service, thanksgiving preponderates; while in the Vesper Service, supplication. The former is more jubilant; the latter breathes the spirit of humble resignation and trust in the divine mercy.

Where congregations, however, are not prepared to use these fixed orders to edification, the Lutheran Church has infinite capacities for adapting the simple truth as it is in Jesus to their varied wants. The service is used as a means to an end, which, like all human arrangements, even when determined by compliance with the impulses of the Holy Spirit, is not an absolute finality. Fixed orders are not used, as though there could be no true worship without them; nor are historical orders repudiated, as though they were obsolete, and no true worship could be found except in that which is born in the present moment.

"Of Rites and Usages, they teach," says the Augsburg Confession (Art. XV.), "that those ought to be observed which may be observed without sin, and which are profitable unto tranquillity. . . . Nevertheless, concerning such things let men be admonished that consciences are not to be burdened as though such observance were necessary for salvation."

Each age has its peculiar wants; and for each age and land God has a special message. The Lutheran Church, therefore, while turning reverently to the sixteenth century to find there the basis for her service, is fully conscious that she cannot rest there, but that the spirit of faith must mingle with the voices of believers in the past, the sincere expression of her own peculiar experiences in the present. Her liturgy, like her hymn-book, represents all ages of the Church, and must continually grow. But this growth can afford permanent results, and contribute to general edification, only as it proceeds upon a well-established historical basis.

BIBLIOGRAPHY.

The following bibliographical list does not attempt to be exhaustive. It aims simply at giving some of the chief works serviceable to a student, who may desire to pursue the subject further:

Daniel, H. A. D., *Codex liturgicus Ecclesiæ Universæ.* 4 vols., Leipzig, 1847. (Vol. II. for Lutheran liturgies.)

Kliefoth, Th., *Liturgische Abhandlungen*, Schwerin, 1854, 2d ed. 1868, 8 vols. (The first five volumes treat of *Die Ursprüngliche Gottesdienst-Ordnung in den deutschen Kirchen lutherischen Bekenntnisses, ihre Destruction und Reformation.*)

Schöberlein, L., *Ueber den liturgischen Ausbau des Gemeindegottesdienstes in der deutschen evangelischen Kirche.* Gotha, 1859.

Schöberlein, L., *Schatz des liturgischen Chor- und Gemeindegesangs nebst den Altarwesen in der deutschen evangelischen Kirche aus den Quellen vornehmlich des 16ten und 17ten Jahrhunderts geschöpft.* 3 vols.

Jacoby, H., *Die Liturgik der Reformatoren.* 2 vols., Gotha, 1876. (Vol. I. Luther; Vol. II. Melanchthon.)

Löhe, W., *Agende für Christliche Gemeinden des lutherischen Bekenntnisses.* 3d ed., enlarged by J. Deinzer. Nordlingen, 1884. (Valuable for its introductions and notes.)

Köstlin, H. A. F., *Geschichte des Christlichen Gottesdienstes.* Freiburg, 1887.

Harnack, Th., Outline of Liturgics in Zöckler's *Handbuch der theologischen Wissenschaften.* 3d edition, München, 1890.

Cantionale für die evangelisch lutherischen Kirchen im Grossherzogthum Mecklenburg-Schwerin. 4 vols., folio, Schwerin, 1886-1887.

Höfling, J. H. F., *Liturgische Urkundenbuch, enthaltend die Akte der Communion, der Ordination und Introduction, und der Trauung.* Leipzig, 1852.

Nitzsch, *Praktische Theologie.* 2 vols., Bonn, 1851.

Zezschwitz, *Praktische Theologie.* Leipzig, 1878.

Siona, A Monthly, devoted to Liturgics and Church Music, published since at Gütersloh (Schöberlein, Herold, Krüger).

Above all, Richter, A. E. L., *Die evangelischen Kirchenordnungen des sechszehnten Jahrhunderts.* 2 vols., Weimar, 1846. Contains most of the chief Lutheran liturgies of the period from 1523-1598.

The Originals in large number may be found in the Liturgical Library at Mt. Airy, Philadelphia.

VI
THE LITURGIES OF THE REFORMED CHURCHES

By the Rev. WILLIAM RUPP, D.D.

Professor of Practical Theology in the Reformed Theological Seminary, Lancaster, Pa.

THE LITURGIES OF THE REFORMED CHURCHES

THERE exists an intimate relation between religious doctrine and worship, or between creed and liturgy. Worship is the expression and action of faith, and faith is the root and motive of worship. Religious faith will always create a system of worship corresponding to its own character; and any system of religious rites and ceremonies will in time give rise to a corresponding creed. Hence the Reformation of the sixteenth century was bound to be equally a reformation of worship and of doctrine.

The Reformers were all agreed as to the necessity of a reformation in worship. The existing abuses and superstitions excited their profoundest indignation and horror. The sacrifice of the Mass especially, and the idolatrous worship of the saints and angels, were, in their view, the very abomination of desolation, now standing permanently in the temple of God. That these abuses must be removed and the existing order of worship reformed, was a proposition to which all the Reformers were agreed. But they differed somewhat in the manner in which they carried out the work of reformation; and so we come to have different orders of worship in different parts of the Protestant Church. In this respect there is a general difference between the churches of the Lutheran and those of the Reformed confessions.

This difference is usually expressed by the proposition that the Lutherans were the more conservative and the Reformed the more radical in the work of reformation. The principle adopted by the Lutheran reformers, it is usually said, was to reject nothing in the cultus of the Catholic Church that was not repugnant to some express statement of the Bible; while the principle adopted by the Reformed was to accept nothing that could not be supported by direct Scriptural authority. Both parties made Scripture the rule of their reforming activity; but they applied this rule with varying degrees of strictness, and hence there arose a difference in their work. With some reservation this representation may be accepted as correct. In reconstructing their worship, the Reformed churches were guided less by the principle of tradition and more by the principle of Scripture, than the Lutheran Church. Hence the Reformed liturgies are characterized by a greater degree of simplicity and unadorned grandeur, but also, in proportion as they drew upon the Old Testament for their material, by something of a legalistic and Judaistic tone, which the student of liturgics will not fail to notice. Nevertheless they all show evidence, more or less plainly, of their origin in the old order of worship, and thus of their connection with the past history and life of the Church. The Reformed churches are not unhistorical creations of the sixteenth century; but in doctrine and worship they are rooted in the old order of Christian life and action within the fields in which they originated.

The Reformed liturgies may be divided into three distinct families or groups, — namely, the *Zwinglian*, the *Calvinistic*, and the *Calvino-Melanchthonian*, or the Swiss, French, and German; the Scotch and English belonging to the second of these groups. They all possess certain elements in common, but differ in special features, according to their national and historical relations. One common feature of all Reformed liturgies, for instance, consists in this, that the public services of God are divided into two kinds, namely, *preaching services* and *communion services*. In the old Catholic Church the Eucharist formed an essential part of every Lord's day service. In the mediæval Church the sermon was suppressed, and the Eucharist, which was now regarded as a sacrifice for the living and the dead, came to be the chief, indeed almost the only, part of Christian cultus. The sacrifice, however, was not a service rendered by the congregation, but by the priesthood in behalf of the congregation. And it could be effectually rendered without the presence of the congregation, and without any communicants. But this was no longer the case when the idea of a propitiatory sacrifice in the Mass was rejected, and when the

Eucharist was again transformed into a common service of the congregation, as it had been in primitive times. In the Protestant sense there can be no communion service without communicants. Nor is the idea of a common congregational service realized, when a few only of the congregation participate in the transaction, while the majority are mere spectators of the solemn show. But the Reformers soon discovered that it was not possible to cause an entire congregation to be present, and get them to participate in the communion service on every Lord's day. What, then, was to be done? Luther proposed to let the communion service stand as a part of the service of every Lord's day, but to make optional the participation in it by the people. Both sides of the Reformation agreed that the ministration of the divine word, the preaching of the sermon, is the central and essential part of public worship; and Luther went so far on one occasion as to say, that there is no use in Christian assemblies where there is nothing but prayer and singing, and where no sermon is preached. But Luther, nevertheless, proposed to let the Lord's Supper remain as an appendix at least to every public service on the Lord's day. If at any time there should be no communicants from among the people, the ministers could commune, and it would still be the communion. This, although a violation of the general Protestant principle, that all acts of public worship must be common acts of the congregation, was adopted at first as the rule of the Lutheran

Church, — a rule, however, it should be added, that did not maintain itself very long in Lutheran cultus. Calvin was at first disposed to retain the celebration of the communion in every Lord's day service according to primitive custom, and to require the presence and participation of the whole congregation on every occasion. He soon found, however, that this was a demand which could not be exacted; and subsequently, while expressing his preference for at least a monthly communion, he agreed to the rule, which Zwingli had already introduced at Zurich, of celebrating four communions in the year, namely, at Christmas, Easter, Whitsunday, and some Sunday in the fall. This came to be the order subsequently in most of the Reformed churches. Thus the communion service was separated from the ordinary Lord's day service, and the latter came to have its chief interest, its centre of gravity, in the sermon. This arrangement, though a departure from all past liturgical traditions, was doubtless justified by the circumstances of the times, and could moreover claim a precedent in the practice of the Apostolic Church. In the early period of the Apostolic Church there were two kinds of Christian assemblies for worship, the one occurring in the temple and other public localities, where nothing took place but prayer and the preaching of the Gospel, the other occurring mostly at night in private houses, where the Lord's Supper was partaken and the love-feast celebrated. The former might be called homiletic, or perhaps better, evangelistic, and the latter eucharistic services. This difference still existed at Corinth at the time when the Corinthian Epistles were written. Agreeably to the modification of the constitution of divine service made by the Reformers, the *liturgy*, which previously signified the order of celebrating the Eucharist, now came to signify for the most part merely the order of beginning and closing sermons. A liturgy, of course, contains other offices, like those for the administration of baptism, of confirmation, of ordination and installation, and so forth; but the office for the conduct of public worship forms its principal feature and determines its character.

The first formal attempt at a reconstruction of the order of Christian worship according to Reformed principles was made at Zurich, in the year 1523, by the composition and publication by Leo Judæ, at the request of Zwingli, of an Order of Baptism, to which was attached an Order for the Beginning and Closing of Sermons. This title is indicative of the change which had taken place in the conception of the liturgy. The order here laid down is very simple, merely containing directions for prayer, which is to be made for the right understanding of God's word, for Christian pastors, for secular authorities, and for those who are in tribulation, directions for the commemoration of those who have recently departed this life, whose names are announced at the beginning of the service, and directions for a general confession of sin. This is in fact a *directory* rather than an *order* of worship; and even as a directory it is incomplete, and was in practice doubtless supplemented by additional forms. It was unsatisfactory, and did not long maintain itself.

In 1525 a new Order of Worship was established at Zurich by public authority. It contains forms for the beginning and ending of sermons, for the administration of the Lord's Supper, for the solemnization of marriage, and for the burial of the dead. The ordinary preaching service begins with a *votum*: "Grace, mercy, and peace be unto you," etc. Then comes the singing of a psalm or hymn. After this we have an exhortation to prayer for the presence and illuminating influence of the Holy Spirit in order to the right understanding of God's word; and this is followed by the Lord's Prayer, and then the general intercessory prayer. After this comes the reading of Scripture, which may be a passage from the Old or New Testament selected by the minister, according to his inclination or judgment. The system of pericopes is abandoned. After the reading of Scripture follows the sermon. And the sermon is followed by a general confession of sin, a prayer of thanksgiving, ending with the Lord's prayer, the publication of the banns of marriage, and of the names of any deceased members of the Church, an exhortation to almsgiving for the benefit of the poor, and the benediction.

The communion service contained in this Reformed Zurich liturgy was prepared by Zwingli himself, and used for the first time on Easter Sunday, in the year 1525. It follows pretty closely the order of the canon of the Gregorian Mass. After the conclusion of the sermon, the minister is directed to stand at the table containing the sacramental elements, and turning his face to the people, he is to say with a loud voice, "In the name of the *Father, and of the Son, and of the Holy Spirit," to which his attendants are to answer, "Amen." Then is to be said the introit, or invocation, a short prayer beginning with the words: "Almighty and everlasting God, whom all creatures justly worship and adore," etc. This is to be followed by the reading of the account of the institution of the Supper in 1 Cor. xi. 20–29, at the conclusion of which the congregation responds: "God be praised." After this the *Gloria in Excelsis* is recited antiphonally by the men and the women in the congregation. Then the minister says: "The Lord be with you," and the people answer: "And with thy spirit." Next the minister announces the reading of another Scripture lesson, namely, John vi. 47–63, which announcement the congregation receives with the response: "God be praised." After the reading the minister kisses the Bible, and says: "Laud be to God, who according to His holy word will forgive us all our sins," and the people respond, "Amen." This is followed by the antiphonal recitation of the Apostles' Creed. After the creed comes an address by the minister, in which the communicants are exhorted to penitence, to faith, and to prayer. Then the congregation kneels, and the Lord's Prayer is repeated, after which another prayer is offered by the minister for the divine blessing and for the grace of sanctification, to which the people respond, "Amen." After this follows the consecration of the elements by means of the words of institution and the breaking of the bread. The elements are then distributed by the deacons to the members of the congregation, who are kneeling in their pews. After all have communed, the 113th Psalm is recited, the minister repeating the first verse, and then the men and women reading antiphonally to the end. Another short collect together with the benediction closes the service.

It will be observed that this whole communion service is an action of the congregation, not an action of the minister in the stead or in behalf of the congregation. But it will be observed also that there is here a striking contrast between the comparative richness of the communion service and the baldness of the ordinary preaching service. This is due doubtless to the lingering influence of mediæval tradition. In the mediæval Church the liturgy or divine service, as we have already seen, meant essentially the offering of the sacrifice of the Mass; and of this preaching was not a part. What preaching there was then took place at irregular times, and was not accompanied by any special ceremonies. Preaching was not a regular and constitutional part of divine cultus. This conception still exercised its influence upon the Reformers. Though the office of preaching was the chief instrument in the work of the Reformation, yet the Reformers found it difficult at first to give it its right setting in the general cultus of the Church. The idea of the liturgy was still associated mainly with the communion service, and the office of preaching stood out by itself without any support from the liturgy. Of course this relation could not long continue. The communion service, with its comparative wealth of ceremony, occurred only seldom, while the office of preaching, with its liturgical baldness and poverty, was performed not only on every Sunday, but often also on week days. Accordingly, the subsequent development of the Reformed liturgies in Switzerland pertained especially to the ordinary service of the sermon. This needed to be enriched and made more popular. The idea of the communion service as being essentially an action of the whole congregation, needed to be extended also to the preaching service. This end was accomplished to some extent by the introduction of additional forms of common prayer, and especially by the introduction of congregational singing. The office of congregational singing did not exist in the Catholic Church of the Middle Ages. This office had to be created by the Reformation; and this was a work that could only be accomplished gradually. But it was the larger extension of this office in the preaching service, and the introduction of additional forms of prayer in which the people could take part, that distinguishes the later liturgies of the Zwinglian type from that which was originally established at Zurich. The Zwinglian type, however, has maintained itself in the various liturgies or agendas of the Swiss churches down to the present day. Zwingli's spirit still lives in the Swiss churches.

The liturgies of the Calvinistic churches have their type in Calvin's "Forms of Common Prayer," published in 1545, as an appendix to the Geneva Catechism, and afterwards used in the churches of Geneva. "Calvin," says Henry, his biographer, "regarded it as most important, for the safety of the Church, to establish a durable order through uniformity in liturgical rites, and thereby to oppose effectually the wilfulness of individuals. But even here he would suffer nothing which was not in strict conformity with the Scriptures. He in all things exhibited the purest antagonism to Rome; and as the papists made the central point of their religious service the Mass, a miracle invented by men, so Calvin employed the exposition of the Bible as the middle point of the devotions of his Church" (Henry's "Life of Calvin," vol. i. p. 410). It is, then, not Calvinistic, in the sense of Calvin himself at least, to reject all fixed forms of prayer as popish fetters of devotion. This Calvin did not do, and would most likely not approve in his followers. But Calvin was the most radical of the Reformers in all things relating to cultus. At least such is the usual judgment of history. While Zwingli, according to Ebrard, may be said to have removed too little of the old order of worship to gain room for things new, Calvin, on the other hand, found everything that was old cleared out of the way, and the ground prepared for an entirely new liturgical creation. Farel, who had preceded Calvin at Geneva, had abolished the whole order of the Catholic Church, and in cultus had left nothing remaining but the sermon, which stood out in entire isolation and nakedness. Here, then, there was room for the architectonic skill of the great Reformer; and the result shows that his skill was indeed of a superior order. It should be observed, however, that Calvin's work was after all not a creation out of nothing. Calvin was evidently familiar with liturgical history. He was acquainted with the forms of worship in primitive times. And his soul was saturated with the spirit of worship which prevailed in the best ages of the Church, — a qualification without which no one will ever be able to produce a liturgy that shall be worthy of the name. He may have been somewhat too coldly intellectual in temper to produce an ideal liturgy; but he was at least not ignorant of liturgical practices, and was willing, moreover, to retain in use the best elements of the old order, such as the Lord's Prayer, the Apostles' Creed, and so forth.

Calvin's originality in the treatment of the order of worship, however, is shown in the very beginning of his common service for the Lord's day. This service begins, as in the primitive Church, with the reading by an assistant of selections of Scripture from the Old and New Testaments, together with the Ten Commandments. After this the minister, having taken his place in the pulpit, begins with an invocation. Then he addresses to the congregation an exhortation to the confession of sin, and invites them to follow him in their hearts while he makes use of a form of confession, which has become the type of confessional prayer in a number of later liturgies. Such a beginning with confession of sin, however appropriate in itself, is something new in the history of worship. No ancient liturgy begins in this way — not even the Sarum Missal. And yet it is the way in which the service begins in the Book of Common Prayer of the Church of England. But this is only one of the many traces of Calvinistic influence in that wonderful work. After the confession of sin, in Calvin's Order, a psalm is to be sung by the whole congregation. A psalm is prescribed, not because Calvin had any objection to suitable hymns of extra-Scriptural origin, but because there were then no suitable hymns in the French language. Luther was a poet of no small power, and exercised his talent in the composition of hymns fit to be sung in the German churches. But poets are born, not made; and Calvin was not only himself not born with much poetical talent, but neither had he a man at his side who was thus endowed. The best, therefore, that he could do was to employ the talents of Marot and Beza in turning the Psalms into metrical French, so that they could be sung by the congregations until something better could be offered them. After the singing of the psalm the minister again leads in a prayer for the illumination of the Holy Spirit, to the end that the word of God may be rightly expounded and rightly received; which ends with the Lord's Prayer. After this comes the sermon; and after the sermon follows a general prayer of intercession, for rulers, for pastors, for all conditions of men, for afflicted persons, for persecuted Christians, and finally for the congregation itself. This again concludes with the Lord's Prayer; and after the Lord's Prayer follows the creed. The service ends with the Aaronic benediction, an exhortation to remember the poor, and the dismission.

We have already seen that, according to the order adopted at Geneva, the Lord's Supper was celebrated four times a year, namely, at the three Christian festivals of Christmas, Easter, and Pentecost, and on some Sunday in autumn. A public announcement of the communion is to be made on the Sunday before its celebration, so that the people may have time for proper preparation. On the day of the communion it is directed that the sermon should have reference, either in whole or in part, to the signification and benefit of this mystery. After the sermon, in addition to the usual intercessory prayer and the succeeding Lord's Prayer, a special prayer is offered, asking God for the grace required for the right and worthy celebration of the sacrament. This is followed by the Apostles' Creed. After the creed comes a lengthy exhortation to the communicants, in which they are further instructed in regard to the nature and meaning of the sacrament, and in regard to the necessary qualification for its salutary reception. After a general sentence of excommunication pronounced against all idolaters, blasphemers, despisers of God, heretics, sectarians, and similarly impious persons, the objective character of the sacrament is explained. It is declared to be as a medicine for those who are spiritually sick; and in order to the due reception of its benefit, there is nothing required on the part of the communicants but a lively consciousness of their sinfulness and misery. The benefit of the sacrament, however, is not connected with the elements of bread and wine. These are only witnesses and signs. The communicants are exhorted to lift up their minds and hearts on high, where Jesus Christ abides in the glory of His Father, that from thence they may obtain food and life from the substance of Christ's glorified being. This is doubtless all very correct in a dogmatic point of view. It is a clear repudiation of the theories of transubstantiation and consubstantiation, and a distinct affirmation of the doctrine of a spiritual real presence of Christ in the sacrament. The only question is whether this is the right place for such instruction. Does not this rather belong to the sermon? The

Sursum Corda of the older liturgies, of which we are reminded by some of the expressions used in this address, is after all something quite different. That is a spiritual and devotional action; this is only an act of intellectual reflection which, in the light of correct liturgical principles, could hardly be said to be appropriate just before the most solemn part of the whole sacramental transaction, namely, the participation of the communion itself. The distribution of the communion takes place at a long table, which stands in the central aisle or nave of the church, and along which the communicants are ranged. At the conclusion of the address just referred to, the minister takes his place at the head of the table; and taking up the bread before him, and repeating the words of institution, he breaks off pieces and hands them to the elders on his right and left; these then take up the bread and pass it along the table, each communicant with his own hand breaking off a small portion, and reverently eating it. In like manner the cup is passed along from one communicant to another. While the communion thus proceeds, a psalm may be sung, or a portion of Scripture read. After all have communed, there is offered a prayer of thanksgiving, the *Nunc Dimittis* is sung, and the congregation is dismissed with the apostolic benediction.

Besides the forms now mentioned, Calvin's liturgy contains offices for the administration of baptism, the solemnization of marriage, and the visitation of the sick, as well as prayers for morning and evening devotion, prayers for use before and after meals, and prayers for times of public calamity. Of these no particular account can here be given. These liturgical forms of Calvin became the type of the various orders of worship in the Reformed churches of France, Holland, Scotland, and parts of Germany. "The Book of Common Order" of the Church of Scotland was first framed, in 1554, by John Knox, for the English congregation at Frankfort. In 1556, it was adopted by the English congregation at Geneva with the approbation of Calvin. Upon the return of Knox to Scotland, his Order of Worship was adopted there by the General Assembly in 1560, as the established order of worship. It continued to be used until it was displaced by the Directory of Worship of the Westminster Assembly, in 1645. The Common Order was modelled closely after the Calvinistic original, though in devotional unction and fervor it probably excelled it. In the Lord's day service we have first a confession of sin; then the reading of Scripture by the minister, and the singing of a psalm by the congregation. After this comes the sermon, and after the sermon a general prayer for the whole estate of Christ's Church, ending with the Lord's Prayer and the Apostles' Creed. After the creed another psalm is sung, and the congregation is dismissed either with the Aaronic or the apostolic benediction. When the Lord's Supper is celebrated, which is directed to be done once a month, there comes, after the part of the service usually following the sermon, an address to the communicants, instructing them in regard to the nature of the sacrament and of the necessity of a proper preparation of the heart for rightly receiving it. This is in a tone somewhat less didactic and more fervently devotional than that belonging to the same part of the service in the liturgy of Geneva. The address is followed by a prayer, which reminds one somewhat of the *preface* of the old Greek liturgies. It is a prayer of thanksgiving for God's goodness, as displayed in the works of creation and redemption, and as it is witnessed especially in the institution of the Lord's Supper for the benefit of unworthy sinners. After this follows the distribution of the elements in Calvinistic fashion. When all have communed, the 103d Psalm is sung, and the congregation is dismissed with the benediction.

One of the best liturgies of the Reformed Church of France is that of Neufchatel. It was formed and adopted in 1713, and belongs, therefore, not to the age of the Reformation. But it is important as indicating the direction of liturgical development in the land of Calvin himself in post-Reformation times. At the time of its formation there was a felt need of a larger number of spiritual hymns fit for use in divine service, and an effort was made to supply this need by the addition to the Psalms of a number of canticles, which may be chanted or read according to circumstances. What may be called the comparative baldness and poverty of Reformed worship is relieved by the introduction of additional responses and antiphonies, and by the rehabilitation of some of the best liturgical elements of past systems of worship. For instance, in the communion service, after the usual explanatory and hortatory address, which is peculiar to the Calvinistic order, we have the true *Sursum Corda:* "Let us lift up our hearts on high, and give thanks unto the Lord our God." Then follows the refrain: "It is just and reasonable, and a very salutary duty, that we should at all times and in all places give thanks unto thee, Lord God, holy and eternal Father." This is followed by the variable preface, according to the order of the Roman Mass. That for Christmas day, for example, reads as follows: "Through Jesus Christ, Thine only Son, our Lord, who at this time was born for us, and who by the operation of the Holy Spirit was made very man, of the substance of the blessed Virgin, His mother, and without any spot of sin, to the end that He might cleanse us from all iniquity." After this comes the *Tersanctus,* as follows: "Therefore with angels, with archangels, and with all the hosts of heaven, we magnify Thy glorious name, singing to Thy glory, and saying, Holy, Holy, Holy, Lord God of hosts, the heavens and the earth are full of Thy glory, O God, Most High." Hereupon follows a prayer for the peace of the world, the salvation of all nations, the protection of the whole Church, the unity and peace of Christians, and finally for the grace required in order to the worthy reception of the communion. This is followed by the Lord's Prayer, and by another prayer for forgiveness of sin, which is but an expansion of the old *Kyrie Eleison.* Hereupon follows the consecration of the elements in the use of the words of institution. After the communion we have, in the following order, the *Nunc Dimittis,* the *Gloria in Excelsis,* an exhortation to Christian fidelity, and the benediction.

The last family of Reformed liturgies are the German. They exhibit evidences of Lutheran, or rather Melanchthonian, as well as Calvinistic influences. The most noteworthy of these are the Hessian, first published in 1539, and afterwards often revised; the Palatinate, published in 1563; and the Netherland, or Dutch, published in 1566. It is only of the second of these that we propose here to give a more particular account. It was prepared for the use of the churches of the Palatinate, by order of the Elector, Frederick III., in 1563. Its authors were Zacharias Ursinus, a pupil of Melanchthon, Caspar Olevianus, who studied theology under Calvin at Geneva, and Emanuel Tremellius, a disciple of Peter Martyr, and at one time professor at Cambridge, England. Thus German, French, and Swiss tendencies are happily and harmoniously combined in the construction of this liturgical book. Its basis was a liturgy prepared by John A. Lasco, for the use of the Dutch and Walloon churches in London, which had itself been based upon an order of worship prepared by Polanus for the foreign Reformed churches of Strassburg. The latter was made the basis also for the liturgy of the Netherlands.

The Palatinate liturgy attests its Reformed character by the distinction which it makes between the communion service and the regular preaching service on the Lord's day, and by the importance which it attaches to the sermon as the principal element in Christian cultus. It contains explicit instructions concerning the preparation of sermons, the source from which their material is to be drawn, and the end which they should have in view. Besides offices for the regular service on Sunday, the Palatinate liturgy contains forms for week day services, which are to be held wherever possible on Wednesday and Friday, and special forms for the Christian festivals, and for days of humiliation and days of thanksgiving. The remaining offices are those for the administration of baptism and the Lord's Supper, for confirmation, or the admission of youths to the Lord's Supper, by prayer and the laying on of hands, for the solemnization of marriage, for the administration of discipline, for the visitation of the sick and of prisoners, and for the burial of the dead. Special offices are provided for the administration of baptism to Anabaptists and Jews.

The service on Sunday morning, in cities, towns, and villages, is to begin at eight o'clock, in country places somewhat later. The service opens with a *votum:* "Grace, mercy, and peace," etc. This is followed by a prayer, consisting of confession of sin and of penitence, and of petitions for mercy, for sanctification, and for saving knowledge of God's word, concluding with the Lord's Prayer. Here follows the sermon, which, according to the rubric, is not to exceed one hour in length. After the sermon comes an exhortation to the confession of sin, and then a confessional prayer, in which both minister and people audibly unite. This is succeeded by the absolution, or the declaration of pardon to the penitent, and the announcement of the retention of sin to the impenitent. Here again follows the Lord's Prayer; and after this the general morning prayer, containing thanksgiving for bodily and spiritual blessings and petitions for the continuation of the same, — petitions for all in authority, for the preservation of the fruits of the earth and the peace of the world, for the prosperity of all men, for the relief of those who are suffering persecution, for the comfort of the poor and of all who are in tribulation and distress. For this prayer, however, others are substituted on special occasions, such as the Christian festivals, for which the liturgy provides suitable forms. The general prayer always ends with the Lord's Prayer, which thus occurs three times in the same service. After the prayer, a short psalm is to be sung, and the congregation dismissed with the Aaronic benediction.

On Sunday afternoon it is ordered that, wherever possible, services are to be held in which a lecture on the Catechism, adapted to the comprehension of the young, is to be the principal feature, but which is to be opened and closed with singing and prayer, forms being provided for this purpose in the liturgy. This liturgy, it should be observed, has no room for extemporaneous prayer in public worship. It furnishes forms for all conceivable occasions, and the rubrics are mandatory in regard to the use of them.

In the order of succession of the various offices in this, as in other Reformed liturgies, the office of baptism comes immediately after that of the preaching service, and before that of the Lord's Supper. This implies that the Lord's Supper is regarded, not as an essential element of all Christian cultus, but as an occasional means of grace and help to piety, the use of which may be deferred to more or less distant intervals according to convenience. It is, however, regarded as an exceedingly solemn transaction, requiring very special preparation for its due and proper observance. The rubric provides that in cities the Supper is to be celebrated every two months, and in towns and villages four times a year, — namely, at Christmas, Easter, Whitsunday, and on the first Sunday in September. On Saturday preceding the communion, a special preparatory service is to be held, when all the members of the church who intend to commune are to be present, and when also the catechumens are to be examined and confirmed. The service on this occasion consists in the usual opening prayer, a sermon dwelling upon the nature and effect of Christ's suffering, and upon the meaning and design of the Supper, and in a series of questions and answers, in which the congregation confesses the sense of its need and misery, its faith in Christ as the only Mediator and Saviour, and its purpose to forsake sin, and to live in newness of life. The service concludes with the Lord's Prayer and benediction. After the dismission an opportunity is given to any members of the church to speak to the minister or other officer in regard to matters pertaining to salvation, about which their minds may be disturbed.

On Sunday, when the communion is celebrated, the service proceeds as usual until after the general prayer. Then the minister takes his place at the table, and reads a very long address to the communicants, in which the history of the institution of the Supper is rehearsed in the words of Saint Paul, the self-examination required in order to its salutary reception explained, the forgiveness of sins announced to the penitent, the impenitent and unbelieving warned not to approach the Lord's table, and the nature and design of the Supper set forth. After the address follows the prayer of consecration, in which the Holy Spirit is invoked to the end that, in consequence of this sacramental transaction, the communicants may be more fully united to Christ their Head. This is followed by the Lord's Prayer and the creed. After the creed comes another address based upon the old idea of the *Sursum Corda*, in which the communicants are exhorted not to let their hearts cleave to the external elements of bread and wine, but to lift them up into heaven, where Christ is in the glory of the Father, that they may be united with Him by the operation of the Holy Spirit. The administration of the communion takes place at the table conveniently placed within the choir of the church, which the members successively approach in order to receive the sacred emblems from the hands of the minister. During the administration of the Supper, suitable Psalms may be sung by the congregation, or appropriate Scripture lessons read. After all have communed, the 103d Psalm may be recited, or a short prayer of thanksgiving offered, after which the congregation is dismissed with the Aaronic benediction.

This Palatinate liturgy may be regarded as the type of a number of German Reformed Agendas, of which it would be impossible here to give any account. They would be found to differ more or less from each other, and to present evidences of development of the liturgical principle in various directions, but they would all be true to their original type.

We have said nothing of the Book of Common Prayer of the Church of England, not because we do not regard the English Church as a Reformed Church, which originally stood in friendly and fraternal relations with the Reformed churches of the continent, exchanging with them both pulpits and ministers, nor because we do not recognize in it

Reformed elements; but, first, because it is too well known to need description, and, secondly, because it forms the subject of a separate lecture in this course. We deem it, however, not out of place to mention in this connection the Order of Worship for the reformed church in the United States, published in 1866. It is a Reformed liturgy resembling in general conception the older liturgies of the German Calvinistic type, but having features in common also with the old Oriental and Roman liturgies. The communion service, for example, while thoroughly true to the Reformed or Calvinistic doctrine of the sacrament, has elements in common with the early Greek liturgies, especially the Clementine of the Apostolic Constitutions. Among these are the *Pax Vobiscum*, the *Sursum Corda*, the invariable *preface*, and the invocation of the Holy Spirit upon the elements of bread and wine in the prayer of consecration. The old responses and antiphonies, the old chants and creeds, the litany, the pericopes, and collects have been restored. The effort has been made to produce a book of worship that should stand in vital continuity with the past, and yet be adapted to the religious wants of the present. As to the success or failure of the effort, it may still be too early to pronounce judgment.

The Reformed churches have in their liturgical treasures a rich inheritance, for which they have reason to be thankful, and which they cannot suffer always to remain unused. But what use shall be made of it? The old liturgies cannot be brought back into the worship of the churches of the present day, in the form in which they were once used. That the old liturgical idea, the idea of a common service in which all the people shall participate, will assert itself again in the churches, we are fully persuaded. There are many tendencies at the present time which point in that direction. The worship of the future will be liturgical. But this does not mean that the Reformation liturgies, in their original form, will again be introduced. There was a reason doubtless for their going out of use in the past; and that same reason will operate against their reintroduction now. Had they fully satisfied the spirit of devotion in the times succeeding the age of the Reformation, they would have continued to direct that devotion. The continued use of the Book of Common Prayer of the Church of England is a fact that should be instructive to other reformed churches. But no work of the past can be true and valuable for all time without undergoing a continual process of transformation and readaptation. The Reformers thought — at least some of them did — that they were bringing back the precise pattern of worship which prevailed in the Apostolic Church. Had they done so, their work would not have suited the age in which they lived, and for which they labored. No one age can be a law for all other ages, either in doctrine or worship. The doctrinal confessions of the Reformation have, indeed, maintained themselves much longer than did the books of worship. But they are now generally beginning to be felt to be inadequate to the demands of Christian faith, and the cry for revision has gone up, which will continue to resound until it shall be satisfied.

But while the past cannot be repristinated, either in doctrine or worship, neither can the present with impunity sever its connection with the past. Continuity in the midst of change is the law of history; and only those productions can be truly valuable to the life of the present which stand in organic connection with the life of the past. Our prevailing unliturgical practices, for instance, are not a development out of the liturgical practices which were once universal; they imply an absolute break with all past principles of public worship. Is not that a reason, perhaps, why the masses among us do no longer attend church? Would, then, the creation of new liturgies, wholly different from anything that has ever been known in the past, meet the wants of the time any better? We think not. Apart from the fact that the man would have to be more than human who should be able to accomplish such a work, it would be a useless work after being accomplished. As the life of the Church at the present moment grows out of the life of the past, so the order of worship that shall satisfy the feelings of devotion now must be the outgrowth of the order of worship in all past ages.

Perhaps the Reformers erred in not sufficiently observing this principle. Did they not in some respects deal too violently with the productions of history, and destroy where they should only have purified and renovated? Did not their hatred of the abuses of the old order and an extreme application of their principle of Scripture, sometimes betray them into violence? Take, for example, their manner of dealing with the Church year. It would not, as is sometimes maintained, be correct to say that they destroyed it, for in principle they accepted it, by accepting the great Christian festivals; but they mutilated it by cutting out those parts which are necessary to connect the festivals into an organic whole of sacred time. Historically they were justified in doing this by the abuse of the sacred year in the Catholic Church, which contained so many holy days that honest people had no longer working days enough to earn their bread. But surely that justification exists no longer now. And the arrangement of the Reformers could not long maintain itself. Either the whole idea of the Church year must be given up, as has happened in some sections of the Reformed Church, or the whole circle must be restored, as has been done in other sections, and is proposed in our own Order of Worship. Again, some of the Reformers at first dealt violently with the altar; for which there was good reason at the time, in the fact that the altar had been made the receptacle for the relics of the saints, many of them spurious, with which much superstitious practice was connected. But Christian worship involves a sacrificial and priestly element, — a God-ward action on the part of the congregation, — and this demands for its full expression the symbol of the altar, just as the prophetic or teaching function of the Church demands the pulpit; and consequently in large sections of the Reformed Church the altar has long since been restored to its place. Finally, the Reformers were generally opposed to the employment of art in worship, because in the old order art had been prostituted to what they believed to be idolatrous practices. But art has its place in worship, and has, therefore, gradually come back into the service of the Church, as we see in the modern styles of church architecture, and in the use of organs, hymns, and music. These changes are evidences of the manner in which the primitive Reformed orders of worship have been developed in modern time. And it must be by still further development and change, making old things new and taking up new things into harmonious union with the old, that the old orders shall again become adapted to the existing wants of worship. The Reformation did not end all liturgical progress, any more than it ended all progress in theology; only the progress that shall be legitimate must be in harmony with the order of the Reformation, as well as with all that was true and good in the old order that went before; and it must produce a work in which all one-sidedness and contradiction shall be overcome, and every element of devotion find its due expression.

It is a question, for example, whether the Reformation has rightly settled the relation between the sermon and the Eucharist in the constitution of Christian cultus, and whether the ideal liturgy of the future will not need some modification at this point. Is the sermon really the central and essential element of cultus, and is the Eucharist properly appreciated when it is regarded merely as an occasional appendix to the service of preaching? As over against the practice of the Catholic Church in the time of the Reformation, there is doubtless a degree of justification for the Reformed view. The Catholic practice had made the sacrifice of the Mass central, and had crowded the sermon out of the regular order of worship altogether. The evil consequences of this neglect of the teaching function of the Church were very apparent in the time of the Reformation, and the Reformers had good reason for emphasizing the office of preaching. But is this emphasizing of the sermon at the expense of the Eucharist with its accompanying services, which may have been right and proper at the time of the Reformation, right and proper now? Is this the ideal of Christian cultus? It is a contradiction of the order of worship of the primitive Church as far back as we know anything of it. Is it in harmony with the fundamental idea of Christian worship? Is not this theory responsible for the prevailingly intellectual and pedagogic character of our church services, which, while they may satisfy the intellect, fail to satisfy the heart? People now "go to preaching," instead of going to church or to divine service; and if the preaching is no longer to their liking, or if it fails to satisfy their intellectual temper, they cease going altogether. Is not this another reason why the Church is losing her hold upon the modern mind? Is there not needed a readjustment of the order of our church services in such way that they shall engage the interest of the heart as well as that of the head? In our opinion, at least, this is one of the pressing needs of the age. The relation of sermon and Eucharist, or the relation of sermon and liturgy, must be readjusted. Neither one may overshadow the other. Neither one may be central in the constitution of cultus. They may be related as opposite poles of the same reality, the one always balancing and supporting the other. Not that the Eucharist needs to be celebrated at every service, but that the central idea of the Eucharist, namely, the idea of collective as well as personal communion with Christ in the Spirit, should be the pervading idea of every service. In this sense the liturgies of the Reformation may need modification in order to adapt them to our time. Our age needs more of worship. The heart needs to be engaged and satisfied as well as the head. And to this end the old liturgical idea and habit need to be brought back to the churches; but it must be the Reformation idea and the Reformation habit enriched and modified by the best liturgical productions of pre-Reformation times, as well as by the liturgical achievements which have been accomplished since the period of the Reformation.

VII

THE BOOK OF COMMON PRAYER

BY THE REV. WILLIAM R. HUNTINGTON, D.D.
Rector of Grace Church, New York City

THE STORY, THE CHARACTERISTICS, AND THE POSSIBILITIES OF THE BOOK OF COMMON PRAYER

IT was Mr. Galton, I believe, who first suggested the ingenious process known as composite photography. Wishing to secure a picture which should represent a class or family rather than any single individual member of such family or class, he hit upon the device of superimposing one negative upon another, until the features of the successive sitters became finally blended in a face that was the likeness of no one of them in particular, but, so to say, of all of them in general.

Only by some such method as this will it be possible for us to make a satisfactory study of the Book of Common Prayer, since, in truth, there are many Books of Common Prayer, each one of which has full right and fair title to be called by that name.

There is the First Book of King Edward the Sixth, the *editio princeps*, the fount and prototype of all the Prayer Books that have succeeded it. That dates from 1549. Then there is Edward's Second Book,— the revision of 1552. Following upon this comes

Elizabeth's Book, then James's. Later still, we have the revised Common Prayer of the Stuart Restoration, and "in the course of human events" the American Book, in its first revision of 1789 and in its latest standard form of 1892. There are still other variants, — as, for example, the Scottish Book, which Laud and Charles endeavored unsuccessfully to force upon the people of the northern kingdom, just before the breaking out of the great rebellion which cost both of them their heads. There is also the Irish Book, the product of the Disestablishment Act of 1870. It would be unfair to take any one of these various readings and to treat it as if it were the alone true and authentic text. The just method would seem to be to approach the subject, first of all, historically: to follow the romantic fortunes of the book from its beginnings until now; and then, but not until then, to attempt the composite photography which is to give us the means of discriminating between transient phase and settled type, accident and essence, ear-mark and birth-mark.

The English Book of Common Prayer came into being as a distinct entity in the year of our Lord 1549. On the Whitsunday of that year it was born; but to discover the genesis of the book's pre-natal life we should have to go much farther back.

It used to be the fashion to say that the Prayer Book was "compiled" by the English Reformers, with the assistance of learned friends brought over from the Continent; but stating the case in that way meant putting a strain upon the words "compile" and "compilation."

The Common Prayer was, and is, not so much a compilation as a product of growth, — interrupted growth, no doubt, dislocated growth, if you prefer to call it that, — but still growth, pure and simple. The English reformers were not as men who got together around a table, saying, "Go to, let us construct a liturgy suited to present-day needs." On the contrary, what they did was this: they took the devotional system to which they and their countrymen had been accustomed from their childhood, and having purged it of what were believed to be superstitious accretions, they sent it forth to do a better work than it had ever done before. Not even for the name upon the titlepage can absolute originality be claimed; for King Edward's first Act of Uniformity begins with the declaration that "Of long time there has been had in this realm of England and in Wales divers forms of *common prayer*, commonly called the Service of the Church." It was apparently, therefore, no new thing for the Service of the Church, as those people already had it, to be called "Common Prayer." What the reformers aimed to do was to make the public prayers really, instead of only nominally, "common" by translating them from aristocratic Latin into homely English, and thus giving to the people their due portion of a worship which had by default lapsed almost wholly to the priests.

We have first, therefore, to inquire what this "Service of the Church" was which Edward's ecclesiastics undertook, midway in the sixteenth century, to remould and refashion into better form.

The service-books in use in the mediæval Catholic Church, although many in number, were all of them reducible to one or other of three sorts, — the Missal, or Mass-book; the Breviary, or Book of Hours; and the Ceremonial, or Book of Rites. No single embodiment of any one of these types enjoyed universal acceptance.

Different countries, yes, even different dioceses, had their own proper missals. There were also breviaries and breviaries; but the variations were of a non-essential kind, the type stood. The Missal was the Office of the Holy Communion, — the Liturgy, strictly and properly so called. The Breviary was a collection of carefully chosen psalms, hymns, and prayers, assigned to the canonical hours of every day in the year. The Ceremonial was a compendium of forms suitable for such occasions as Holy Matrimony, the Burial of the Dead, Exorcisms, Confessions, and the like. A distinction was made, to be sure, between such rites and ceremonies as came within the province of the parish priest and those that only a bishop could lawfully perform; and so there was a special book, known as the Pontifical; but, not to burden the memory unnecessarily, it suffices to say that the Missal, the Breviary, and the Ceremonial were the standard books, — the great devotional manuals of the Church.

Were we disposed to go into the philosophy of the

matter, we might find here the grounds for a very interesting study in evolution. The proposition is a defensible one that these three sorts of service-books correspond to ritual uses even more ancient than the Christian Church itself, — uses, in fact, which may be traced back to synagogue and temple. The central feature of the Hebrew worship was sacrifice, an action which had, as we know, its carefully prescribed method or ritual. We find the antitype to this in the commemoration of the sacrifice of the Son of God upon the Cross, the eucharistic expression of which is the service of the Holy Communion, known in mediæval times and among Roman Catholics to this day as the Mass.

But besides its sacrificial system the Jewish Church had also its scheme of daily psalmody and prayer. Peter and John, for instance, went up together into the temple at "the hour of prayer"; and it is evident, from the many musical rubrics of the Book of Psalms, that sacred song played no small part in the temple worship. The Psalter, with its ordered sequences and responsals, was practically the Hebrew's breviary. But besides their acts of sacrifice and their offices of daily prayer and praise, the Jews had other religious usages that called for liturgical accompaniment; and these we naturally classify under the distinct head of rites and ceremonies, — such would have been, for instance, the official cleansing of the leper by pronouncement of the priest, the receiving of children into the fellowship of the congregation, and the like.

Of course, it is easy to say that all this was only part and parcel of the semi-pagan sacerdotalism which Christ came to sweep away and to replace. That is a question by itself, — a very grave question, no doubt, but not the question with which we are busy just at this moment. At present I am only seeking rationally to account for the existence in the Christian Church of the particular sorts of service-books which, in point of fact, were everywhere in use among the faithful before the Protestant Reformation, and to account for it with due deference to that principle of continuity which is to-day as much the watchword of historical, as it has long been of geological and biological investigation. But, be this as it may, the fact remains that by the middle of the sixteenth century the multiplicity of the service-books had become, in the eye at least of the northern portion of European Christendom, an intolerable nuisance.

It should be remembered that in what I have been saying as to Missal, Breviary, and Ceremonial, I have been speaking of *genera* rather than of *species*. Had these three books existed only as three volumes, the mental hardship of familiarizing himself with their contents would have been no greater for the mediæval Christian than was involved in that mastering of Holy Scripture which the Reformers demanded of him if he inclined to become a Protestant. In reality, however, the mingle-mangle of the service-books was much more perplexing than our classification would suggest; and it was only trained ecclesiastics who could so much as pretend to understand the ins and outs of public worship.

But this was not the only grievance, nor was it the most serious. The era of the invention of printing was the last of all times when we should have expected impatience at the number of service-books in use to become the provoking cause of a liturgical revolt. The real trouble lay deeper. The intelligence of the age had awakened to discern the childishness and senselessness of much that the old formularies of worship contained, and there was a prevalent demand that the winnowing-fan be set in motion, the melting-pot made ready. The men to whom new worlds were opening, both overhead and over seas, could not be put off much longer with old wives' fables read to them from the lives of the saints. The times were waking up. Cervantes was born. Presently his gentle knight, the representative of a belated mediævalism, would be laughed off the stage of secular affairs; why should not the equally superannuated priest Mumpsimus Bumpsimus be expelled the sanctuary as well? A cry for veritable fact was on the air. Men were clamoring for the pure word of God, and their demand was that it should be given them in the vernacular. All this the scholars who adventured the remodelling of the devotional system of the Church of England well and clearly perceived and knew.

Present-day Anglicans are, many of them, very mealy-mouthed indeed when it comes to any criticism of old-time methods in religion; but the broad-minded ecclesiastics who took up liturgical revision in the year of our Lord 1549 were of a more robust temper. The fact that a lie was masquerading in venerable raiment gave it no sanctity in their eyes; and whatever in the old usages seemed to them "superstitions" they did not scruple to brand with that offensive name. If you have an appetite for racy English, look up, some day when opportunity serves, the First Prayer Book of Edward VI., and read the Preface. You will find there the frankest possible statement of the burdens under which English Christians in that day must needs stagger if they would arise and go unto their Father and say unto Him anything. Take a few sentences, picked out here and there, for a sample of their style: "Whereas St. Paul would have such language spoken to the people in the Church as they might understand and have profit by hearing the same, the service in this Church of England, (these many years) hath been read in Latin to the people, which they understood not, so that they have heard with their ears only, and their hearts, spirit and mind have not been edified thereby. . . . Moreover . . . the manifold manglings of the service was the cause that to turn the book only was so hard and intricate a matter, that, many times, there was more business to find out what should be read than to read it when it was found out."

"These inconveniences, therefore, considered," they go on to say, "here is set forth such an order whereby the same shall be redressed; . . . because here are left out many things, whereof some be untrue, some uncertain, some vain and superstitious."

"Furthermore, by this Order," and here the national instinct of thrift betrays itself, "the curates shall need none other for their public service but this book and the Bible, by the means whereof the people shall not be at so great charge for books as in times past they have been. And where, heretofore, there hath been great diversity in saying and singing in Churches within this realm, some following Salisbury use, some Hereford use, some the use of Bangor, some of York and some of Lincoln, now, from henceforth, all the whole realm shall have but one use."

With such honest, sane, and pithy sentences as these was the Book of Common Prayer launched upon its eventful voyage. But the ship, to continue our nautical figure, was scarcely out of port before she found herself temporarily grounded upon a bar.

The more advanced among the English reformers were not entirely satisfied with the Book as it stood, and presently they began to agitate for revision. Their movement was successful; and after three short years of use Edward's First Book gave place to his second; otherwise known as the Book of 1552. This second Book was even shorter-lived than the first, for it had scarcely been set forth and made obligatory before Mary came to the throne, and at a stroke overthrew, for the moment, the whole Reformation fabric. But the labor expended upon the second Book was by no means wasted; for Elizabeth's divines chose to make it, rather than the first Book, the basis of their recension, and thus what had seemed abortive turned out fruitful. Almost, if not quite, all of the changes made in the second Book, differencing it from the first, had been in what may fairly enough be called the Protestant direction. Prayers for the dead were omitted; certain vestments were disallowed; the prefatory portions of the Morning and Evening Prayer were amplified; the word "Table" was substituted for "Altar," the public reading of the Decalogue was enjoined, and various transpositions were effected in the Office of the Holy Communion. There were other alterations, but these that I have mentioned were among the more significant. Slight as they may look from one point of view, from another they may be said to have influenced the whole course of English Christianity from those days to these. Elizabeth's Prayer Book has been twice revised, — once under King James after the Hampton Court Conference, and again under Charles the Second after the Savoy Conference; but neither of the Stuart monarchs in his day laid so strong a hand upon the text as the Tudor queen had done in hers. Substantially, the Prayer Book of the Church of England to-day is what the age of Raleigh, of Bacon, and of Shakspeare made it. Conceivably some Victorian pen might have ministered to the devotional needs of the modern English more effectively than the Elizabethan has made out to do, but most lovers of their mother tongue will doubt it.

Time presses; but I cannot forbear detaining you a moment for a look at the two Conferences just mentioned, seeing that they count among the more noteworthy of the lost opportunities of history.

A little way out of London stands the charming old palace of Hampton Court, a house of many more than seven gables, and compassed about with a perfect paradise of trees and shrubs. Hither, at the invitation of King James, shortly after his accession, came divers Puritan divines, the representatives of more than a thousand petitioners, " groaning," as they declared, "under a common burden of human rites and ceremonies." This common burden was none other than the Common Prayer. His Majesty set over against these champions of reform a brave array of ecclesiastics, — to wit, one archbishop, eight bishops, seven deans, and two doctors of divinity; but with characteristic Scottish shrewdness the British Solomon was careful to retain the chair for himself. The Puritans made their complaints, the Anglicans their rejoinders, the King his caustic observations, — in fact, to use his own rather piquant language, he "peppered the Puritans soundly," but nothing, or next to nothing, came of it. Yes, something came of it; something always does come of futile negotiations for peace. The grievance rankled, and when next the Puritans set their hand to the revision of the Common Prayer, it was not in kings' houses that they gathered, but on the field, their pen a trooper's sword. Just one and forty years after the fiasco at Hampton Court, an ordinance passed both houses of Parliament whereby it was enacted that any persons found using the Book of Common Prayer, either publicly or in their families, were to forfeit five pounds for the first offence, ten pounds for the second, and a year's imprisonment without bail for the third. Clearly the pepper-pot had changed hands. But England wearied of the Directory, even as it had wearied of the Common Prayer; and presently we find ourselves lookers-on at a fresh Conference. Again, ominously enough, the council chamber is a palace, — the palace of the Savoy in the Strand. It is the year 1661. The Stuarts are once more in the saddle; and with the fond hope that the King is at last in some measure favorable to their views, the Presbyterians have come to meet the Episcopalians, ostensibly for peace. This time the two sides are more fairly matched in point of numbers than they were at Hampton Court; for each delegation counts twelve principals and nine assistants. But again, alas! the thing turns out a flash in the pan. Richard Baxter, saint and scholar though he is, makes the unaccountable blunder of proposing to substitute a liturgy of his own impromptu manufacture for the already venerable Book of Common Prayer; the bishops show themselves imperious, not to say revengeful, certainly anything but "easy to be entreated," and the Conference perishes in collapse.

A large number of unimportant changes were made by Convocation in the text of the Prayer Book while the Conference was still in session, but few, if any, of them were in the direction of the Presbyterians' desires.

Twenty-eight more years passed, and yet another attempt was made to promote a better liturgical understanding. It was in the reign, this time, of William and Mary; and again there was good hope felt in some quarters that Englishmen might come to at least an approximate agreement in the matter of their prayers. But, no, "this great and good work," to quote the language of the Preface to the American Prayer Book, "miscarried," and all things continued as they had been from the beginning of the Restoration. Yes, all things thus continued, so far as England was concerned; but see what happened next, for it is a most striking illustration of what we may call the reprisals of divine Providence.

"The shot heard round the world" was fired at Lexington, the little group of thirteen Colonies that fringed the Atlantic coast fought its way to nationality, and the long quarrel of the European powers over the partition of North America ended in the establishment of a great English-speaking Commonwealth. What did all this portend for the Book of Common Prayer? It portended the reversal, in great measure, of the judgments pronounced at Hampton Court in 1604 and at the Savoy in 1661. Let us quote again from the Preface to the American Prayer Book, for it gives the whole story in a nut-shell: —

"When in the course of Divine Providence, these American States became independent with respect to civil government, their ecclesiastical independence was necessarily included; and the different religious denominations of Christians in these States were left at full and equal liberty to model and organize their respective Churches and forms of worship and discipline in such manner as they might judge most convenient for their future prosperity, consistently with the laws and Constitution of their Country.

"The attention of this Church was, in the first place, drawn to those alterations in the Liturgy which became necessary in the prayers for our civil rulers in consequence of the Revolution. And the principal care herein was to make them conformable to what ought to be the proper end of all such prayers, namely, that 'Rulers may have grace, wisdom and understanding, to exercise justice and to maintain truth;' and that the people 'may lead quiet and peaceable lives in all godliness and honesty.' But while these alterations were in review before the Convention, they could not but, with gratitude to God, embrace the happy occasion which was offered to them (uninfluenced and unrestrained by any worldly authority whatsoever) to take a further review of the Public Service, and to establish such other alterations and amendments therein as might be deemed expedient."

So far, the American revisers of 1789. Their words present a sober and modest estimate of what they had just been doing in convention assembled. It might look, from their own account of the matter, as if they had not accomplished very much in the line of improvement; but if you will be at the trouble of laying an American Prayer Book open by the side of an English one, and will compare them page for page, you will find that almost all of the more serious liturgical grievances alleged at London in the seventeenth century were redressed at Philadelphia in the eighteenth. I say "serious grievances," for very many of the criticisms brought against the Prayer Book by the Puritan party at Hampton Court, and by the Presbyterians at the Savoy were of a sort which the ecclesiastical descendants of those who brought them would be, to-day, the first to declare frivolous and petty.

"The thoughts of men are widened with the process of the suns;"

and many things that loomed large before the eyes of Puritan and Churchman two hundred years ago look insignificant enough to you and me.

As to the very latest of all the revisions of the Prayer Book, I mean the one made in this country and brought to a conclusion four years ago, any extended remark is uncalled-for. The changes effected were none of them of a doctrinal character, but were consented to on grounds of practical expediency, as likely to heighten the book's usefulness under the present conditions of American life. Whether the authorities, in their anxiety "to keep the mean between the two extremes of too much stiffness in refusing and of too much easiness in admitting any variation," erred most on the side of boldness or on the side of timidity, it must be left to the critics of a future generation to decide.

Our swift review of the history of the Common Prayer concluded, I suggest that we pass next to a study of the book's characteristics, literary and theological, beginning with the former of the two. And here let me say that I welcome the fact that I am addressing an audience not supposed to be particularly alive to the excellences of the Prayer Book, because it will help to safeguard me against that tendency to indiscriminate eulogy which so many Anglicans betray when once you start them on the subject of their "incomparable liturgy." To hear some people talk, one would suppose that the doctrine of verbal inspiration, driven from the biblical precincts, had taken up its abode in liturgical quarters. It is worth our while to remember that the worship of any book whatever, whether a book of Holy Scripture, a book of prayer, or a book of destructive criticism, is "bibliolatry."

Of course there are inequalities of style in the Prayer Book, and divers varying grades of literary excellence. As well go through the Pitti and Uffizi galleries affirming that all the Raphaels you may happen to find possess one and the same artistic value simply because signed by the same hand; as well insist that "The Surgeon's Daughter" is as good a novel as "Ivanhoe," or "Troilus and Cressida" as great a play as "Hamlet," or "The May Queen" as fine a poem as the "Ode on the Death of the Duke of Wellington," as try to make it out that in point of loftiness, dignity, and fervor all portions of the Common Prayer are of a piece. The General Exhortation and the General Confession, for instance, stand next to each other in the Offices of Morning and Evening Prayer; they are so near that they actually touch; yet is the one as far removed from the other in style-value as silver is from gold.

The notes of the style of the Common Prayer are simplicity, majesty, and tenderness. Of course I do not mean that we everywhere find these characteristics conjoined; it is not to be expected or desired that we should; all I say is that they are noticeable features when we look at the book as a whole with a view to appraising its value and fixing its place. The simplicity is almost everywhere present; the majesty comes out whenever it is a question of addressing the Throne; the tenderness reveals itself in all that is said of God's disposition towards the penitent soul, and in every reference to the sorrows and calamities of the mortal lot.

The simplicity of the language may be accounted for on more grounds than one. A chief reason for putting forth the book at all had been the demand for a worship which the common people could understand. As in the case of the translated Bible, the object was to get as far away from the Latin tongue as possible. This explains, perhaps, the marked contrast as respects the proportion of Saxon to Latin derivatives, between the Bible and Prayer Book on the one hand, and on the other not a few of the masterpieces of English letters produced at the same period. The secular authors, even though writing English, were not wholly loath to have the gold thread of their latinity reveal itself pretty freely in the texture of their homespun; but Tyndale and Cranmer had another aim in view altogether, being more anxious that the ploughboy should understand them than that the ear of the university don should detect nothing amiss. Take as an illustration the following prayer from the Matins of Edward the Sixth's First Book. I have chosen it almost at random: —

"O Lord, our heavenly Father, Almighty and everliving God, which hast safely brought us to the beginning of this day; Defend us in the same with thy mighty power; and grant that this day we fall into no sin neither run into any kind of danger; but that all our doings may be ordered by thy governance to do always that is righteous in thy sight, through Jesus Christ our Lord."

Here out of seventy-one words, only three — namely, "defend," "ordered," and "governance" — are Latin derivatives. It is probable that an analysis of the whole book would show a similar ratio.

Another guarantee of simplicity was supplied by the healthy realism characteristic even of those corrupt forms of devotion which Cranmer and his colleagues had before them as working models in their task of reconstruction. Superstitious as many of the old formularies were, they could not be charged with indifference to things in the concrete. Hence we find throughout the Book of Common Prayer a careful avoidance of figurative speech, and a jealous clinging to what is substantive and real. An exception should be made with respect to such imagery as has the sanction of the Bible writers, — though even this is very sparingly employed; but of metaphors not Scriptural, there are, in the more ancient and best-loved portions of the book, very few indeed. The Litany, which a justly honored and beloved professor in this Seminary, the late learned Dr. Shedd, once told me he regarded as the most wonderful compend of intercessory prayer to be found in the whole range of devotional literature, — the Litany is devoid of figurative language altogether. It might seem, at first, as if this banishment of trope and figure, simile and metaphor, must involve a costly sacrifice of beauty, — but no, that does not follow. Massiveness has a beauty of its own. The interior of Durham Cathedral is severe, profoundly so; nothing could be further removed from those tremendous pillars and those solemn Norman arches than the airy grace of the churches which exemplify the decorated Gothic of a later period; and yet it never occurs to anybody to speak of Durham as lacking the element of beauty. It is a grave and serious beauty which reveals itself under that high vault, but it is beauty. A liturgy which is to live on, from generation to generation, must possess the sort of beauty which wears. What is fascinating upon occasion does not necessarily meet our every-day need. Eloquent prayers, tense with imaginative thought and vibrant, in a good sense, with poetic feeling, are, as a rule, eloquent only for once. Try to repeat them and they pall. The most marvellous burst of eloquence I ever listened to in my life was the extemporaneous prayer made by Phillips Brooks at the Harvard Commemoration in 1865. Even the splendors of Lowell's Ode paled, for the moment, in the presence of that flame. It was the very utterance for which the great occasion called. But it, or any adaptation or paraphrase of it, would be simply preposterous in a liturgy. You may reply that if this be so, its being so is the condemnation of liturgics. Yes, perhaps so, if the conditions which made that prayer possible could be counted upon to reproduce themselves every Sunday in the fifty-two that punctuate a year, and you were sure of having a poet-orator in every pulpit.

I spoke of majesty of speech as characterizing more particularly those portions of the Common Prayer in which we are invited to draw near to God for purposes of adoration. I had especially in mind the usage which there obtains, of linking some attribute with the name of Deity in the opening sentence of every prayer, and thus imparting a certain sublimity to the very act of crossing the threshold of worship. "O God, who showest to them that are in error the light of thy truth"; "O Almighty God, who alone canst order the unruly wills and affections of sinful men"; "O God, who never failest to help and govern those whom thou dost bring up in thy steadfast fear and love"; "O God, who hast prepared for those who love thee such good things as pass man's understanding,"— these are illustrations of what I mean. We shall all of us agree that there is a quiet dignity about this method of approaching the Most High in worship which, without argument, commends itself to a reverential mind. But not only in the prayers, majesty is the distinguishing mark of the praises as well. The *Te Deum* is majestic: "We praise thee, O God, we acknowledge thee to be the Lord." The *Gloria in excelsis* is majestic: "O Lord God, Lamb of God, Son of the Father, that takest away the sins of the world, have mercy upon us." The *Ter sanctus* is majestic: "Holy, Holy, Holy, Lord God of Hosts, heaven and earth are full of thy glory. Glory be to thee, O Lord most High."

The other characteristic of which I spoke was tenderness. The tone of the Prayer Book in its approaches to the human soul is gentle, winning, compassionate. There is nothing anywhere between the covers that even remotely resembles gush. There is no shilly-shallying with the awful fact of sin. In the Office for the Visitation of the Sick there is no suggestion that opiates are a good substitute for a quiet conscience, and in the Office for the Visitation of Prisoners the words addressed to criminals under sentence of death are in refreshing contrast to the maudlin sentimentalism which, with a strange perversity, too often seeks to divert sympathy from the person wronged and to transfer it to the unrepentant doer of the wrong. For tenderness of this morbid type, the Prayer Book has no indulgence; but towards all who sorrow, and for all who "suffer according to the will of God," its tone is everywhere gentle, sympathetic, pitiful, compassionate. It not only asks that the merciful Lord will strengthen those who do stand, it pleads with him to comfort the weak-hearted and to raise up those who fall; it remembers all who are in danger, necessity, and tribulation, all sick persons and young children, the prisoners and the captives, the fatherless and the widowed, and all who are desolate and oppressed. Simplicity, majesty, tenderness, — yes, these are certainly the features that we should wish to see looking out upon us from a manual of worship, a book purporting to teach us how to pray.

Having discussed style, we pass next to the more difficult question of doctrine. What is the theology of the Book of Common Prayer? Pray observe that this is a matter quite apart from the Thirty-nine Articles of Religion. The Thirty-nine Articles bear an important doctrinal relation to the Church of England and to the American Episcopal Church; but we are not discussing these Churches, we are discussing the Prayer Book, and the Articles are no part of the Prayer Book, they make a book of themselves. The theology of the Prayer Book must be gathered from within its own covers. If we look there to find a system of theology thoroughly well bolted and riveted, we shall look in vain; but this is by no means an admission that the language of the formularies is that invertebrate and undogmatic thing which some would like to see it made. Far from it; for not only are the ancient creeds, in one or other of their authenticated forms, made a frequent feature of worship, the very prayers themselves are redolent of dogma. And yet it is rare indeed to hear anybody, except an extreme liberal, complain of the dogmatic feature of the Prayer Book worship as a grievance. And why? Simply because the dogma has been, if I may be allowed to coin a word, devotionalized. In liturgies, as elsewhere, much depends upon the way of putting things. By way of illustration, suppose we take some orthodox statement of doctrinal truth and lay alongside of it a devotionalized form of the same thought. We are bent, for example, upon setting up a barrier against the arch-heretic Pelagius and his vicious doctrine of human merit. Very well, here is one way of doing it, the systematic way: "Albeit that good works, which are the fruits of faith and follow after justification, cannot put away our sins and endure the severity of God's judgment, yet are they pleasing and acceptable to God in Christ; but works done before the grace of Christ and the inspiration of his Spirit are not pleasant to God." This of course throws the mind of the listener into a critical and argumentative mood at once; but attend to the same thought in the attractive form in which it comes wooing us through the lips of prayer on the Fifth Sunday after Easter: "O Lord, from whom all things do come; Grant to us thy humble servants, that by thy holy inspiration we may think those things that are good, and by thy merciful guiding may perform the same, through Jesus Christ our Lord."

Most will agree, I think, that the liturgical method of inculcating the truth is, for the ordinary lay mind, at any rate (and the laity are much in the majority), the more persuasive of the two. I do not for a moment pretend to affirm that the Prayer Book is always equally felicitous in its attempts to clothe the hard skeleton of dogma with the warm flesh and blood of a personal devotion. There are marked exceptions. The opening invocations of the Litany, and the Proper Preface, so called, for Trinity Sunday in the Communion Office are well-meant endeavors to fasten the Nicene dogma in the affections of the worshippers; but the same end would have been more effectively served, and the purposes of devotion far better met, by a few quotations from that strangely neglected liturgical treasure-house, the Revelation of St. John the Divine. There need have been no real fear that the interests of Trinitarianism would suffer. The Prayer Book is Trinitarian through and through, warp and woof. You would have to put it under axes and hammers, as was once done in Boston, to get the Trinitarianism out of it.

Again, the theology of the Prayer Book is preeminently a biblical as contrasted with a systematic theology. In saying this I do not mean to assert that the Prayer Book is always true to the teachings of Holy Scripture (though personally I believe it so to be), for that, in this presence, would seem too much like begging the question; but what I mean is that the Prayer Book ever shows itself more solicitous that its utterances shall square with the utterances of the prophets, the apostles, and our Lord Jesus Christ than that they should be absolutely consistent in their relations to one another. In a "system," whether of theology or of philosophy, the great point is to avoid self-contradiction. All things must hang together logically; there must be no broken link in the coat of mail, no gap between gorget and cuirass wherethrough the point of sword or lance may pierce. But the Bible writers do not seem to have felt this sort of anxiety. First they stated one truth, and then they stated another; and the listener was left, notably in the case of the Sermon on the Mount, the most divine of all discourses upon ethics, to discover for himself the articulation of the truths enunciated. If they seemed to him contradictory, so much the worse for him.

I have already once referred to the doctrine of merit by way of illustration; let it again serve us as a case in point. What a very Arminian sound, to speak theologically, has the following sentence from the Apocrypha which the Prayer Book orders to be read at the Offertory, or Alms-gathering: "Be merciful after thy power, if thou hast much give plenteously, if thou hast little do thy diligence gladly to give of that little, for so gatherest thou thyself a good reward." Here there seems to be a very evident eye to some recompense for our deserts. On the other hand, Calvin himself would have been satisfied with the predestinarian import of a petition which occurs in the very same office, later on, where the order of request is that the suppliants may be given grace to do such good works as have been " prepared " for them " to walk in."

Another striking instance of the Prayer Book's utter indifference to logical consistency, when it is a question of faithfully reflecting the teachings of Holy Scripture, is afforded by its eschatology. With respect to the great central verity of the resurrection to eternal life, there is no uncertain sound; but as to lesser points, and especially as to the temporal relations between death and the judgment, we find in the Prayer Book the same ambiguity that perplexes us in the New Testament. How much better this than an attempt to be wise above what is revealed!

It remains to say something about the sacramental aspects of the theology of the Common Prayer. It is here that we come into closest contact with that great doctrinal quarrel which underlay the whole sixteenth century movement. On its political side, the Reformation was a protest against absolutism centred at Rome; on its doctrinal side, it was a protest against an overstrained and exaggerated sacramental system, or, as Froude bluntly puts it, an assertion on the part of the laity of their own intrinsic spiritual rights.

The attitude of the Prayer Book towards Roman error under this head is not so much polemical as it is independent and self-respecting. Those were not the days when Anglicans waited with bated breath to hear what Rome might have to say as to the validity of their orders. The men who framed the Prayer Book had a mind of their own, and did not think it necessary to cross the mountains to search out what was Catholic and primitive. It is true that a slight panicky feeling betrays itself in the famous suffrage of King Edward's Litany, "From the tyranny of the Bishop of Rome and all his detestable enormities, Good Lord deliver us"; but this is offset by the courage and good sense which Elizabeth showed in expunging the supersensitive clause while as yet the embers of the fires which her sister had kindled at Smithfield were scarcely cold.

The unquestioned prominence which the Book of Common Prayer assigns to sacramental doctrine and sacramental practice is not adequately explained by the hypothesis of a sort of half-way covenant with Rome. This is a method of dealing with the fact more popular than profound. Journalists and littérateurs may be pardoned for taking that view, but serious-minded theologians will scarcely be content with it. The true explanation of the emphasis that the Prayer Book lays upon sacramental obligation and sacramental privilege is to be found in a conviction toward which many independent lines of present-day thought converge; namely, the conviction that religion is, after all, far more an affair of personal allegiance and personal intercourse than it is the acceptance of a syllabus of sacred truths, however well authenticated or accurately dovetailed. St. Paul's aspiration was not "that I may know about Him," it was "that I may know Him."

It might seem to be expecting a great deal of a Church to ask it to retain within its confines two such contrasted and apparently irreconcilable minds as Pusey and Maurice. Yet each of these two men is found exalting to a very lofty place in his religious system the sacrament of the body and blood of Christ. What worthier explanation can we frame for the occurrence of so unlooked-for a truce between hostile temperaments than to suppose that both men have discovered the emptiness of mere intellectuality in religion, and, weary of what one of them was so fond of stigmatizing as "a Gospel of notions," are fleeing, hungry and thirsty, to the presence of the personal, the true, the living Christ.

The truth is, that so far from carrying any taint of Roman error, the Prayer Book Office for the Holy Communion is probably, of all the formularies which the book contains, the one least obnoxious to such a charge. The doctrine of the Eucharist was known to be the critical point in the Reformation's line of defence, and it was guarded with a corresponding jealousy. That the Prayer Book Office still retains this bulwark character is sufficiently evidenced by the fact that those who seek to make it do duty as High Mass are compelled to mutilate and dislocate it before it can be forced to lend itself to their questionable purpose.

I have spoken of the history and of the characteristics of the Prayer Book; bear with me a little longer until I shall have said a few words about its possibilities in years to come.

It would rightly have appeared a poor requital of the courtesy which I began by acknowledging, had I come here to exploit the Prayer Book as the special possession of the Communion in which it happens to be my own privilege to serve, or to make boast of its excellences in the spirit of a monopolist. Such has not been my attitude of mind, and I should be unhappy if I thought that any one of you who have so kindly listened to my imperfect setting forth of a great subject had so imagined. I hold the Common Prayer to be the common property of the whole English-speaking race. It was originally promulgated with the intention of its being that. By what disabling statute or repealing clause, I should like to ask, has right of ownership been since limited to any narrower constituency? There are, to be sure, certain corporate bodies that hold the book in trust, as it were, for the several nationalities into which the Englishry of the sixteenth century has, under God's providence, wonderfully developed, — there is a standard edition according to the use of England, another according to the use of Ireland, and another according to the use of the United States; but on the book's titlepage, high up above these particulars of lesser moment, stands the generous and inclusive superscription, "The Book of Common Prayer, and Administration of the Sacraments and other Rites and Ceremonies of the Church." What Church? England's Church? Ireland's Church? No;— the Holy Catholic Church, the Congregation of Faithful Men, the Body of all those who have been baptized into the Holy Name. Do not imagine that I am about to close a cool survey with a perfervid rhapsody. I have no extravagant expectations for the future of the Prayer Book in this country, though in common with many others I entertain some, perhaps not wholly unreasonable, hopes. In the light of the post-Reformation history, covering now almost four centuries, it does not seem likely that liturgical worship will ever again become universal throughout Christendom, least of all that it will do so in a country like this. If the Church to which an eminent Presbyterian divine has given the felicitous title of "The United Church of the United States" ever grows into reality, the probability is that we shall see within its borders public worship conducted with high ritual, with low ritual, and with no ritual, by liturgy or by directory, according to the needs, demands, and aptitudes of particular communities.

The Church of England is the only national Church in Christendom that ever undertook to enforce absolute uniformity in public worship, and England's attempt has been a conspicuous failure. Ritualists and Evangelicals succeed in making one and the same liturgy speak in very different tones; while non-conformity, standing beyond the pale altogether, contrives to say its prayers without the help of any book at all, and yet keeps up, strange to say, a fair show of good works.

But let that pass. What I am seeking to emphasize in these closing words is the common and undivided interest which all English-speaking Christians already possess in the ancient Common Prayer if they have a mind to claim it. There are no copyright restrictions hedging the book; no ecclesiastical treasury derives a royalty from its sale. Why should not congregations of whatever name that feel the need of a liturgy take it and use it, or so much of it as they care to use, instead of setting committees at work compiling formularies which after all would have to shine mostly by borrowed light? Scruples about the ordination service need not be an obstacle; for no more than the Thirty-nine Articles is the Ordinal a part of the Prayer Book. The Prayer Book proper ends with the Psalms of David, as a glance at its table of contents will show. And these are the words with which it ends: "Let everything that hath breath praise the Lord."

BIBLIOGRAPHY.

Palmer, Rev. Wm., *Origines Liturgicæ.*
Freeman, Rev. Philip, *Principles of Divine Service.* 2 vols.
Breviary, Salisbury.
Breviary, Aberdeen.
Breviary, Quignonian.
Breviary, Mozarabic.
Muratori, *Liturgia.* 2 vols.
Gee and Hardy, *Documents illustrative of English Church History.*
Primers, The Three, of Henry VIII.
Keeling, *Liturgiæ Britannicæ.*
Parker, James, *First Prayer Book of Edward VI.* compared with the successive Revisions.
Parker, James, *Introduction to the History of the Successive Revisions of the Book of Common Prayer.*
Maskell, Rev. Wm., *Ancient Liturgy of the Church of England.*
Maskell, Rev. Wm., *Monumenta Ritualia Ecclesiæ Anglicanæ.*
Walton and Medd, *First Prayer Book of Edward VI.*
Pickering, W., *Reprints of Books of Common Prayer, from Edward to Victoria.* 7 vols.
Cardwell, Dr. E., *Two Books of Common Prayer of Edward VI. compared.*
Henry Bradshaw Society, Liturgical publications of.
Wheatley, Rev. Chas., *Rational Illustration of the Book of Common Prayer.*
Sanderson and Wrenn, Bishops, *Fragmentary Illustrations of the History of the Book of Common Prayer from Manuscript Sources.*
Blue Book of House of Commons, containing Revised Liturgy of 1689.
Hall, Rev. Peter, *Reliquiæ Liturgicæ.*
Hall, Rev. Peter, *Fragmenta Liturgica.*
Baxter, Rev. Richard, *A Petition for Peace with the Reformation of the Liturgy.*
Blunt, Rev. J. H., *Annotated Book of Common Prayer.*
Cardwell, Edward, *History of Conferences and other Proceedings connected with the Revision of the Book of Common Prayer.*
Luckock, Rev. Canon, *Studies in the History of the Book of Common Prayer.*

Daniel, Rev. Canon, *The Prayer Book, its History, Language, and Contents.*
Proctor, Rev. F., *History of the Book of Common Prayer.*
Campion and Beaumont, *The Prayer Book Interleaved.*
Hole, Rev. Chas., *Manual of the Book of Common Prayer.*
Black-Letter Prayer Book of 1636, Zinco-photographic facsimile.
Manuscript Prayer Book of 1662, Photographic facsimile.
Jebb, John, *The Choral Service of the Churches of England and Ireland.*
Stephens, A. J., *Book of Common Prayer with Notes Legal and Historical.*
Purchas, Rev. J., *Directorium Anglicanum.*
Convocation Prayer Book.
Bright and Medd, *Liber Precum Publicarum.*
Scudamore, *Notitia Eucharistica.*
Maurice, Rev. F. D., *The Prayer Book and the Lord's Prayer.*
Goulburn, Dean, *Collects of the Day.*
Selborne, Earl of, *Notes on some Passages in Liturgical History of the Reformed English Church.*
Sprott, *Scottish Liturgies of James VI.*
Huntington, Rev. W. R., *Short History of the Book of Common Prayer.*
S. P. C. K., *Commentary on the Prayer Book.*
Barry, Rev. Wm., *Teacher's Prayer Book.*
Wright, Rev. John, *Early Prayer Books of America.*
M'Garvey, Rev. Wm., *Liturgiæ Americanæ.*
The Book Annexed, Philadelphia, 1883.
The Book Annexed, as modified, New York, 1885.
The Standard Prayer Book of 1892.

VIII

THE BOOK OF COMMON ORDER AND THE DIRECTORY FOR WORSHIP

BY THE REV. ALLAN POLLOK, D.D.

Principal of the Presbyterian College, Halifax, N. S.

THE BOOK OF COMMON ORDER AND THE DIRECTORY FOR THE PUBLIC WORSHIP OF GOD

JOHN KNOX'S views on the subject of public worship may be found in a letter written to the Protestants of Scotland from France in 1556 — *four* years before the Scottish Reformation. In this he advises for their ordinary assemblies: *first*, Prayer with confession of sins and invocation of the Spirit of the Lord Jesus: then, the reading of the Scripture, plainly and distinctly: then, the interpretation. In reading the Scripture, he adds: "I would ye should join some books of the Old and some of the New Testament together, as Genesis and one of the Evangelists, Exodus with another and so forth, ever ending such books as ye begin: for it shall greatly comfort you to hear that harmony and well-tuned song of the Holy Spirit speaking in our fathers from the beginning." He then recommends that common prayers and intercessions be made for princes, rulers and magistrates, for the "liberty of the Gospel, the comfort of the afflicted, and the deliverance of persecuted churches." This letter contains the first rough sketch of the worship of the Reformed

Church of Scotland. We must not suppose that this subject was new to the Scottish reformer, or that in the enthusiasm of his anti-Romish iconoclasm he had entirely overlooked public worship. On his release from the French galleys, he had been employed by the English Privy Council preaching in the north of England. After two years' service there he was appointed one of King Edward's chaplains-in-ordinary — a most important office, which he retained till the king's death in 1553. Thus, during *four* years he must have been familiar with the liturgy of Edward VI., both in its first form and subsequent revision. Such an important work as the revision of the *first* book could not but have occupied much of his attention. As a matter of fact, Knox was called up to London and consulted on the subject, and by his influence significant changes were made in the communion office of the Book of Common Prayer. It is important to notice that the Scottish reformer had formed opinions on this subject before he made the acquaintance of Calvin or the Continental divines. In the beginning of 1554 he sought safety and found leisure in Geneva, which he described as "the most perfect school of Christ that ever was upon earth." There Calvin had fully established the Reformed doctrine and worship, and here he directed the movement all over Europe. But soon Knox was invited to take charge of a congregation of English exiles, who had been permitted to worship in Frankfort upon condition of conforming as nearly as possible to the worship of the French church. These Englishmen accordingly agreed to omit the surplice, the litany, audible responses, and other ceremonies of the Book of Common Prayer, but discord had begun when Knox arrived, and, notwithstanding all his efforts, it continued till he left, and with even increased vehemence after his departure. In the course of these disputes between those who were *for* and those who were *against* the use of Edward's book, Knox, along with some others, had composed what was afterwards known as the Book of Geneva — a service not the same as the Genevan order but closely resembling it. The name — the Book of Geneva — was derived from the fact that, upon Knox's return to Geneva, it was printed and used by the English Kirk of Geneva, of which John Knox was minister. The title of the first edition states that it was approved by the famous and learned man, John Calvin. From the preface, as given in Dunlop's Confessions, we find that the date of this first edition is the 10th of February, 1556. This is the book afterwards known as the Book of Common Order, but commonly and not very inaccurately called, Knox's Liturgy. We thus find that, in the rough sketch addressed to the Scottish Protestants in 1556, Knox wrote from long and sometimes unpleasant familiarity with the subject. As was conspicuously the case with Calvin, we find in all Knox's writings carefully composed prayers. Neither of these great men could have had the least objection to written prayers, and both were familiar with liturgical composition. How could they be otherwise when the Bible is so full of prayers?

Knox returned to Scotland in 1559, and the Scottish Reformation was accomplished in 1560. In the interval between 1556 and 1560, and for *four* years afterwards, the Book of Common Prayer was used in meetings of the Reforming party. In 1557 the Scottish Lords of the Congregation resolved: "That the Common Prayers be read weekly on Sunday and other festival days, publicly in the parish kirks with the lessons of the Old and New Testaments, conform to the Book of Common Prayer." The book referred to here was unquestionably the *second* book of Edward as resumed and slightly amended at the accession of Queen Elizabeth. This was afterwards disputed. However, not only does the wording of the resolution imply it, but it is established by contemporary testimony. There is not the least doubt that they would have preferred the Book of Geneva, but few copies of this were available and copies of the other could easily be procured from England. In the First Book of Discipline, prepared by the famous *five Johns*, John Winram, John Spottiswood, John Douglas, John Row, and John Knox, and embodying the church principles of the Scottish Reformers, the Order of Geneva is spoken of as "used in our churches." In 1562 the General Assembly enjoined its uniform use in the administration of the sacraments, solemnization of marriage, and burial of the dead. In 1564 it was enlarged and the Psalter completed. In this form its use was enjoined upon every minister, exhorter, and reader. In 1567 it was by order of the General Assembly translated into Gaelic for the use of the Highlanders. Probably it was thus the first book printed in the Gaelic language. It is constantly referred to in Acts of Assemblies as the settled and legalized form of worship down to the year 1645, when the Directory was authorized by the Scottish Estates.

In a copy of this book, printed at Aberdeen in 1635 — that is, shortly before the St. Giles's riot in 1637 — I find the following contents: a calendar of the movable feasts, a short and admirable Confession of Faith, used in the English congregation of Geneva, an extract from the First Book of Discipline concerning ministers, their election and duties and the assemblies of the Church, the form of ordination of ministers, the order of discipline in excommunication, repentance and absolution with all the prayers prescribed for such services, the order for the visitation of the sick, confessions and godly prayers for the daily service and special occasions, forms for the communion, baptism, and marriage, a treatise on fasting, with Scriptures and prayers to be used at such fasts. The prayer for the whole estate of Christ's Church, as in all the liturgies, *follows* the sermon. It is concluded with the Lord's Prayer. Then followed the recitation of the Apostles' Creed, after the following preamble: " Almighty and everlasting God, vouchsafe, we beseech thee to grant us perfect continuance in the lively faith, augmenting the same in us daily, till we grow to the full measure of our perfection in Christ, whereof we make our confession, saying, I believe in God, the Father Almighty," etc. This was followed by the benediction, either from Numbers or from 2 Corinthians. The Psalms in metre, along with a music score in four parts and marginal notes to aid the worshipper in singing with the understanding, occupy two-thirds of the book. Thus it must be seen that a worshipper in the Scots church, for nearly a hundred years after the Reformation, went to church well provided for its services. So far as congregational worship is concerned, we have, in losing these forms, not advanced but retrograded.

On the special features of this form of service, I must restrict myself to but a few observations. The peculiar title, "Book of Common Order," was well chosen, for various reasons. *Ordo* is a word which, from the eighth century, was applied to rubrical directions for the guidance of priests in the administratration of the sacraments. It accurately describes services which were sometimes discretionary in their parts but never in their order. The term "Common" might suggest a comparison, perhaps a contrast, with the Book of Common Prayer, previously in use. It was "*common*" because it was not only a service *by* the people and not by priests alone, but because it was *for* the people in every church throughout the nation.

The word expresses the meaning which, in the following century, was conveyed by the word "*uniform.*" The churches throughout the land were to have a service common to all. The whole form is in close conformity with the Genevan liturgy of 1543, which became the model for all the Reformed liturgies except that of the English Church. The Book of Common Prayer borrowed much from them, but they borrowed nothing from it. Calvin was preceded in Geneva by Farel, who had swept away every vestige of the ancient worship, so that his successor was able to go directly back to the Holy Scriptures for guidance and authority. The Genevan morning service for the Lord's day began with the reading of the *appointed* chapters of Holy Scripture and the Ten Commandments; then, after a very brief formula of invocation and a single sentence of exhortation, with the confession. After a psalm had been sung, a prayer for illumination followed. For this the minister might take a form provided or one composed by himself. The sermon was followed by the prayer for all conditions, the Lord's Prayer, the recitation of the Apostles' Creed, and the benediction. The service was long neither as a whole nor in any of its parts. The minister was rigorously tied down to this service once a week, — that is, on Sunday mornings; but ample provision for free prayer was made by the rubric that "On week days the minister useth such words in prayer as may seem to him good, suiting his prayer to the occasion and the matter whereof he treats in preaching." Such is substantially the service now maintained in all the Reformed churches of the European continent. All this was reproduced in the Book of Common Order; except that the prayer after sermon might be varied, according to a rubrical permission, — a liberty of which Knox often availed himself in his conflicts with the Court. In the services for baptism, the communion, and marriage, everything is prescribed, and no latitude is given to the minister. The communion was to be ministered once a month, or as oft as expedient, and baptism and marriage were to be in church on the Sabbath day in presence of the congregation.

The fundamental principle of all the Reformed liturgies, the Anglican excepted, is the conjunction of free with prescribed prayer. The advantages and disadvantages in each were balanced by using both. But there was a common *Order;* so that in the substance and succession the worshipper always knew what was coming, and confusion and surprise were prevented. At the same time, as it was not accordant with primitive Christianity to restrain all expression of the free spirit, free prayer was allowed in one part of the daily service and encouraged in all other meetings of the Church. The rubrical directions for baptism, the communion, and marriage, allowed no deviation; because these were of the nature of vows or engagements. A very special feature was the extensive use made of the *psalms.* Calvin clearly perceived that the psalms were the Church's response to the Divine message. This response burst from human hearts in a warm tide of emotion diversified by all kinds of experience. The psalmist might speak in the *first* person, but he spoke as a representative believer and an organ of inspiration. The psalms are the voice of the Church. They everywhere breathe a churchly spirit, and they were written not to be read or recited but to be sung, and if possible sung responsively. It may be confidently affirmed that this collection of sacred song can never with propriety be omitted from the services of the Church of that God whom its devout aspirations bring so near to the human soul, or that anything can be found on earth to take its place. When we hear it merely read by the minister, the psalm strikes the ear with a kind of inverted majesty. It must in some way be uttered by the Church which has been divinely furnished with this voice in which to call upon and cry out to the living God. The minister's part in the service was confession, intercession, and preaching, to which the people replied in the psalms by adoration, praise, and exhortation. The minister's prayers contain only confession and intercession, and without the psalms would have furnished an incomplete service. Calvin wholly rejected audible responses without musical expression as fitted not to awaken but to disturb devotion. The psalms were translated into metre by Clement Marot and Theodore Beza and set to plain tunes which could easily be followed by the whole people. Knox adopted the same method, using for this purpose the version of Sternhold and Hopkins. This psalm singing was so marked a feature that the whole Book of Common Order was usually called "The Psalm Book" not only in common speech but in Acts of Assembly. The liturgy and the psalms in Geneva and Scotland were invariably bound together. All the prayers in the Book of Common Order and in the Geneva liturgy are models of simplicity and comprehensiveness, but the daily offices are especially beautiful. The morning prayer was being heard by Coligny when the assassins burst into his chamber; and the evening prayer was read to John Knox two hours before he expired. When asked if he had heard it, he replied, "Would that you and all men had heard as I have heard it. I praise God for that heavenly sound."

The last edition of the Book of Common Order was issued in 1644, and the Directory was adopted by the General Assembly in 1645. In a work, known to be by Alexander Henderson, published in 1641, and intended to correct an impression prevalent in England that the Scots had no settled forms of worship, he describes the worship in his day. The churches were open every day for the reading of prayers, and on one day of each week there was a regular service with sermon. On Sundays at 7 o'clock a bell was rung to warn the people to prepare for public worship. Another bell at 8 o'clock served to assemble the congregation. Each person on entering the church bowed in silent prayer. As there were no pews, the men stood while the women sat on chairs or stools. The reader read from the lectern the common prayers and gave out psalms to be sung. The singing was always concluded with the "Gloria Patri." He then read chapters from the Old and New Testaments. After an hour another bell announced the entrance of the minister, who bowed as the people had done. Many have wondered at the ringing of three bells in Scotch churches on Sunday mornings and inquired what it is done for. It is simply a survival of the old worship. We have lost the prayers, and for our comfort or vexation we have the bells. The minister began with a conceived prayer, which was understood to be for illumination. Then followed the sermon, the prayer for all estates, the Lord's Prayer, the Creed, and the benediction — all forming a service, scriptural in character, logical in structure, and in harmony with the order of all Reformed churches on the European continent. It was not tedious, as the age of long sermons and long prayers had not arrived. The Scots church would have retained it substantially till now but for the violent interference of the authorities of another church and another people.

At the accession of James I., a Presbyterian king, the Puritan members of the Church of England hoped for some relief from obnoxious ceremonies; but their most reasonable requests were contemptuously rejected. He told them that they must conform, or he would harry them out of the land. Under Charles I., persecution more and more increased till the meeting of the Long Parliament, when the situation was reversed, and Laud was sent to the prison to which he had consigned so many conscientious men. The Scots, in defence of their despised and insulted worship, had invaded England, and when their Commissioners were treating with the king at Ripon, Commissioners from the Long Parliament arrived for a similar purpose. It was at this point that the Scots and English began to co-operate. In 1643 — a year after the civil war had begun — English Commissioners appeared at the General Assembly in Edinburgh and proposed a league between the two kingdoms. As the Scots desired a religious covenant also, the Solemn League and Covenant was subscribed by both nations. It was in consequence of this conjunction that Scottish Commissioners went to the Westminster Assembly — an English Council called by the Long Parliament to reform the English Church. We do not know what reforms the English divines might have made in the Church of England, nor what kind of polity or worship or discipline they would have established without the aid of the Scots, but we do know that it was in consequence of this treaty that the Scots gave up their ancient Book of Common Order and adopted the Westminster Directory.

It may be well to review the situation at this juncture. The grand aim of the Court had been to reduce the Church of Scotland to the English pattern, and in this there was some progress made, for bishops had been established in Scotland for twenty-eight years.

Uniformity in both kingdoms was the dream of James and Charles and Laud, and they fondly hoped to have it realized. But worship touched the feelings of the Scottish people more than polity, and when a new liturgy was forced upon them and their old one was superseded, then the Scots threw down bishops, abolished the Perth Articles, and cancelled all the offensive legislation from 1605 to 1638. Along with this movement in Scotland, Charles and Laud were forcing, by the most cruel penalties, uniformity in England. When the Scots took up arms to fight for their religion, the necessities of the king compelled him to summon a parliament which at once took cognizance of the *religious* grievances of the English nation. Thus the king had arrayed against him the religious people of both nations. Uniformity was still aimed at, but now the parties had changed places. By the Solemn League and Covenant, the Scots sought uniformity, but it was Scotch Presbyterian uniformity, with which they hoped to bless England. With such views and expectations, the Scots Commissioners came to the Westminster Assembly in the autumn of 1643. As representatives of the Scots church and nation, they were received with much respect by the members of what has been called the most grave and learned Assembly of the Church since the days of the Apostles. Upon the 12th October, the Lords and Commons ordered the Assembly to commence the work of framing a Directory of Public Worship. Previous to this the Solemn League and Covenant had been taken by the

House of Commons, the Lords, the Assembly of Divines, and the Scots Commissioners, in St. Margaret's Church, Westminster, and had been sent back to Edinburgh to be subscribed throughout the kingdom. It was under this conjunction and covenant that Puritan and Presbyterian now united in framing a form for public worship and Church offices. The Scots Commissioners, six in number, sat as a body of assessors, with voices but no votes, treating in the name of Scotland for uniformity with England, and they took more than their share in the debates of an Assembly which sat without intermission for five and a half years. Their influence arose, not from their number, which was small, nor from their talents, which were great, but from their representing the Scotch nation. The preparation of the Directory was intrusted to a small committee consisting of Marshall, Palmer, Goodwin, Young, Herle, and the Scots Commissioners. From this it might be expected that the Directory would be more Scotch than English in its cast. In fact, the important sections on prayer, preaching, and the administration of the sacraments were ultimately left to Henderson and his fellow Commissioners alone. The thirteenth volume of Lightfoot's works, containing his "Notes" and Baillie's letters, give the most distinct account of the debates on the Directory, which are recorded under fifty-four sessions in the end of the second volume, and twenty-one at the beginning of the third of the Minutes. Not only had they the co-operation of thirty lay assessors from the Long Parliament, but their decisions were submitted to that body for confirmation or amendment. The sentiments of the English parliamentary government were thoroughly Erastian, and they did not scruple to make important corrections upon drafts of the Directory as passed by the divines. The work was continued throughout 1644, completed in December, and sanctioned by Parliament. In February, 1645, the Scottish Estates ratified and approved it in all the heads and articles thereof. It ought to be noted that the Scots General Assembly passed it with two reservations — one relating to the Lord's Supper, in which they say that there must be a table and the communicants must distribute the elements among themselves, and the other maintaining the order and practice of the Scots Kirk in all matters, except where they are otherwise ordered and appointed in the Directory. These are important reservations. The Scots were stiffly opposed to the Independents in their manner of distributing the elements to the people in their pews, as well as to the Anglican method of the minister giving them to each communicant. They held, as true Presbyterians, a place between these two extremes. The second reservation betrays their attachment to their own ancient service and their desire to preserve as much of it as they possibly could.

The Preface of the Directory, which sets forth the views and aims of the Divines, should be carefully studied by all who would understand this formulary. It refers almost solely to England and the English

Church. They say, "We have resolved to lay aside the former liturgy with the many rites and ceremonies formerly used in the worship of God, and have agreed upon this following Directory for all the parts of public worship at ordinary and extraordinary times," etc. It is called a "Directory" to distinguish it from a liturgy, wherein all is set down to be followed without change and no discretion is allowed. Here the general heads, the sense and scope of the prayers, are given "that there may be a consent of all the churches in those things that contain the substance of the service and worship of God." The meaning of this is that, though the majority desired a fixed order in all the churches, the Independents did not wish even a Directory, but entire and unrestricted liberty—which some may think to be the *beau idéal* of public worship and of which we now have enough and to spare. The name "Directory" implies that the rubrics and forms were to be strictly followed, except in parts where latitude is allowed. Clauses or expressions conceding liberty in some parts surely imply that in other cases the minister is bound by the rubric. Without this restraint the book could not be even a Directory. Those who do as they please follow, not the Presbyterians, but the Independents. Also in the matter of order the minister is not left *free*, except where an alternative is allowed. This rule applies to the order of topics in prayers and exhortations. For example, along with the prayer of confession before sermon is the prayer for all conditions; but the rubric allows the latter to come after the sermon and change places with the thanksgiving. As it was designed by having a Directory that the worshippers should always know what part to expect next, the *order* of service and of topics was not discretionary. The Preface was debated for six sessions principally upon the point whether the prayer-outlines might be moulded into prayers or not. The Independents were against this, and to satisfy them it was left indefinite; so that each minister might decide this for himself. Lightfoot, the Rabbinical scholar of his age, said that "it was dangerous to hint anything against a form of prayer." Curiously, there is no mention of the posture of the worshippers in prayer, but historical testimonies prove this to have been either kneeling or standing, and *never* sitting, except during Communion. The long prayer before sermon is referred to by Baillie as "a new fancy of the Independents" — "contrary to all the practice of the church, old or late." This outline, consisting of confession and intercession, admits of easy separation into two distinct prayers. The public reading of passages from both Testaments is enjoined as an act of worship. The Scriptures must be read in course, and no comments are allowed till the reading is ended, lest the word of God should be intermingled with the word of man. Private prayer on entering the church is presupposed by the rubric which says that "if any be hindered from being present at the beginning, they ought not, when they come into the congregation, betake themselves to their devotions." Here the exception clearly establishes the rule. The minister also bowed on entering the pulpit, until this also was abandoned to please the Brownists and their followers, and so, when the minister gave up this becoming practice, the people did the same. This custom, the use of the Gloria and the Lord's Prayer, long used in Scotland, were surrendered by the Scots, to the sorrow of a great many devout ministers and people. But regard for the Directory might have preserved one of them, for it says: "And, because the prayer which Christ taught his disciples is not only a pattern of prayer but itself a most comprehensive prayer, we recommend it also to be used in the prayers of the Church." Notwithstanding these words, it is not long since it was scarcely ever heard in our churches. The compilers, following the Book of Common Order, intended it probably to be introduced as a conclusion to the last prayer, which is the prayer of thanksgiving and Christian hope. It has been thought very strange, especially in these days, when singing often occupies so much of the time in public worship, that so little place is assigned to it in the Directory. It is referred to incidentally after the reading, and again after the last prayer it is said: "Let a psalm, [not part of a psalm], be sung, if with conveniency it may be done." There is reason to believe that, as expressed in the first Book of Discipline, singing was regarded as "a profitable but not necessary part of worship." This may have been the prevalent feeling in England, but it was not so among the Scottish presbyters, who had long been accustomed to the singing of the Psalms as an indispensable part of Presbyterian worship; and hence, when Rouse's version had, after considerable amendment, been sanctioned by the divines and the Long Parliament in 1646 and sent down to Scotland for adoption, the Scots were not as compliant as formerly. They continued to correct and compare it with their own and other versions, and to ask for the advice of presbyteries — in fact to take the utmost pains to secure a suitable version and it was not till 1650 that our present version of the Psalms was finally passed. It was thus not part of the covenanted uniformity and it can only with a qualification be called Rouse's version. It is to this that we owe the preservation of the old versions of the 100th Psalm by Wm. Keith, the old 124th by Whittingham, the brother-in-law of Calvin and the noble second versions of Psalms 102, 136, 143, and 145, by John Craig, the friend of Knox and minister of Holyrood.

Coming to special services, baptism must be administered in church and in the face of the congregation — that is, not in a font at the door. Sponsors are dispensed with, but, in the necessary absence of the father, the child may be presented by a Christian friend. This is accordant with Westminster doctrine: that a child's title to baptism is its federal holiness in right of descent from those who were by profession under the covenant of grace. The form contains no profession of faith, no creed, no vows, and no questions; but a promise for the performance of duty is required. These seem to have been either excluded or expunged by the Independents — perhaps by the long Parliament. However, in the Book of Common Order there is no promise required, but the Apostles' Creed is rehearsed and expounded. In the absence of any formal and explicit engagement, the instruction is very carefully worded and was meant to be used as a form. It embodies the doctrine of the Westminster divines, that, though the grace of baptism is not tied to the time of its administration, it ought to be desired and prayed for as a blessing to be conferred in God's own time, whether then or afterwards. If the seal has no connection with the sign, we cannot justify the baptism of infants at all. The whole Order is most complete, and wholly opposed to views which are more Socinian than Catholic or Presbyterian. It is a manifest defect that there is no Order for the baptism of adults. As to the mode: *sprinkling* was preferred, but dipping was not excluded. There was much debate in this matter, but it was not as to the one right mode, but as to the exclusion of the other. The exhortation to the people to improve their baptism is a special feature. The whole service, including the prayers, is most impressive and well worthy of close adherence.

As the communion signalized the differences between the Scots and the English, and especially the Independents, the debates upon this section were long and ardent. It took up eighteen sessions. They at last agreed upon the word "frequently" and left the frequency to be determined by each congregation. The qualification was reduced to the smallest dimensions, probably, by the House of Commons. Only the ignorant and scandalous are excluded. In the rubric a table is mentioned, but the Independents were for what has been called "simultaneous communion" — to which the Scots would never consent. The phrase "about it or at it" expressed compromise, and each nation held fast by its own way. The Scots table-services, once universal, have now nearly disappeared, and have carried away many holy associations and sweet remembrances with them. The Scots way, which continued under sometimes very trying circumstances — in the church and in the wilderness — for three hundred years was nearest to the Institution. At the risk of being called a *laudator temporis acti* I must say that I would much prefer it still. The change which the divines could *not* make has been the work of church builders and building committees who made no provision in the pews for this ancient mode of celebration. In this we have gone completely over to the Independents. There must be an address, called sometimes fencing, before the prayer of consecration. There is no liturgy in modern times without it. The prayer includes the three elements of thanksgiving, a profession of faith, and an invocation. There was a debate as to the distribution. In the Scottish practice the communicants handed the elements, the one to the other. In the rubric this matter is left undecided. The prayer at the close is a prayer of thanksgiving. In Scotland the post-communion prayer has always included intercession for all ranks and a strong expression of Christian hope of reunion with departed saints. This is a natural conclusion to a service which not only expresses but ought always to be a communion of saints — a remembrance of the living and the dead. Such a prayer in the morning service would be premature, would interrupt the preparatory work and would make it tedious, so that, on communion Sundays, it should be kept till the close. On ordinary days, if the rubric is followed, the *first* prayer would be the prayer of faith, the *second* the prayer of charity, and the *last* the prayer of hope.

Thus was the most important part finished and sent up to Parliament. The rest refers to the sanctification of the Lord's day, marriage, fast days and days of thanksgiving, the visitation of the sick, the burial of the dead, and the singing of psalms. Marriage is to be in church, and, contrary to the Book of Common Order, it is recommended that it be not on Sunday. In many places where Presbyterians began to celebrate marriage in church, they were denounced as innovators and imitators of another church. The marriage service, both in its rubrics, address, and prayers, is most admirable, and it is not long. The word "obey" is not omitted from the formula, and it need not be, as probably the persons addressed will, as of yore, rejoice in doing just as they please. The words, "without any further ceremony," refer to the custom of giving the ring, which, so far as the minister is concerned, is discharged. There is no service permitted at funerals, but some word of exhortation is allowed. This rigor was too severe to last, and prayers at the house forced themselves into our practice under the pretext of giving and returning thanks where refreshments were common. Now a reasonable impulse has brought in prayers also at the grave. No former abuses could justify such a stringent prohibition of religious expression when earth opens its mouth to fulfil the primeval curse, when we stand round the grave as more than conquerors through Him that loved us, and God has opened up such an opportunity for admonishing the living. This is certainly one of the most serious omissions in the Directory,— a book which may be old, but is not antiquated, — may be neglected, but is not obsolete. In all its ritual it embodies Westminster doctrine, and, even without such emendations as the Church might and should make, a more strict observance of its forms would be an improvement upon much of our present practice. In Scotland the Directory was adopted in evil times. Montrose, an apostate from the Covenant and its legislation, was slaying thousands of its people. If he had been successful, he would have restored the Book of Common Order. Betwixt 1645 and the

Restoration, all was confusion, and the book was only imperfectly brought into use. From the Restoration to the Revolution, matters were worse, and neither prelatists nor Presbyterians had any fixed form. They were in that happy state which many think the best. Both prayed entirely without book, as long or as short and in whatever order they pleased. The Directory was not legally sanctioned at the Revolution, which was a compromise in all respects. Only the confession was adopted, and the Church was left without even a catechism or a form of worship. By repeated Acts, however, down to 1856 the General Assembly has endeavored to strengthen the authority of the Directory; so that it is at this time the only proper standard of public worship. As all this took place before the divisions in the Church of Scotland, the Directory occupies the same position in the non-established Churches in Scotland and England, two of which have marked their desire for improvement by authorizing forms for special services. The book issued by the United Presbyterian Church is of such a character that it must be a great help to ministers and people of that large and respectable body of Christians. The Euchologion, or Book of Common Order, first published by the Church Service Society in 1865, and now in its fourth or fifth edition, has wrought a reformation in the worship of the Church of Scotland, as well as other Presbyterian churches. The professed object of this Society has been not *innovation* upon the present, but *restoration* of the past. It has been dominated by a spirit of reverence for old Presbyterian forms. The existence of associations in all the *three* Presbyterian churches in Scotland and the Presbyterian Church in England, having similar ends in view, and discussing such subjects as not only an amended Directory but also an optional liturgy with some responses, the rehearsal of the Lord's Prayer and the Apostles' or Nicene Creed, and the reading of the Ten Commandments, shows plainly how the current of opinion is flowing. In the United States the Directory was *adopted* in 1729, and recommended to be used "as near as circumstances will allow." The Rev. Charles W. Baird, in his most instructive little book on liturgies, mentions that when the Synod of Philadelphia revised its Constitution in 1788 it renewed the adoption of the Directory, with the instruction that it was to be followed as each minister "shall think meet," and *threw out* a number of forms of prayer — for the invocation before sermon, before and after baptism, at the Lord's table, upon exercising discipline, at the solemnization of marriage, in the sick room, at ordinations, and nine prayers for the family, which had been drafted by its own committee. He gives specimens of these rejected forms, which are fine liturgical compositions and show that the Synod's committee were men of taste as well as devotion, and were well acquainted with that kind of literature. We may speculate upon what effect the adoption of their draft *might* have had upon the public worship of the Presbyterian Church of the United States. In

Canada the Directory is part of the basis of union in 1875, and it is similarly part of the constitution of the Irish Presbyterian Church. The acceptance is universal, and so also are the deviations from its explicit directions.

Thus the Reformers in all countries declared for fixed forms combined with free prayer. These forms both in Knox's book and the Directory were supplemented by the Psalms, which are an essential part of Presbyterian worship. As the Assembly of 1645, in their zeal for the ancient worship, resolved to retain whatever was not otherwise ordered in the Directory, it would only be right and lawful in our present circumstances to restore the use of the Apostles' Creed, the Ten Commandments, and the Lord's Prayer as the most concise expression of the elements of the Christian Religion, — doctrine, duty, and devotion. For the daily service the Directory provided regularity of order, and for special services a prescribed form. By this method the divines, though they have signally failed, honestly endeavored to control the love of novelty and to check the presumption of ignorant and thoughtless men. They sought to keep a middle place between the rigorous monotony of the Book of Common Prayer and that unbridled license in worship which was the delight of the sectaries. Indeed, experience proves that without sacramental forms the true doctrine of the sacraments will be perpetually misstated or misapprehended, and their benefits may be lessened or lost to the partakers. To adopt any Directory with the proviso that it is to be followed as far as circumstances allow, is to defeat its purpose. When any latitude is given, more will be taken than was given. For proof of this, we have merely to point to the aspect of all Presbyterian churches at the present time. A Directory compiled by the most representative divines of their age, assisted by lay-assessors, revised by both Houses, and accepted by the Scots civil and ecclesiastical authorities, might well claim some attention; but all its provisions are systematically violated. Infinite diversity prevails, and confusion extraordinary. The Directory does indeed require enlargement; but as far as it goes, its order is simple, scriptural, and free from all ambiguous and unauthorized symbolism; but all this diversity means not only that we differ from the formulary, but that we have a most depraved delight in differing from one another. It would be too tedious to enumerate these profuse and unprofitable variations. Any one who pleases may do this for himself to some extent — but only to some extent, for such knowledge is too wonderful for any one individual. This diversity ranges through all degrees, from sheets distributed among the pews for each service to the curtailed worship of the last generation. A partial remedy is commonly sought by a written order being kept in each pulpit for the use of the occasional supply, — an arrangement very trying to the preacher for the day, who has to learn a new ritual; and who, when he has enough to think about, is haunted with the fear that he may be breaking through an order which he does not know. This irregularity may be expected to increase by ministers using different manuals of their own selection; and all the while the Church does nothing but gather hymns and hymn-tunes of all kinds, and bind them for our use in volumes larger than our Bibles; and when any attempt is made to reform matters, some of our most devoted ministers and laymen are met with all sorts of dark suspicions calculated to excite prejudice and prevent people from arriving at a correct opinion on a most important subject, and with the well known cry for what is called the *good old way*. It may be well to ask, What is that way [since there are so many ways]? The Book of Common Order is one way, and the Directory is another. A way might be good without being old, and it might be old without being good. Probably such complainers, by the "good old way" mean *their own way*. They *think* that it is old, and, because it is theirs, it must be good, not only for themselves but for all others. But it is not always good for people to have their own way, — especially when it is not very old and may not be very good, and when so many love it, not so much for its own sake as for the delightful sensation of forcing it upon other people. But Church-rulers should always remember that the people have an option; and that *they* can take their own way too. When persecuted in one city they can flee to another. When they do not find, and cannot get, what they want in one church, they can seek it elsewhere. Under ordinary circumstances, the Presbyterian Church must appeal very strongly to the sympathies of religious people who are reasonable and don't delight in extremes. It looks for its polity where it finds its doctrine and discipline, — nowhere but in Scripture. In *polity* it stands between Prelacy and Independency, and in worship it ought to stand, where it stood long ago, — both in the sixteenth and seventeenth centuries, — between Ritualism and Radicalism. It ought to allow some freedom, but it ought to be a *regulated* freedom, lest it may fail in securing such respect for its ordinances as may produce respect for itself and for religion. Extempore prayer being allowed, it might be well to interpose such questions as the following: Can it ever be a prayer not offered *to* but *by* an ordinary congregation? Can the people supplicate before they know or feel the want? Can such an exercise rise higher than a meditation? Can the people ever be more than hearers? Are they not often critics? and, since the exercise *stimulates* curiosity, can they well help this undevout attitude of mind? Is not the pleasure experienced in such an exercise rather the delight of being witness to a succession of pious reflections and emotions in another without any participation of these in themselves, or any thought of this? Does not the leader in this exercise succeed best when he forgets the presence of others, and, becoming wrapt in himself, pours forth his own rapturous experience or desires to God? — that is, forgets or ignores the true nature of an exercise in which he is supposed to be representative and to express the average wants and feelings of human beings and of Christians? Does not all this give too much a mediatorial character to the Christian ministry? Can such prayer ever be the voice of the Church? Is there, or can there be, in this world any exercise so difficult for any mortal man? Prayer is not a string of Scripture passages, but the highest result of faith, — the rich flower and fruit of pious thought and experience, — a holy secretion of digested thought and life. These are questions of immense moment. I hope American Presbyterians, with their predominating good sense, are destined to answer them and practically solve them for us all as they have done in many other cases; and I cannot but think that a lecture course on this subject, in this, one of the greatest and most progressive of the American theological schools, is a bright augury of some change which may be an improvement in our worship, by which Presbyterians all over the world will be gainers.

IX

WORSHIP IN NON-LITURGICAL CHURCHES

BY THE REV. GEORGE DANA BOARDMAN, D.D., LLD.

*Honorary Pastor of the First Baptist Church,
Philadelphia, Pa.*

WORSHIP IN NON-LITURGICAL CHURCHES

WORSHIP is a human instinct. Wherever travellers have penetrated (whether into the polar regions, the heart of the Dark Continent, or the most isolated isles of the seas), they have never found a tribe so degraded that it did not worship something, — God, man, beast, demon, thing. On the other hand, there has never been a nation so civilized that it did not have its own divinity or divinities; recall Baal of Assyria, Osiris of Egypt, Brahm of India, Ormuzd of Persia, Jupiter of Rome, Zeus of Greece, Jehovah of Canaan. True, there are in our own favored land a few who profess themselves to be atheists. Nevertheless, even these gentlemen have some kind of a god of their own; if it is not the personal Jehovah of the Bible, it is some impersonal Absolute of Law, of Force, of Existence, of Something or other. It is said that even Voltaire prayed in an Alpine thunderstorm. No man was ever born an atheist; if he has become one, it is because he has suicidally emasculated his own moral nature. This innate worship of God is one of the few relics of the Paradise that has been; it is also one of the many auguries of the Paradise that is to be: "They have no rest day and night, saying:

> Holy, holy, holy, is the Lord God, the Almighty,
> Who was and who is and who is to come!"
> — *Revelation* iv. 8.

Man worships as instinctively as he breathes.

And the God of Revelation made provision for this instinct in His covenant with His ancient people. Listen to Jehovah as He spake unto Israel through His servant, saying:

"Let them make me a sanctuary; that I may dwell among them . . . There I will meet with thee, and I will commune with thee from above the mercy-seat, from between the two cherubim which are upon the ark of the testimony." — *Exodus* xxv. 8, 22.

Observe what Jehovah declares to be the precise purpose of His tabernacle: He did not appoint it as the place where His people might gather together to worship Him; He appointed it as the place where He would enshrine Himself and meet His worshipping people. This phrase — "tabernacle of the congregation" (or "tent of meeting," as it is rendered in the Revised Version) — did not mean the meeting-place of man and man in worship, so much as it meant the meeting-place of God Himself and man. It is curious to recall how the Established Church of England paid an unconscious tribute to "dissenters" by styling their places of worship "meeting-houses" or "conventicles." No, Jehovah appointed His ancient tabernacle to serve as the shrine for Himself; the congress of Godhead and manhead; the convention of the Infinite and the finite: "There I will meet with them, and commune with them from above the mercy-seat, from between the two cherubim." Accordingly, when the tabernacle was dedicated, the Shechinah, or dazzling symbol of Jehovah's presence, which had been hovering for many weeks over Sinai, majestically swept downward into the plain and covered the tent of meeting, and the glory of Jehovah filled the tabernacle.

But Jehovah not only appointed the tabernacle for His own enshrinement and communion with Israel; He also appointed an elaborate system of worship by which Israel could meet Him in humble adoration, thanksgiving, confession, supplication, consecration, communion. This was the meaning of the priesthood with its minute details of vestments, ablutions, sacrifices, oblations, festivals, Levitical ritual, and the like, — all this being scrupulously arranged according to a divinely shown pattern. Thus this whole elaborate system of ancient worship was a divinely prescribed liturgy. True, it appealed to the eye rather than to the ear, being, so to speak, a pictorial service or dramatic liturgy. Nevertheless, the chief point is this, — for fifteen hundred years Jehovah's ancient chosen people worshipped according to a divinely appointed liturgy.

But that ancient sanctuary, with all its elaborate

ritual, has been abolished in Christ. Recall the story of Jesus at Jacob's Well: —

"The woman saith unto him, Sir, I perceive that thou art a prophet. Our fathers worshipped in this mountain [pointing to Gerizim towering hard by]; and ye say, that in Jerusalem is the place where men ought to worship. Jesus saith unto her, Woman, believe me, the hour cometh, when neither in this mountain, nor in Jerusalem, shall ye worship the Father. Ye worship that which ye know not: we worship that which we know: for salvation is from the Jews. But the hour cometh, and now is, when the true worshippers shall worship the Father in spirit and truth: for such doth the Father seek to be His worshippers. God is a Spirit: and they that worship Him must worship in spirit and truth." — *John* iv. 19–24.

I know not that even the Son of God ever made a more majestic annunciation. This proclamation by Jacob's Well forms a momentous epoch in the moral history of mankind; it marks a colossal stride in the unfolding of the ideal of worship. It is as though the divine prophet had said, —

"Henceforth worship is not to be a thing of place and time and rite. Believe me, woman, the hour is coming when men will neither on your Gerizim nor on our Moriah worship the Father. You Samaritans are worshipping blindly. What though you accept the five books of Moses? You do not catch their meaning. But we Jews know what we worship. We understand the meaning of paschal lamb; day of atonement; holy of holies; mercy-seat. We know that the promised Messiah is to come of Jewish stock. As then between Moriah and Gerizim, Moriah must take precedence. Yet our system of worship, although divinely ordained, is only provisional. The hour has already come in which all who truly realize the ideal of worship will worship the Father in spirit and truth, — in spirit as opposed to form; in truth as opposed to type. For such kind of worshippers does the Father of spirits seek. Being Himself of a spiritual nature, He yearns toward what in us is spiritual. All true worship is but response to our Father's yearning."

What sublime teaching for a Galilean carpenter!

Alas! how slowly the Church has been learning this sublime lesson of the spirituality of Christian worship! To this day the confessors of the Prophet of Jacob's Well are debating about Gerizim and Moriah, — about little matters of vestments, canons, re-ordination, rebaptism, terms of communion, and the like. One might almost fancy that the story of Jacob's Well were altogther a myth, and that the Divine Man had never been born. No, worship is no longer a question of form, — henceforth worship is a question of spirit; no longer a matter of Jewish distinctions of meat and drink, — henceforth a matter of righteousness and peace and joy in the Holy Ghost.

"Are we then (I hear you asking) to dispense with all forms of worship? Must we understand our Master as teaching that there is no need of church-organizations, and sacraments, and set seasons of worship?"

Certainly not. We need all these, and such as these, as helps to worship, and therefore we must have them. For the body is the spirit's home, vehicle, organ, inlet, outlet. Accordingly, body and spirit act and react on each other. No matter how exalted our ideal of a Christian life may be, no matter how exalted our Christian character actually is, a quite certain thing is this, — the possibility of a genuine spiritual worship at any given time does depend greatly on our environment: for example, on the state of our bodily health; the comfortableness of the temperature; the thoroughness of the ventilation; the freedom from noise and distraction; the manner of the preacher; the religiousness of the music; and the like. Even the character of the architecture affects the case of spiritual worship, — many persons being really aided in their devotions by

> "The high embowed roof,
> With antick pillars massy proof,
> And storied windows richly dight,
> Casting a dim religious light."
>
> — *Il Penseroso.*

As a simple matter of fact, we cannot, even if we would, at least while we remain in this world, get rid of our bodies; we must take them with us whenever we go to church, and be more or less affected by them during our worship. Here in fact is one of the reasons of the incarnation or enfleshment of Deity. Just because we are perforce more or less swayed by our bodily organisms, it pleased the Father that in Jesus Christ His Son all the fulness of the Godhead should dwell bodily, body-wise. The incarnate career of the Son of God is Deity in sensible outflow and manifestation. The visible Jesus, because moving in the realm of our senses, helps us to see the invisible Father. Herein also lies the meaning of the ordinances of baptism and communion. These are outward acts, palpable to the senses; and therefore have been appointed to help us, body-invested as we are, to grasp the spiritual truths which they visibly symbolize. Forms of worship then are necessary. But they are necessary merely as means; they are not themselves ends. The great thing then is to use forms intelligently, conceiving them as being only aids to worship, mere ladders by which the soul may climb to her eternal habitation. For God is spirit; and therefore they that worship Him must worship in spirit and truth. Nevertheless, we are still in the body; and therefore even spiritual worship must take on some kind of form or liturgy. Beware then of that pantheistic philosophy which, to use the words of one of its most distinguished champions, teaches that

"Religion demands no particular actions, forms, or modes of thought; man's plowing is as holy as his praying, his daily bread as the smoke of his sacrifice, his home as sacred as his temple; his week-day and his Sabbath are alike God's day."

On the other hand, Horace Bushnell never said a more sensible thing than when in his sermon entitled "Routine Observance Indispensable" he declares that

" We need to keep fixed times, or appointed rounds of observance, as truly as to be in holy impulse; to have prescribed periods in duty as truly as to have a spirit of duty; to be in the drill of observance, as well as in the liberty of faith." — *Sermons on Living Subjects*, xvi.

Yes, I believe in Sabbaths and sanctuaries and hymns and prayers and sacraments. Were it not for these, and such as these, I honestly believe that true personal godliness would soon perish from the face of the earth. The consecrated temple, the gathered multitude, the devout posture, the humble invocation, the sacred melody, the holy reading, the reverent adoration, the hearty thanksgiving, the lowly confession, the fervent supplication, the generous intercession, the ardent aspiration, the glowing consecration, the grateful offering, the uplifting sermon, the solemn baptism, the peaceful communion, the gracious benediction, — these, and such as these, are the stately buttresses and graceful shafts on which the Master of assemblies rests the temple of His truth, and from which His righteousness goes forth as brightness, and His salvation as a lamp that burns. It is as true to-day as it was in the days of the psalmist Asaph, God's way is in the sanctuary.

And as a matter of fact, even non-liturgical

churches do have some form of liturgical service. Indeed, this whole question of liturgy is largely a question of degree rather than of nature; ranging all the way from the simplicity of the Quaker meeting to the elaborateness of the Roman ritual. The comparative bareness of the service in our non-liturgical churches is not so much a denial of the principle of a liturgy as it is a recoil against the excessive liturgy of ritualism. In fact, do not we ourselves, non-liturgical ministers though we are, have in our pulpits a printed "Order of Service."—indeed, a little Breviary of our own,—varying, it is true, in different pulpits, yet serving as a sort of chart for such sons of Levi as may honor us with their friendly exchange, and particularly for those ecclesiastical peripatetics who are ever walking through dry places, seeking rest, and find none? No, the question is not so much a question of substance as it is a question of degree. We all do have some kind of liturgy. And the problem is,—How much shall we have? Where shall we stop?

What provision liturgical churches have made for worship in their respective communions has already been eloquently set forth by my honored predecessors in this course. "Worship in Non-Liturgical Churches" is the topic your courtesy has assigned me. And in discussing this topic, I must remember that in the audience which I have the honor of addressing there are many students for the Christian ministry, the larger part of whom are doubtless looking forward to service in non-liturgical churches. Accordingly, I presume, it is expected of me that I should say something about what I conceive to be a proper manner of conducting worship in churches which have no prescribed liturgy. Not that I am so conceited or stupid as to presume to prescribe rigid rules or modes of worship. All that I may presume to undertake is to offer some hints suggested by a somewhat long and varied observation and experience.

Let me then, young brothers, say to you first of all that your responsibility in this matter will be very serious. For devotions, or acts of homage, constitute the chief part of worship. Beware, then, of falling into the irreverent habit of regarding the devotional services as merely subsidiary, degrading them into what are profanely styled "preliminary services, mere accessories," and the like. In fact, the devotional part of public worship is even more important than the preaching part; for the preaching part is to men, but the devotional part is to God. Do not then let the devotional part drift. Arrange it as orderly and progressively as you would arrange the movements of your sermon. Poet and scientist alike sing "Order is Heaven's first law." Listen to Ulysses as he stands before Agamemnon's tent:

> "The heavens themselves, the planets, and this centre
> Observe degree, priority, and place,
> Insisture, course, proportion, season, form,
> Office, and custom, in all line of order."
>
> — *Troilus and Cressida.*

It is particularly true in the sphere of public worship. Indeed, it was public worship which St. Paul had in mind when he wrote to the Corinthian Church, —

"Let all things be done decently and in order" (decorously and orderly). — 1 *Corinthians* xiv. 30.

If ever we are to deport ourselves with reverent decorum, it is when we stand in the presence of the King of kings in His own appointed audience-court.

"Keep thy foot when thou goest to the house of God; be not rash with thy mouth, and let not thine heart be hasty to utter anything before God; for God is in heaven, and thou upon earth: therefore let thy words be few."
— *Ecclesiastes* v. 1, 2.

How then shall we as a congregation of worshippers express our worship? Unitedly, as one congregation; or isolatedly, as a congregation of one? Before undertaking to answer this question, permit me to say that I have the painful conviction that the worshippers in our non-liturgical churches are allowed too small a part in the public worship of Almighty God. With the exception of the responsive Bible readings now prevailing in some of our churches, and also of the singing (alas, even this privilege is in many instances artistically denied us), everything is done by a vicarious worshipper. No voice but the preacher's is heard in adoration, thanksgiving, confession, supplication, intercession, aspiration, communion. So far as the vocal act of homage goes, the preacher alone worships. Should some angelic visitor enter one of our sanctuaries and observe the silence of the congregation, I am not sure but that he would imagine that some calamity like that which befell ancient Zacharias in the temple had befallen Christ's churchly priesthood to-day, and he would wonderingly ask what sin this people had committed that they should thus be struck dumb. Enter any Roman Catholic sanctuary while the service is going on. The priest is everything; the laity is nothing. From beginning to ending, excepting the organist and choir, it is the priest who carries on the entire worship; the congregation remaining as voiceless as an asylum of mutes or a graveyard of the dead. Enter one of our non-liturgical churches, and the same scene in its essential features is re-enacted. From beginning to ending, with the exception of the singing, and it may be of the responsive reading, it is the minister who is everything; the congregation is nothing. It is the minister who does the preaching; and this of course is right. But preaching is not, strictly speaking, a part of worship. Preaching means exposition, instruction, warning, entreaty, comforting, building up of the body of Christ. As such, and in its own place, preaching is of supreme importance, and indeed indispensable. But preaching in itself is not a part of worship. The addressing men on the subject of their duties and privileges is not worship; except in the general sense that all life, alike on Sunday and on week-days, in closet and market, ought to be a ceaseless liturgy. Public worship means the direct adoration of Almighty God and the direct supplication of His favor. It means the personal soaring of each individual worshipper toward his heavenly Father. Alas! this individual privilege of each member of the congregation we allow the minister to appropriate to himself. He alone lifts the veil, and enters the holy of holies, and communes before the mercy-seat; while the congregation stands mute in the outer court. The New Testament doctrine of the rent veil and the priesthood of all Christians gives way to the Old Testament doctrine of a sacerdotal order; or, what is worse, to the Roman heresy of a priestly caste and a priestly worship. Even the pulpit has been removed from the side to the centre; so that the preacher is perpetually in the foreground, while the worship of Almighty God is consigned to a comparatively subordinate niche. How painfully true this is may be seen in the fact that while it is not considered rude to enter the sanctuary during the earlier parts of the service, such as the singing or the Bible reading, — that is to say, be it observed, during that part of the service which is distinctly liturgical or worshipful, — it is considered rude to come in or go out while the minister is preaching, as though, forsooth, the main thing in worship were ignorant, feeble, sinful man, instead of Jehovah of hosts. What we need is a return to the ancient ways, even the good old paths of our fathers, falling in line with the venerable and saintly past, worshipping liturgically, as did the church of Knox and Luther, Anselm and Chrysostom, Peter and Isaiah, David and Moses.

On the other hand, we must guard ourselves against falling into mere routine worship. Remember what our Master Himself has said in this very matter of worship:—

"In praying use not vain repetitions, as the Gentiles do: for they think that they shall be heard for their much speaking: be not therefore like unto them: for your Father knoweth what things ye have need of before ye ask Him."—*Matthew* vi. 7, 8.

Does our Lord then mean to forbid all repetitions of the same words? Certainly not. He Himself bids repetition: "When ye pray, SAY"; then follows the Lord's Prayer according to the Evangelist Luke; moreover, He Himself thrice repeated the same prayer in Gethsemane. What, then, does our Lord forbid? Evidently the senseless repetition of prayers for repetition's own sake; substituting quantity for quality; vaporizing verbal requests into monotonous iterations and reiterations. And this is a characteristically heathen habit. Thus prayed Baal's prophets on Carmel in Elijah's time, calling on the name of their god from morning even until noon, saying: "O Baal, hear us!" Thus pray Buddhist monks to-day, ceaselessly repeating for whole days the sacred syllable, "Um! Um! Um!" But is this much worse than the rosary of our Roman Catholic friends, which requires that each of its fifteen decades shall begin with a Paternoster, be continued with ten Ave Marias, and end with a Gloria Patri? Is it much worse than the ritual of our liturgical friends, which requires that on the recurrence of a certain day in each succeeding year precisely the same prayer shall be recited? Nay, more, is this Gentile custom of using vain repetitions much worse than the stereotyped prayers of not a few of us non-liturgists, — prayers in which the round of particulars and the very phraseology may be predicted with almost as much certainty as the eclipses or the tides? Ah, if we cannot do better than this, — if we must use vain repetitions as the heathen do, — it would pay for us to buy one of the devotional machines of the Thibetan Lamaists, and, cranking the wheel, set our prayers a-going.

And now, to revert specifically to the question in hand, how shall we conduct worship in non-liturgical churches? Of course I cannot go into minute particulars, — questions, for example, of order of service, selections for Bible reading, holy days, saints' days, posture, costume, and the like. I must content myself with general suggestions. The chief elements of public worship are two, — Praise and Prayer. And just here the Model Prayer[1] is our

---

[1] Observe, I do not say, "the Lord's Prayer;" for, although the Lord dictated it, and although it is familiarly and dearly known to us as "the Lord's Prayer," yet it is not His prayer in the sense that He

divine pattern. Observe how the first half, —

> "Our Father who art in heaven,
> Hallowed be Thy name:
> Thy kingdom come:
> Thy will be done
> As in heaven, so on earth," —

consists in praise to God. Observe how the second half, —

> "Give us this day our daily bread;
> And forgive us our debts,
> As we also have forgiven our debtors;
> And bring us not into temptation,
> But deliver us from the evil one," —

consists in prayer for men. And observe particularly that the praise comes before the prayer, — the angels of our worship ascending before descending upon the ladder of the Son of man. This divinely given order of thought in praise and prayer deserves

Himself used it. For although entering sympathetically into human woe and guilt, — Himself taking our infirmities and bearing our sicknesses, — yet He was evermore holy, harmless, undefiled, separate from sinners. How, then, could He, who did no sin, and in whose mouth was found no guile, ever pray for Himself as though He were a fellow-sinner with us, saying, "Forgive us our debts, as we forgive our debtors?" No; it is the seventeenth chapter of St. John's Gospel, — that wonderful, sublime, blessed chapter which records the Lord's own prayer, first, for Himself (verses 1-5); secondly, for His Apostles (verses 6-19); and, thirdly, for His Church Universal (verses 20-26). It is this seventeenth chapter of St. John which is in the strictest sense the Lord's Prayer; whereas the prayer which our Lord dictated to His disciples for their use, — "After this manner pray ye"; "When ye pray, say," — this is the Church's, or the Model Prayer.

profound pondering. In studying it, let us reverently follow the same divine order.

And first, what does praise mean? To answer in general outline, praise means adoration, thanksgiving, aspiration, consecration, offering, communion, and the like. Now the question is, — How shall we as a congregation of worshippers express our praise, our service of adorations, thanskgivings, aspirations? Let an inspired apostle answer our question: —

"Speaking one to another in psalms and hymns and spiritual songs, singing and making melody with your heart to the Lord" (speaking one to another responsively, in psalms and hymns and odes pneumatic; chanting and psalming with your hearts to the Lord). — *Ephesians* v. 19.

No wonder that Pliny, writing to his master Trajan about the close of the first century, describes the early Church as accustomed to assemble before daylight, and sing alternately one to another, praising Christ as God: —

"Ante lucem convenire, carmenque Christo quasi Deo dicere secum invicem." — *Epist.* x. 97.

The exile of Patmos describes the worship in heaven itself as liturgical (see Rev. iv. 8–11; v. 9–14; vii. 9–12; xv. 3, 4; etc.).

For all deep feeling, especially the feeling of praise, is essentially poetical, instinctively yearning for the rhythmical accompaniment of sound. In fact, the truest devotion is also the highest poetry. It has been so in all lands and in all ages. Recall the pæans of Miriam, Deborah, Hannah, David, Isaiah, Mary, Zacharias, Simeon; even the great Hallel, or Hallelujah, of our Lord's final Passover. The Delphian Pythoness herself was wont to breathe forth her oracle in hexameter. Even the Quakers, although they disallow music, yet preach intoningly, in a singsong way. In brief, music is the natural outlet of devotion. What does not the Church owe in way of worship to the hymns of Greek Anatolius, Latin Ambrose, French Bernard, Italian Aquinas, German Luther, English Watts, American Palmer? Ay, here is the real concord of the ages; here is the true ecumenical. I do thank God that the Christian hymns, of whatever communion, are the common property of Christ's Church of all communions. Here at least the non-liturgical churches are themselves liturgical; for they join in praising God congregationally and synchronously by using together the same hymnal formulas.

But we are not only to praise God by speaking to one another in hymns and spiritual songs; we are also to praise Him in Psalms, chanting and psalming with our hearts to the Lord. In fact, the Psalter of the Bible ever has been, and I trust ever will be, the chief praise-book of the Church. Indeed, many of the Psalms were composed for a distinctively liturgical purpose; for example, Psalms xcii.-c. Accordingly they have an antiphonal or responsive structure; that is, the lines or strophes were to be chanted alternately, for example, by sections of the choir responsively to each other, or by Levite and congregation. For while English rhythm is the rhythm of metre, and English rhyme is the rhyme of sound, Hebrew rhythm was the rhythm of statement, and Hebrew rhyme was the rhyme of sentiment; or, as Ewald beautifully expresses it, "the rapid stroke as of alternate wings," "the heaving and sinking as of the troubled heart." Viewed in this light, Hebrew poetry is as much nobler than modern as rhyme of thought is nobler than rhyme of sound. When will our colleges teach Job and David and Isaiah as well as Homer and Virgil and Dante? Now this musical burst of soul and its responsive echo — this deep calling unto deep — is quite lost in our Authorized Version, and also in the Psalter of the Book of Common Prayer; for in these versions the parallelism of sense-rhythm or thought-rhyme is ruptured into verses so-called, which, however, are not so much verses as fractures. I confess that the responsive readings of Scripture, whether in the Psalter of liturgical churches or in the Bible selections of some of our non-liturgical, have never impressed me deeply; for they are painfully mechanical, suggesting neither the thought-rhythm of Hebrew parallelism nor the sound-rhyme of modern hymnals. One of the great boons which the revisers of our English Bible have conferred on us is their printing the

Psalms (as also they ought to have printed many of the prophecies) in lines instead of "verses" so-called; thus helping to preserve the parallelism so exquisitely characteristic of Hebrew poetry.

And herein, as it seems to me, lies the superiority of chanting. For while in certain respects it is said to be more difficult than singing, yet in other respects it is the simplest form of religious music, and therefore it offers least temptation to pride of artistic execution. Moreover, chanting is intelligible; and this is certainly an advantage. For, according to a master of spiritual music, —

" Even things without life, giving a voice, whether pipe or harp, if they give not a distinction in the sounds, how shall it be known what is piped or harped? For if the trumpet give an uncertain voice, who shall prepare himself for war? So also ye, unless ye utter by the tongue speech easy to be understood, how shall it be known what is spoken? for ye will be speaking into the air."
— 1 *Corinthians* xiv. 7-9.

Once more, chanting is probably the most ancient form of temple music. To the reflective worshipper few things are more inspiring than the sense of joining in strains centuries old. What can awaken a sublimer feeling of worship than to join in chanting, for instance, the *Benedicite*, the *Magnificat*, the *Benedictus*, the *Gloria in Excelsis*, the *Nunc Dimittis*, the *Gloria Patri*, the *Tersanctus*, the *Te Deum Laudamus?* What could be auguster than for a congregation to rise at the beginning of worship, and join in chanting *antiphonally* the *Venite, exultemus Domino?*

"O come, let us sing unto Jehovah;
  Let us make a joyful noise to the rock of our salvation.
  Let us come before His presence with thanksgiving,
  Let us make a joyful noise unto Him with psalms.
  For Jehovah is a great God,
  And a great King above all gods.
  In His hand are the deep places of the earth;
  The heights of the mountains are His also
  The sea is His, and He made it;
  And His hands formed the dry land.
  O come, let us worship and bow down;
  Let us kneel before Jehovah our Maker;
  For He is our God,
  And we are the people of His pasture, and the sheep of His hand." — *Psalm* xcv. 1-7.

Now when this responsive chanting or antiphonal recitative of the Hebrew parallelism shall become more familiar in our worship, and take the place due it in the musical part of our service, then shall the Hebrew Psalter become still more than ever the great praise-book of the Church. True, to chant well is a difficult art; but it can be learned. In my judgment, music composers could hardly do a more sacred thing than to set the liturgical psalms to simple and fitting chants; nor could music teachers do a richer service to the Church than to teach the children of our congregations (not merely a "boys' choir") how to chant the psalms; thus singing in the temple Hosannas to the Son of David, and out of the mouths of babes and sucklings perfecting praise. Let our children of this generation be thus trained to chant the melodies of the Psalter; then the worshippers of the next generation will indeed be, like the sons of Korah in the ancient temple, singers to the Chief Musician.

But prayer, not less than praise, is a part of worship. Indeed, to praise without praying is to worship as worshipped Cain and the Pharisee. And now our question is, — How shall we as a congregation of worshippers express our prayers, our service of confessions, supplications, intercessions, aspirations? Shall each worshipper pray silently, following the minister as he prays for the congregation? Or shall the minister and the congregation pray together, joining their voices in familiar and appropriate formulas? In brief, shall the congregation pray directly; or shall it pray by proxy? Both directly and by proxy is my answer.

On the one hand, we need extemporaneous prayers. Observe, however, that when I say "extemporaneous," I do not mean unpremeditated. For no minister has a right to undertake to lead his people in their devotions, and at the same time to allow himself to drift before God in his praying. If ever a pastor should carefully arrange his thoughts beforehand, asking the Spirit's guidance in his preparation, it is when he undertakes to present his flock before the Chief Pastor, voicing for them their manifold desires and needs. No; by extemporaneous prayers I mean prayers that are unwritten, or at least unread. And such prayers, when duly premeditated, are apt to be fresh, specific, appropriate, sympathetic, fervent, unctional. Just here, as I venture to think (may my dear brethren of the liturgical churches forgive me for saying it!), is one of the serious defects in their noble form of worship. Profoundly convinced as I am of the need and the beauty of liturgical forms of worship, I would never surrender the precious privileges and spiritual worth of extemporaneous prayers in the house of God. But as this is already one of our established usages, I need not descant on it further.

On the other hand, we need forms of devotion as well as the spirit of devotion. Young brethren, the older I grow, the more incompetent I feel for attempting to lead the people's devotions extemporaneously. As the flying years bring with them more of experience and observation, the more I shrink from the possible disasters incident to extemporaneous prayers, — for instance, grammatical blunders; tortuous movements; forced retreats; explanatory parentheses; ill-timed allusions; unfortunate reminiscences, and oblivions as unfortunate; unintentional exaggerations; personal idiosyncrasies; capricious moods; theological processes; conscious mentalities; in one word, egoism. And therefore I thank the Master of Assemblies that He has at sundry times and divers manners moved saintly men of all communions to provide prayers for the use of His Church,— prayers which are choice in thought; brief in statement; comprehensive in range; manifold in variety; specific in details; reverent in expression; hallowed in associations; reverend in antiquity. For prayers, like hymns, are the common heritage of all Christ's people in all lands and all times and all communions. Our brethren of the Greek Church have no more right to monopolize the Prayer of St. Chrysostom than our brethren of the Methodist Church have the right to monopolize Charles Wesley's "Jesus, Lover of my Soul." If it is right to praise God by singing together the same hymns, why is it not right to pray to God by joining together in the same prayers? Is prayer less solemn than praise? Oh, brothers, why take such pains to elaborate our written sermons before finite and sinful men, and yet presume to extemporize our prayers before infinite and sinless God? Of whom shall we be the more afraid, — them who can kill the body, and after that have no more that they can do; or Him who has power to destroy both body and soul in Gehenna? Yea, I say unto you, Fear Him.

But while all this is true, we must take care lest in our use of collects and liturgical prayers we allow ourselves to become slaves to a ritual. Laws which alter not may have become heathen Medes and Persians: they hardly become the followers of Christ; for where the Spirit of the Lord is, there is liberty. Appropriate, beautiful, devout, uplifting as many of the collects are, they must not be allowed to supplant liberty of conscience or freedom of emotion and expression. Minister and people must stand fast here in the liberty wherewith Christ set us free, lest we be entangled again in some yoke of bondage which our liturgical fathers or our non-liturgical contemporaries may have imposed. Having thus insisted on the right of Christian liberty here, I feel free to say that while extemporaneous prayers and liturgical prayers are both allowable, they are hardly equally allowable, my judgment leaning, in the majority of cases, to the use of appropriate and hallowed formulas. Doubtless the wisest course here is to have a liturgy which is flexible, judiciously blending the stateliness of ancient formulas and the tenderness of modern adjustments.

Glancing back at the territory through which we have sped, let me re-indicate some of the points where we halted for special inspections. We have seen that worship is a divine instinct; that the God of Revelation made provision for this instinct in His liturgy for ancient Israel; that Israel's liturgy was abolished under and in Christ; that, notwithstanding this abolition, forms of worship are still indispensable; that liturgy is a question of degree rather than of substance; that devotions are the chief parts of worship; that worship in non-liturgical churches tends to be vicarious; that we must guard against vain repetitions; that "the Lord's Prayer" is our model for worship; that the two chief elements of worship are praise and prayer; that music is the natural outlet of praise; that the Psalter is the Church's chief praise-book; that chanting is the noblest form of church music; that extemporaneous prayers have certain immense advantages of freshness, adaptedness, personality, sympathy, fervor, unction; that liturgical prayers have also certain immense advantages of variety, brevity, specialty, reverence, preciousness, and above all, concord.

To sum up as compactly as possible: Worship in non-liturgical churches should have a liturgy that is flexible; thus joining the stability of the golden altar with the mobility of its soaring incense. So shall the two pillars of our praise and prayer in the temple of our God be called "Jachin" (that is, "He shall establish") and "Boaz" (that is, "In it is strength").

After all, young brothers, daily life is the real worship; daily character is the true liturgy. Listen to Jerusalem's great Pastor: —

"Pure religion ($θρησκεία$, worship, ritual) and undefiled before our God and Father is this, to visit the fatherless and the widows in their affliction, and to keep himself unspotted from the world." — *James* i. 27.

> "There are in this loud, stunning tide
> Of human care and crime,
> With whom the melodies abide
> Of the everlasting chime;

> Who carry music in their heart
> Through dusky lane and mart,
> Plying their daily task with busier feet,
> Because their secret souls a holy strain repeat."
> — KEBLE'S *Christian Year*.

Be it for you and me thus to worship. Thus worshipping, we shall be admitted to that nobler service, in that purer realm, wherein there shall be no longer need of sun or moon, church or rite; for the Lord God, the Almighty, is the temple of it, and the Lamb is the liturgy thereof.

"Almighty and merciful God, of whose only gift it cometh that Thy faithful people do unto Thee true and laudable service; grant, we beseech Thee, that we may so faithfully serve Thee in this life, that we fail not finally to attain Thy heavenly promises; through the merits of Jesus Christ our Lord. Amen." — *Collect*.

X

THE IDEAL OF CHRISTIAN WORSHIP

BY THE REV. THOMAS S. HASTINGS, D.D., LL.D.

*President of the Faculty of Union Theological Seminary,
New York City.*

THE IDEAL OF CHRISTIAN WORSHIP

THIS course of lectures began with an admirable presentation of the Principles of Christian Worship. Then followed historical discussions of the chief representative liturgies, showing an evolution which prepared the way for the final theme, — *The Ideal of Christian Worship.*

The terms are simple, and yet there may be help in definition. What is an ideal? An ideal is the superlative, the uttermost degree of excellence, of beauty, and of power of which a thing is capable. It is that toward which all development tends: it is the goal of progress. The value and power of the ideal can hardly be overestimated. In his *History of Rationalism in Europe*, Lecky says[1] that it is "the assimilating and attractive influence of a perfect ideal," which has been "the main source of the moral development of Europe." To some the ideal is only a visionary thing. It savors of building castles in the air. But, as Thoreau says,[2] "If you have built castles in the air, your work need not be lost: that is where they should be. *Now put foun-*

---

[1] Vol. i. p. 336.   [2] *Walden*, p. 346.

dations under them." That touches the vital point. We *must* build castles in the air, but can we, will we put foundations under them? Without the ideal there would be no aspiration, no progress.

The other term to be defined is worship. In the most general sense it is the natural or instinctive recognition and assertion of our divine kinship; it is the uplifting and outgoing of the soul toward the author and the end of its being. Not impression but expression is its main object, its characteristic idea. Worship is the expression to God of the soul's convictions and emotions; — it involves reverence for God in Christ, penitence, faith, love, joy, gratitude, hope, aspiration and holy desire. It is the expression of the inward faith and love of the believer by methods and forms corresponding to the nature of the soul. Vinet says:[1] "Worship is the more immediate expression, the purely religious form of religion. It is the internal or external act of adoration, — adoration in act. Now adoration is nothing else than the direct and solemn acknowledgment of the divinity of God, and of our obligations to Him." It is important to remember that there are two sides of worship, the divine and the human. In prayer man draws near to God, and God draws near to man. The divine spirit co-operates with the human spirit in every true prayer. It has been beautifully said that "Worship is the *dialogue* be-

---

[1] Vinet's *Pastoral Theology*, p. 178.

tween God and the soul "; or, as another [1] puts it, true prayer is "a part of God's soliloquy." If the divine participation be wanting, it is because the human service is not genuine. In real worship God and man are together, and are co-operating.

The question will be asked, — How much of our public service is to be considered as comprehended in worship? Vinet says,[2] "Public worship, otherwise called *service* or *divine office*, comprehends, according to the ordinary idea, whatever is performed during the time in which an assembly remains together in the name of God and for the cause of God." But our question was more fittingly answered in the opening lecture of this course. We were told that there are seven elements in public worship, — "the hymn, the Scripture, the belief, the prayers, the oblation, the teaching, the sacraments." This is the general and prevailing view. And yet there are some who deny that the sermon is really a part of the worship. But it should be remembered that the true object of a sermon is to feed the fires of devotion, of consecration, and of service. Devotional feeling must have a basis of knowledge, thought, and conviction. Emotion is secondary; it must be fed, or it will soon burn out. Instruction feeds the flame of worship, and through it comes that necessary increment of knowledge which is fuel for the altar fire of worship. Sometimes the tendency has been

[1] *Radical Problems*, p. 89.
[2] *Pastoral Theology*, p. 198.

to crowd out the sermon by the predominance of other parts of the service; at other times the sermon by its length has lessened the time for reading, song, and prayer. Luther went to an extreme in this matter. He said, "The greatest and most important part of all the worship of God is the preaching and the teaching of God's Word." He even went so far as to say, "Wherever the Word of God is not preached, there it is better neither to sing, nor to read, nor to assemble together." On the other hand, the Presbyterian *Directory for Worship* says,[1] "As one primary design of public ordinances is to pay social acts of homage to the most high God, ministers ought to be careful not to make their sermons so long as to interfere with or exclude the more important duties of prayer and praise; but preserve a just proportion between the several parts of public worship." Those are wise words. The ideal of worship requires that this "just proportion" of its several parts be carefully preserved. Ritual and liturgy must not crowd the sermon and so limit its usefulness as a means of promoting a thoughtful and an intelligent worship. On the other hand, the sermon must not be permitted to subordinate praise and prayer, or the reading of the Word. In the non-liturgical churches the sermon is generally too long; while in the liturgical churches it is apt to be too short.

It would be quite impossible within the limits

[1] Chapter vii. 4.

assigned to this lecture to speak at length of all the seven elements of public worship which have been named. A few words may be said concerning some of these elements, and then a more extended consideration of the others will be undertaken. I shall not follow the order of the seven elements, because the first, "the hymn," and the fourth, "the prayer," require the chief places in our discussion.

The second element in worship is "the Scripture." The reading of the Divine Word is a part of the worship, not as bibliolatry, but as a homage to the recorded will of God. The ideal is that the Word shall be read with such intelligence, clearness, and emphasis that its meaning shall be apparent, and its power and beauty shall be felt by the people. Responsive reading makes *good* reading impossible. It breaks the exquisite rhythm and the fine coherence and continuity of the Scriptures. Another element in the ideal of this part of the worship is, that as much as possible of the Word should be read in the course of each year in the public services. A Lectionary, or table of selections from Scripture, would serve an excellent purpose. It would insure a far more comprehensive public reading of the Bible than is possible while the minister is left, as now, to make his selection with reference to his sermon, or to be guided only by his taste and feeling. The Bible is a large book, much larger than any one minister. Its public reading should not be circumscribed by the small limitations of any one man. The ideal is to have the whole of the Scriptures as fully represented from year to year in the public reading as may be consistent with the maintenance of a due proportion of the several parts of the worship.

The third element of public worship is "the belief." That venerable and beautiful symbol, the Apostles' Creed, of course belongs equally to all the churches, and deserves a place in all public worship at least once on the Sabbath. It should be repeated in unison by the whole body of worshippers standing together before God.

The *oblation* was named as the fifth element of public worship. The Psalmist cries, "Give unto the Lord the glory due unto His name; *bring an offering, and come into His courts.*" (Ps. xcvi. 8.) The ideal worship will no more be empty-handed than it will be songless or prayerless. The gold, frankincense, and myrrh wise men will bring whenever they gather to worship the incarnate Lord. Instead of occasional contributions, there will be in every service free-will offerings as inseparable from worship as are songs and prayers. The treasury of the Lord will then be full. Giving will be a delight; not a hesitant and reluctant answer to arguments and appeals, but a glad and grateful, a spontaneous and habitual offering unto God.

The Sacraments constitute the crowning element of worship. Only a few words may be said concerning the Holy Communion. This beautiful symbolic ordinance deserves a high place in public worship.

To put its observance at the close of an ordinary service is to endanger its spiritual value, unless it can be made the culmination, and not the mere hurried conclusion of such a service. One thing should be emphasized: the celebration of the Eucharist is not by any means a fitting occasion for didactic or for evangelistic talk. It is not the fitting occasion for instructing or exhorting believers, much less for warning unbelievers. It is pre-eminently a Communion Service, in which fellowship with Christ and with one another should characterize the worship; and this fellowship should be full of praise, of gratitude, of gladness, and of hope. To my mind it would be ideal if all churches could agree to be visibly one in the celebration of this ordinance, both as to the time and as to the mode of its celebration. It would indeed be inspiring to feel that the whole believing host is at the same time and in the same way commemorating the sacrifice of our common Lord and Saviour. Surely we might — God grant that we may — agree, in all branches of the Church, upon some common order for at least this one delightful service. This order should not be *made* by any one church, but should be compiled from the usages and from the historic treasures of all the churches, both liturgical and non-liturgical. Could we reach such an agreement, it would be an ideal movement toward the inviting goal of Church Unity. It would be a thrilling scene to angels and to men, if all believers, in holy concert of the common faith, would thus unite in celebrating the Supper of the Lord.

Thus far all of the seven elements of public worship have been considered except the first and the fourth, the hymn and the prayer. To these our attention shall now be given.

The Hymn. — The ideal is that as many as possible shall take at least some part in the service of song and of prayer. Neither the minister nor the choir should be so prominent as to dishonor or to discredit the true priesthood of the body of believers. Christians are "an holy priesthood to offer up spiritual sacrifices acceptable to God by Christ Jesus"; they are "a royal priesthood, an holy nation, a peculiar people, that they should shew forth the praises of Him who hath called them out of darkness into His marvellous light." (1 Pet. ii. 5, 9; cf. Isa. li. 6; Rev. i. 6.) As Pearsall[1] says, "The complaint of many intelligent Christians is not that we have too much of the voice of the minister, but too little of the voices of the people, — that too much is done *for* them, and too little *by* them. There is an excess of *listening* in our devotional services." This complaint, of which Mr. Pearsall thus speaks, is becoming more and more general and imperative. The people are willing that the minister and the choir should in some fitting measure represent them in song and in prayer, but they rightfully claim that their own voices shall be heard in the services. This claim cannot safely be disregarded.

[1] *Public Worship; the Best Methods of Conducting it*, p. 160.

Jonathan Edwards took the deepest interest in this part of public worship, and he uttered these pungent words, which the Church of to-day sadly needs to hear: "As it is commanded of God that all should sing, so all should make conscience of *learning* to sing, as it is a thing that cannot be done decently without learning. *Those therefore who neglect to learn to sing live in sin, as they neglect what is necessary to their attending one of the ordinances of God's worship.*"[1] These words convict most of the churches of to-day as living in sin in neglecting systematic instruction in church music. In the early Christian centuries the Church recognized its duty in this regard. Gregory the Great established singing schools in Rome, and often attended them himself. In this country, especially after the Revolution, singing schools were common and characteristic. But during recent years such schools are scarcely known, and are not in any way recognized as necessary for the proper equipment of the Church, or for the maintenance of such singing in the sanctuary as, to use Edwards's words, "cannot be done decently without learning." Meanwhile the reading of music at sight is almost a lost art, so that for the most part the singing of God's praise must of necessity be done by proxy, except so far as the old tunes, learned by ear, are retained, to the deep and restless dissatisfaction of the young and of

---

[1] Quoted by the Reverend J. Spencer Pearsall in his *Public Worship*, p. 109.

all who love good music. The churches of course must suffer for this neglect of duty, and they deserve no sympathy whatever for the endless troubles they are having with choirs and with those who want something more and better than "Windham," "Dundee," and "Balerma." In England, Scotland, and Wales the situation is by no means so bad. Under the influence of the Curwens, of Dykes, Barnby, Smart, Monk, and of many others, there is an active interest in the promotion of the practical training of congregations in church music. Mr. Curwen says,[1] "The example of every church whose psalmody has reached a high degree of congregational power and beauty shows that the key to success is hard and sustained work in teaching the congregation." Then this author tells us how this work is done in many different churches through "Psalmody Improvement Associations"; through large elementary classes in which congregations are taught to read music; and through regular "practices" (or rehearsals), "Psalmody Classes," and Praise Services. This educational work, we are told, has yielded excellent and delightful results.

We are living in the era of the Hymn-Tune Book. Our forefathers had only psalm-books, and would tolerate nothing else. Sternhold and Hopkins, Rouse, Tate and Brady, Ainsworth's Psalms, the Bay Psalm-book, and then Watts's Psalms and Hymns, — this is the familiar succession. Isaac Watts is

[1] *Studies in Worship Music*, by J. Spencer Curwen, p. 162.

styled the "Inventor of Hymns." But in all the editions of Watts's Psalms and Hymns, a sharp distinction was maintained between psalms and hymns; they were separated. But that distinction and separation are practically lost. For convenience of adaptation, the Hymn-Tune Book has mingled the psalms and the hymns together, and gradually the rapid multiplication of hymns has been steadily crowding ✓ out the psalms from our repertoire. For the last forty years, that is, throughout the era of the Hymn-Tune Book (which began in 1856), this process has been steadily going on. What will be the result? It is to be hoped that the best and noblest of the versions may be retained. We cannot afford to lose them. But probably metrical versions of the Psalms will be to a great extent succeeded by a revival of chanting, which, though a low order of music, has this great advantage, that it preserves and honors the exact language of the Psalter. Hymns must have place and recognition, for it is the inalienable right of each age and generation to make and to sing its own songs of praise. Dr. Watts said:[1] "Moses and Deborah, and the princes of Israel, David, Asaph, and Habakkuk, and all the saints under the Jewish state, sung their own joys and victories, their own hopes and fears and deliverances; and why must we, under the Gospel, sing nothing else but the joys, hopes, and fears of Asaph and David? Why must Christians be forbid all other melody but what arises

[1] *Works*, iv. 116.

from the victories and deliverances of the Jews? David would have thought it very hard to have been confined to the words of Moses, and sung nothing else on all his rejoicing days but the drowning of Pharaoh in the fifteenth of Exodus." Of course Dr. Watts was right. We must have our own hymns. Demand will regulate supply. Ephemeral hymns and tunes will intrude themselves for a time, but will disappear as the level of education is lifted.

I have said nothing of instrumental music as an aid in worship. The organ has come to stay, for it deserves to stay. Dr. Bushnell said of it:[1] "This is the instrument of God, and so in fact it now is. The grandest of all instruments, it is, as it should be, the instrument of religion. Profane uses cannot handle it. It will not go to the battle, nor the dance, nor the serenade; for it is the holy Nazarite, and cannot leave the courts of the Lord."[2] But are we to have other instruments in the sanctuary? Who shall dare

[1] *Work and Play*, p. 460.
[2] In 1735, the Dean of Berkeley presented an organ to the town which bears his name, but in a public meeting the people voted that "An organ is an instrument of the Devil, for the entrapping of men's souls"; and so they declined to receive the generous gift. (*Studies in Worship Music*, by J. Spencer Curwen, p. 62.) The violoncello was the first instrument to invade the sanctuary. It was sneeringly called "the Lord's Fiddle." It drove many people from the churches. Even Dr. Emmons left the pulpit, and refused to preach, when he heard the violoncello in the choir gallery. The churches were distracted and divided by the innovation, and in the language of that day were known as "Catgut" or "Anti-catgut" churches. Comp. Hood's *History of Music in New England; The Sabbath in Puritan New England*, by Alice Morse Earle.

exclude them if they can aid the service of song? Read the last Psalm in the Psalter as the best and briefest treatment of this point. "Praise ye the Lord. Praise God in His sanctuary; praise Him in the firmament of His power. Praise Him for His mighty acts; praise Him according to His excellent greatness. Praise Him with the sound of the trumpet; praise Him with the psaltery and harp. Praise Him with the timbrel and dance; praise Him with stringed instruments and organs [or "the pipe," as the Revision has it]. Praise Him upon the loud cymbals; praise Him upon the high sounding cymbals. Let everything that hath breath praise the Lord. Praise ye the Lord." This would seem to justify a whole orchestra in the church, if thereby the praise of God may be promoted. The best and highest that we can bring to the altar we owe to Him whom we worship. Art must be subordinate; must serve and not dominate. Architecture and music we *must* have. Painting and sculpture we *may* have, if only they can serve and not rule.

One principle must be emphasized as bearing equally both upon praise and prayer. While we deprecate the entire silence of the people in public worship, it must not be assumed by any means that they cannot join in song or in prayer except as they join with their voices. That would be a monstrous assumption against which all churches, liturgical and non-liturgical, must alike protest. Worship may be silent. There should be some singing in which the people do not join with their voices, but only with their hearts. Introits, Anthems, Psalms, and Hymns, in some parts of the service, may be so sung by the representatives of the people that the singing shall be both an education and a spiritual help to the silent worshippers. It can be wisely claimed only that the people shall have some vocal participation both in song and in prayer.

Now can we give the ideal of this part of public worship? The ministry will be so trained in the theological schools that they can intelligently guide and elevate the praises of the sanctuary. The Church will feel that she must systematically promote and maintain such musical education as will make the praise of God in his house a delight and a service worthy of His holy name. There will not only be schools and classes for instruction, but there will be gatherings of the congregations for special practice, tuition, and rehearsal. As all can be taught to sing, all will be taught to sing. I know that some will question this statement; let me fortify it by high authorities. Curwen says:[1] "The question may be asked, Do you really mean that all persons can be taught to sing? What about those that have no voice, or no ear? To this I reply, that although natural capacity for singing differs greatly in different people, I believe that, speaking generally, all persons can be taught sufficient to enable them to take their natural part in the chants and hymn-tunes of

[1] *Studies in Worship Music*, p. 155.

the service. Dr. Hullah[1] is never tired of reiterating his disbelief in the common talk about people having no ear, and no voice. It is, of course, easier for a boy to learn to sing than a man; it is easier for some men than for others; but it is impossible for so very small a minority, that we may safely say it is possible for all." Then the people will praise the Lord in the beauty of holiness. Is there any other being so sensitive, so refined, so delicate in taste and feeling as is the God we worship? He who has made the forms and colors of the flowers so fine and fair, and the songs of the birds so varied and sweet, He surely should have the choicest and best offerings of our minds and hearts, of our hands and tongues. He longs for the faith, the confidence, and the overflowing affection of his worshippers; for as that exquisite Scripture puts it, "The Lord taketh pleasure in His people." (Ps. cxlix. 4.)

The remaining element in public worship which we have to consider is prayer.

Two types of worship have characterized Protestantism, — liturgical and non-liturgical services.[2]

---

[1] John Hullah, LL.D., Professor of Vocal Music in Queen's College and in Bedford College, London.

[2] A few books may be named in two classes. 1st. For those who are opposed to liturgies : Miller on *Public Prayer ;* Henry on *Prayer ; Worship of the Old Covenant;* Willis's *Pulpit Prayers by Eminent Preachers ; The Worship of the Presbyterian Church,* D. D. Bannerman ; *The Worship and the Offices of the Church of Scotland,* Dr. G. N. Sprott. 2dly. For those who favor liturgies : *Translations of the Primitive Liturgies,* Neale and Littledale ; *The Book of Common Order,*

All who desire the unity of the Church should seek to blend these two types in one. That is the ideal. Some one has said, "The Gospel edition of Leviticus is comprised in a single verse, ' God is a Spirit, and they that worship Him must worship Him in spirit and in truth.' " All will agree with that. Worship is a matter of spirit rather than of form. But form and spirit are not antagonistic. They belong together, and form may serve and help spirit, and spirit may subsidize, beautify, and glorify form, transfiguring it as on the mount of vision. My limits forbid a full review of the history of what the Presbyterian Church has done with reference to this subject. Only some necessary points shall be touched. In 1787, a committee, appointed the year before to revise the "Book of Discipline and Directory for Worship," reported to the Synod of New York and Philadelphia a collection of devotional forms, specimens of what the public prayers should be. A majority of the Synod, however, decided that only *directions*, and not forms, should be given. Against this action some of the ablest and wisest men in the

commonly known as John Knox's Liturgy; Eutaxia, or the Presbyterian Liturgies, and *A Book of Public Prayer, compiled from the Authorized Formularies of the Presbyterian Church, as prepared by the Reformers, Calvin, Knox, Bucer, and others,* both by Dr. C. W. Baird; *A General Liturgy and Book of Common Prayer,* Dr. S. M. Hopkins; *An Order of Worship, with Forms of Prayer for Divine Service,* B. B. Comegys, LL.D.; also, by the same author, *Public Worship, partly Responsive; Scriptural Prayer Book for Church Services; A Presbyterian Prayer Book.* Other books will be named as reference is made to them.

Church at that time — Doctors Rogers, McWhorter, Ashbel Green, and others — protested, desiring that at least some forms should be given to the churches. It should be noted that forms of prayer were not forbidden, but they could not be *imposed* or *enjoined*. I quote the language of the Directory: " But we think it necessary to observe that, although we do not approve, as is well known, of confining ministers to set or fixed forms of prayer for public worship; yet it is the indispensable duty of every minister, previously to his entering on his office, to prepare and qualify himself for this part of his duty, as well as for preaching. He ought by a thorough acquaintance with the Holy Scriptures, by reading the best writers on the subject, by meditation, and by a life of communion with God in secret, to endeavor to acquire both the spirit and the gift of prayer."[1] Going back still further, I would emphasize the fact that in 1543, Melancthon and Bucer prepared the Cologne Liturgy, a translation of which was published in London four years later. From this Cologne Liturgy, says Archbishop Laurence, in his work on the Thirty-nine Articles, pp. 377, 378, "Our offices bear evident marks of having been freely borrowed, liberally imitating, but not servilely copying it." That is the Anglican statement of the case. The Presbyterian statement is more definite and comprehensive. It is claimed that the whole Lord's day service, as usually celebrated, "contains but a single prayer (and even

---

[1] *Directory for Worship*, chap. v. section iv.

this exception is doubtful) that can be traced to a distinctively Episcopalian origin. In the occasional offices of baptism, matrimony, visitation of the sick, and burial of the dead, the question of authorship lies between the Calvinist and the Lutheran, or between the French and the German Protestant, rather than between the Presbyterian and the Episcopalian."[1] *The Book of Common Order*, prepared by John Knox (1564), had much in common with the Anglican Liturgy, and was formally adopted by the General Assembly. The Scotch Prayer Book, substantially agreeing with the Anglican Liturgy, was authorized by the General Assembly in 1637. This would doubtless have been generally acceptable, but for the attempt of Charles I. to force the liturgy upon the Church. This attempt led to the Solemn League and Covenant, which was the bold and decisive assertion of such liberty as Presbyterians have always loved and maintained. After the Restoration, the Book of Common Prayer would have been adopted by the Presbyterians if it had been changed in some particulars, as Charles II. promised that it should be. The Savoy Conference failed to bring about an agreement, and then followed the famous Act of Uniformity in 1662. Two thousand Presbyterian clergymen thereupon at once surrendered their livings, and went forth penniless and homeless, because they would not be *compelled* to use a liturgy. The

---

[1] *Presbyterian Book of Common Prayer*, edited by Professor Charles W. Shields, D.D., LL.D. *Liturgia Expurgata*, p. 55.

lessons are obvious. The Book of Common Prayer cannot be considered as the exclusive property of any one branch of the Church; it really belongs to the Church Catholic. It is a legacy, not from Cranmer alone, but also from Calvin and Melancthon and Bucer and John Knox. Presbyterians have a historic right to use a liturgy, but its use must be discretionary, and not required.

Whether prayer be free or prescribed, its quality and character will correspond with the quality and character of the Church and of her ministry. So Van Oosterzee says,[1] speaking of Germany: "As regards the contents, we see reflected also in the Church prayer, whether free or prescribed, the different periods which were passed through in the sphere of Church and theology. Orthodoxism petrified it; Formalism lengthened it; Rationalism diluted and watered it; Crypto-Catholicism restored it in a form harmonizing with its own aspirations; but happily also, sincere devotion animated and raised it, in accordance with the wants of the time, to be the worthy expression of the highest life of the soul."

In recent years there has been a growing uneasiness with reference to this subject, both in the liturgical and in the non-liturgical churches. The former want more liberty, — at least some room for free prayer; the latter want less liberty and more uniformity. In 1880, in his brilliant paper read before

[1] *Practical Theology*, by Professor J. J. Van Oosterzee, D.D., p. 406.

the Presbyterian Alliance in Philadelphia, the late President Roswell D. Hitchcock, D.D., LL.D., said: "Now in all liturgical churches, or nearly all, the liturgy is no longer servant, but master. There is too much of it for constant repetition. Liberty of omitting portions not always apposite, is unwisely denied. The absolute exclusion of extemporaneous petitions is equally unwise. And the overshadowed, dwarfed discourse would be a great misfortune were good discourse otherwise more likely to be had. . . . One of these days, though probably not till we are all gone, there will be a form of public service, which shall suit the matured and cultured none the less for suiting the immature and uncultured. . . . No existing Prayer Book satisfies any good Presbyterian. Still less would any good, wise Presbyterian ask to have a new Prayer Book made up out of materials that are new. The materials mostly are old; some of them very old, such as the ' Gloria in Excelsis,' the ' Tersanctus,' and the ' Te Deum.' Christendom could better spare any treatise of Athanasius than the prayer ascribed to Chrysostom: ' Fulfil now, O Lord, the desires and petitions of thy servants as may be expedient for them, granting us in this world knowledge of thy truth, and in the world to come life everlasting.' The farther we get down the centuries, the more precious will be to us the long unbroken melodies of praise and prayer."

I have quoted these words of my honored predecessor, because with his main positions I heartily agree;

but I cannot quite agree with what he said about existing Prayer Books, and this may be because, in Dr. Hitchcock's view, I am not a good Presbyterian. I certainly do not want all that is found in any existing Prayer Book, or Ordinal, but as certainly I could find in the Book of Common Prayer all the forms which I would crave for the use of our non-liturgical churches. And I would far rather have the selections made from that venerable and beautiful liturgy, than to have new forms made by any ecclesiastical body, or by any association. I am not unmindful of the excellent work which has been done by the "Church Service Society" in Scotland. That Society was formed in Glasgow in 1865. The first edition of its *Book of Common Order*[1] was published in 1867, and the sixth edition in 1890, at which time it was reported that there were five hundred and six ministers and one hundred and thirty laymen in the membership of the Society, representing more than sixty different Presbyteries. The Editorial Committee of this Society has searched the libraries of the great Universities to draw from all the liturgical literature of the centuries contributions for their work. Their methods have been scholarly, their labors abundant, and the results are of exceed-

[1] Εὐχολόγιον. *A Book of Common Order, being Forms of Prayer and Administration of the Sacraments, and other ordinances of the Church; issued by the Church Service Society.* William Blackwood and Sons, Edinburgh and London. The volume contains a Lectionary intended to secure in the public reading of the Scriptures the fullest and most comprehensive representation of the whole Bible.

ing value. A similar society, bearing the same name, has been organized in this country.[1] But is it wise

[1] Dr. Louis F. Benson, of Philadelphia, is the President. The statement of the principles of this American "Church Service Society" is as follows: —

"I. The Church Service Society of the Presbyterian Church in the United States of America stands upon the basis of that doctrine of the Church, the Ministry, and the Sacraments, which is set forth in the Westminster standards; including within its province all matters and things which pertain to public worship.

"II. The society proposes as its first object an inquiry into the present conduct of public worship in the Presbyterian Church, and the various orders of worship in actual use.

"III. The society proposes to study the modes of worship which have been in use in the different branches of the Church, and especially in those Churches known as the Reformed, of which we are one; and thus to recognize the importance of this branch of historical theology, to make its lessons clear to the mind of the Church, and to strengthen in our services the links which bind us to historic Christianity.

"IV. The Society aims to follow this study of the present conduct and past history of the worship of the Church by doing such work in the preparation of forms of service in an orderly worship as may help to guard against the contrary evils of confusion and ritualism, and promote reverence and beauty in the worship of God in His holy House, unity and the spirit of common praise and prayer among the people."

The Provisional Constitution of the American Church Service Society is added: —

"I. The name of the Society shall be The Church Service Society of the Presbyterian Church in the United States of America.

"II. The object of the Society shall be the improvement of public worship in the Church upon the basis set forth in the Statement of Principles.

"III. The officers of the Society shall be a President, a Vice-President, a Secretary, a Treasurer, and a Committee of Twelve, all of whom shall be elected for the term of three years, and shall form a Board of Management for the Society.

to multiply forms of prayer? In his Introduction to his *Systematic Theology*, Dr. Charles Hodge says:[1] "So legitimate and powerful is this inward teaching of the Spirit, that it is no uncommon thing to find men having two theologies, — one of the intellect, and another of the heart. The one may find expression in creeds and systems of divinity, the other in their prayers and hymns. It would be safe for a man to resolve to admit into his theology nothing which is not sustained by the devotional writings of true Christians of every denomination. It would be easy to construct from such writings, received and sanctioned by Romanists, Lutherans,

"IV. Clergymen and male communicants in good standing in the Presbyterian Church in the United States of America may be admitted to membership by the votes of a majority of the Board, upon the applicant's approval of the Statement of Principles.

"V. Members shall make an annual payment of one dollar to the funds of the Society.

"VI. Any person who is in sympathy with the objects of this Society and will subscribe the Statement of Principles, may be admitted to associate membership by a vote of the Board, and upon payment of the annual dues shall be entitled to receive a copy of the publications of the Society, but without the privilege of voting.

"VII. Meetings of the Society for the election of officers and for other purposes shall be called by the Board. Members may send their ballots through the mails.

"VIII. Changes in the Constitution may be made by a majority of ballots cast at any meeting, provided that one month's notice of the proposed change has been given in writing to all members.

"IX. Changes in the Statement of Principles shall be made only by a three-fourths vote of all the members of the Society, three months' notice of the proposed change having been given in writing to all members."

[1] Vol. i. pp. 16, 17.

Reformed, and Remonstrants, a system of Pauline or Augustinian theology, such as would satisfy any intelligent and devout Christian in the world." This statement may be assumed to be orthodox. Accordingly, Christians of "every denomination" may be asked and expected to unite with a good degree of uniformity in their "prayers and hymns." So the historical spirit, the tradition of the churches, the common longing for church unity, the sacredness and the beauty of the affluent liturgical literature which we inherit from the centuries, and the confessed deficiency and inadequacy of the average extemporaneous prayer, — all these things unite in a common demand for some prescribed forms of worship.[1] The Lord's Prayer, all will agree, should have place and prominence, and it should be repeated in unison by the whole congregation. In Rhenish Prussia, and elsewhere, the beautiful custom has prevailed of tolling the bell when the Lord's Prayer is repeated in the public worship, so that those who are detained from the house of God by sickness or other causes may join in the common service. The Commandments should be read, combining duty with

---

[1] In an article in the "New Englander" for August, 1855, the late Dr. Leonard Bacon, with characteristic positiveness, made this statement: "The responsive reading of the Psalms and of other devotional parts of Scripture, between the minister and the congregation, or the repetition of the Lord's Prayer by the whole assembly, would be quite certain to break down if attempted in any of our churches. Anything of that sort, we are sure, will be a failure." This reads strangely now. "We are sure" the good Doctor has not proved a good prophet.

devotion, and, as I said before, the Apostles' Creed should be repeated in unison. To these should be added the "Te Deum," the "Tersanctus," and the "Sursum Corda," the latter in connection with the Communion serivce. So far as this most are willing to go. The ideal, however, demands something more. The opponents of all forms of prayer assume that one man can be large enough to comprehend and to represent five hundred men. This seems a monstrous assumption. No one man can reasonably be expected to be large enough or elastic enough to comprehend so much. The priesthood of the people must not be overshadowed and suppressed by the excessive and false assumption of priesthood by the minister who is only a *minister*. So the ideal of prayer calls us further. Nothing could be more beautiful and appropriate for the beginning of the Sabbath worship than such Scriptures as introduce the "Order for Daily Morning Prayer": — "The Lord is in His holy temple; let all the earth keep silence before Him. I was glad when they said unto me, We will go into the house of the Lord. Let the words of my mouth and the meditation of my heart, be alway acceptable in thy sight, O Lord, my strength and my redeemer. Grace be unto you, and peace from God our Father, and from the Lord Jesus Christ." Then a form of confession, another of general thanksgiving, a prayer for the President of the United States and for all in authority, and another for "all classes and conditions of men," might be used in common by all the churches of all denominations, and such unison and uniformity seem to me ideal. It may not be best that these forms should be taken from the Book of Common Prayer, though this would be my preference; it may be better that they should be compiled from that and also from other existing liturgies. The important thing is not to add to divisiveness and confusion by *making new forms*. Added to these forms there should be free prayer, in which the pastor's heart may intercede for his people under the pressing consciousness of their immediate and characteristic wants. It would be the ideal of worship if all Christians of all denominations could be outwardly one at least in song and in prayer. Thus on the one hand might be avoided the danger which freedom in public worship involves, — the danger of lawlessness, disorder, and narrow inadequacy; and on the other hand might be avoided the danger which fixedness in public worship involves, — namely, the danger of formality, monotony, and restraint. The ideal must be the combination or the interblending of the two methods which have obtained so long, the liturgical and the non-liturgical. The best things in each method should be adopted and unified. Then and thus the real oneness of all believers would be proclaimed and emphasized; then and thus the churches which differ in polity or in doctrine would be visibly one before the throne of grace.

The ideal of Christian worship, — feeble and inadequate must be the attempts of any one man to set forth such a theme. Even an archangel could not do it, for he could not know and feel the *Christian* element in worship. The fallen and the believing, and only they, can realize that ideal. We try to do it; we long to do it; we vie with animate and inanimate nature to swell the volume of adoration which this stricken and struggling earth is ever sending up to the throne of the Eternal, and God is always listening and is always gracious.

> " From hill to hill, from field to grove,
> Across the waves, around the sky,
> There 's not a spot, or deep or high,
> Where the Creator has not trod,
> And left the footstep of a God.
> But are his footsteps all that we,
> Poor grov'ling worms, must know or see?
> Thou Maker of my vital frame,
> Unveil thy face, pronounce thy name,
> Shine to my sight, and let the ear
> Which Thou hast formed, thy language hear.
> Where is thy residence? Oh! why
> Dost Thou avoid my searching eye,
> My longing sense? Thou great Unknown,
> Say, do the clouds conceal thy throne?
> Divide, ye clouds, and let me see
> The power that gives me leave to be.
> Or art Thou all diffused abroad
> Thro' boundless space, a present God,
> Unseen, unheard, yet ever near?
> What shall I do to find Thee here?
> Is there not some mysterious art
> To feel thy presence at my heart?

To hear thy whispers soft and kind,
In holy silence of the mind?
Then rest, my thoughts; no longer roam
In quest of joy, for heaven's at home." [1]

[1] Watts's *Works,* iv. 510.

www.ingramcontent.com/pod-product-compliance
Lightning Source LLC
Chambersburg PA
CBHW030000240426
43672CB00007B/765